Applied Big History

A Guide for Entrepreneurs, Investors,
and Other Living Things

William Grassie

ISBN-13: 978-1719853071
ISBN-10: 171985307X

Version 1.2

Please send corrections, comments, and feedback to
grassie@metanexus.net

Metanexus Imprints
New York, NY

Table of Contents

Foreword by Mitch Julis

During college and graduate school, my focus of study was mainly in the areas of economics, finance, statistics, demography, psychology, political economy, international relations and policy, management, and the law. Aside from an introductory physics class at Princeton with famed Professor John Wheeler, there was no excess of physics chemistry, biology, and geology in my higher education and certainly not much paleoanthropology, anthropology, or neuroscience. Over the last ten plus years, however, my areas of interest began to expand as a result of my learning relationship, friendship, and partnership with Professor John Sterman of MIT who heads the system dynamics program at The Sloan School and The Institute for New Economic Thinking, where I was previously a board member. This phase of my continuous learning, so necessary in the ever-changing field of investment, logically led me to Big History.

Investors, regardless of preferred strategy, face an increasingly complex world and require an effective and creative multi-disciplinary approach to embrace that complexity. As William Grassie shows in this important book, the origin story and evolution of the universe, our planet, life generally, and humanity specifically has a lot to teach us about how to identify, analyze, capture, and create value in business and finance. Moreover, for micro investors in complex situations and securities, the crucial importance of understanding macro structures and dynamics has become painfully evident in the aftermath of the Great Financial Crisis of 2008. Big History and the related areas of systems thinking and complexity economics are about as macro a framework as one can adopt in sorting out the patterns and dynamics of complexity and its relevance to allocating capital.

I first met William Grassie in 2015, when I invited him to speak on Big History, at the suggestion of one of the discipline's key thought leaders, David Christian, at our firm's annual internal research retreat. I asked him specifically to discuss why Big History might matter to value investors. I was certainly intrigued by this religion scholar who studied in Jerusalem, spoke Hebrew (among other languages), taught German students about the Holocaust, and wrote academic books and articles primarily about science. Grassie was such a great opening act for our research team with his compelling lecture that we invited him back the next year. I challenged him to enhance his understanding of economics and finance as a part of *his* continuous learning too. That was the start of a yearlong collaboration, sharing and discussing a stream of essays, articles, and books. And so began this project, *Applied Big History*, in which I am pleased to have played a small role in instigating and supporting.

As renowned investor and Vice Chairman of Berkshire Hathaway, Charlie Munger, points out, "no one can know everything, but you can work to understand the big important models in each discipline at a basic level so they can collectively add value in a decision-making process." According to Munger, a multidisciplinary approach allows us to simplify complexity, remove blind spots and see reality more clearly in order to bring about a better outcome. In practical terms, investors need to understand how companies function in diverse sectors of an interdependent global economy, as well as how the changing macroeconomic context impacts the performance of those enterprises. The focus on short-term returns in business and finance can blind us to the larger drama playing out over human history. It is a timeline of booms and busts, ups and downs, but against the backdrop of escalating long-term growth. Big History is one of several distinct but related mental models that deal effectively, in my view, with this complexity on the macro and micro scale. As the broadest macro lens, Big History captures the origin of our universe, solar system, planets, and *us* – human beings who as a species have the distinct capability of collective learning. It draws appropriately from multiple subjects and branches of knowledge to reframe and solve problems outside of their usual parameters. This strategy is key to embracing complexity at the micro and macro levels and applying that understanding to complex situations and securities.

The Great Acceleration of the last hundred years, as documented in this book, is a stunning achievement—many more humans living longer with vastly more and better health and wealth. In my six plus decades, the human population has tripled, from 2.5 to 7.5 billion people accompanied by an eighty-fold increase in Global World Production, from an estimated $1 trillion to over $80 trillion today (World Bank Data). These dramatic increases over the last decades are highly dependent on scientific discovery, technological innovation, and enhanced cooperation between humans. With our species' tremendous success comes also daunting, new challenges—environmental, cultural, political, economic, scientific, and philosophical. These are best understood and addressed with the help of Big History.

It is a story of emergent complexity. Hydrogen and helium fuel solar furnaces that give rise to heavier elements. Elements join together to form molecules. Molecules become living cells. Cells become organisms. Organisms create ecosystems. Ecosystems evolve with the cells and organisms. As bigger organisms and bigger ecosystems evolve, they achieve economies of scale and in rare moments increasing rates of return. The process is epigenetic, meaning that it is structured by dynamic interactions between gene expression and the environment in the development of organisms.

Such is a similar case in economics. Individuals are consumers and producers. Individuals join together to form communities and companies in order to achieve economies of scale and network effects. Companies cooperate and compete in the market. The market landscape is analogous to an ecosystem, one that is also dynamic and evolving. Businesses struggle to profit, grow, adapt, and survive in economic environments. The process is similar to epigenetics in which causal pathways are bottom-up, top-down, and side-to-side. Many companies bottom-up and side-to-side contribute to the macro-economic context, while the macro-economic context constrains top-down the development of companies.

In this book, Grassie gives us intellectual tools to understand Big History at different times and scales. He fleshes out the dynamics of emergence in nature in the first two chapters—"The Great Matrix" and "The Economy of a Single Cell." These chapters are expansive and memorable recaps of fundamental science. Critically, he develops our understanding of energy, matter, and ingenuity in the evolution of biological complexity and by extension economic growth. A lot to grok, as Billy likes to say.

Energetics is a big theme throughout the book, which Grassie understands to be "the currency of the Universal Central Bank, as guaranteed by the Laws of Thermodynamics." On offer are "variable rates of losses in a predictable flux that impacts every domain at every scale. Energy dissipates. Entropy grows. That's not a problem. That's the singular opportunity." He suggests that the prime directive of evolution, one we replicate in the evolution of our technology and societies, is to "minimize entropy and maximize creativity." Ingenuity is how we minimize while maximizing.

In chapter four, Grassie turns to "Complexity Economics," using the insights, scales, analogies, and metaphors from the earlier chapters to interpret economic theory and history as an exponential flux of energy, matter, and ingenuity. Along the way, he introduces concepts like complex adaptive systems, turbulence, chaos, feedback, tipping points, energy density flow, information density, economies of scale, exponentiality, natural and economic selection, Goldilocks gradients, creative destruction, energy regimes, instability, and resilience. He argues that instability is an endogenous feature of economic markets, much as storms are essential features of the weather.

The story of Big History is also the story of human evolution. In a chapter titled "Your Hunter-Gatherer Brain," Grassie show how cognitive biases evolved over hundreds of thousands of years in the survival and reproduction of our hunter-gatherer tribal ancestors and continue to influence our thought and behavior today. Investors beware.

As mentioned in the introduction, Grassie wonders how humans in the Great Acceleration of the last hundred years, have come to cheat the logic of Malthus and Darwin. In a chapter titled "The Big Lollapalooza," Grassie explores how a number of big historians try to account for the dramatic and accelerating rise of our species— collective learning, network effects, artificial instincts, energy capture, exponential ingenuity, and gene-culture coevolution. Humans cooperate to compete and compete to cooperate.

Past performance is no guarantee of future success, as they say in the investing business. This is also true of our species. Grassie devotes a chapter to "Existential Threats," in which he offers a short list of man-made and natural threats to human wellbeing and survival. He explores in depth two "contrarian" case studies—peak humanity and climates changing. He encourages readers to thoughtfully prepare for all manner of disasters, but to also not let "negativity bias" cloud judgement. Similarly, he encourages businesses and investors to have staying power, such that they can re-enter markets after major disruptions. At the species level, staying power for humans means passing on knowledge and knowhow to survivors on the other side of future evolutionary bottlenecks.

In the last chapter, The Bottom Line, Grassie draws conclusions and precepts from this expansive book. In life and in economics, we are all capturing and creating value in the need to energize complexity, growth, maintenance, repair, and reproduction. While innovation and entrepreneurship are the engines of capitalism, Grassie points out that finance also plays a critical role in preventing the engines from freezing up. At 7.5 percent of US GDP, Grassie argues that finance, including the insurance industry, are relatively efficient lubrication in functional economies.

As one might expect of a philosopher and religion scholar, the last chapter takes a broader understanding of "values investing" than I learned in business school. "Sacred, moral, and aesthetic values transcend cost-benefit analyses," writes Grassie. "And while there is much disagreement about what counts for good, true, and beautiful values around the world, these are potent categories that profoundly shape human behavior beyond the ken of transactional economic analyses."

Grassie's exposition is careful, concise, informative, and engaging in telling and applying this origin story to the investment world. One of the many virtues of this book is the sheer number of experts that Grassie cites. The references in *Applied Big History are* thus a great guide for further study on a wide variety of topics.

Big History, along with systems and design thinking, complexity economics, behavioral finance and other related disciplines are all aspects of what I call "artisanal intelligence" in contrast to artificial intelligence. Artisanal intelligence as applied by value investors answers Munger's call for a "latticework of mental models" to make better decisions, by identifying complexity as a core principle to be analyzed and actualized.

For example, from the perspective of Big History, the stock and flow dynamics of micro and macro balance sheets interacting and evolving fundamentally can be seen as the accumulation and channeling of energy and matter through information and ingenuity to create value and wealth. Big History views the universe as islands of low entropy and organized complexity amidst the vast presence of increasingly high entropy and disorganization. This concept is an important way of framing value and wealth creation, preservation, and destruction in business and finance. Value investors in complex situations and securities are often faced with gaps and cracks on both sides of micro and macro balance sheets — that is, holes and discontinuities in the economics and finances of consumers, businesses, countries, etc. The way in which these holes constantly and dynamically appear and disappear, as well as grow and shrink, can be likened to the capture of the stock and flows of energy and matter enabled and transformed by information and ingenuity — collective learning, creativity, socialization, etc. To this point, as technology and artificial intelligence assume a larger share of automated tasks, the relentless data flow and processing power in this age of technological acceleration spark innovations and disruptions that are unplanned, uncontrolled and incomprehensible. Big History can help investors prepare for and interpret these events along with the endogenous and exogenous risks characteristic of a complex, evolving world.

The overarching question is whether Big History, specifically and artisanal intelligence, generally enhance an investor's understanding of the wealth preservation and creation process and the earnings and staying power of companies and investment portfolios. Further, does that understanding lead to better risk and return performance. I am of the affirmative view. William Grassie's book provides the micro and macro origin story that underpins the wealth creation process of the investment landscape. He grounds economic theories in the fundamentals of physics, chemistry, biology and history, giving us a realistic picture of how things work from the bottom-up and the top-down. He helps us identify and observe fit patterns common in business and nature and understand emergence, chaos and complexity in economics and evolution. Grassie uses economic metaphors to explain cell biology and biological metaphors to understand economics. These are among the themes *Applied Big History* tackles.

This book won't replace the skilled, detailed, and situation specific work of valuing and investing in particular securities, financial structures, businesses, industries and geographies. Big History, notes Grassie, "gives us little contextual insight into the diverse pathways actualized in any particular evolutionary or economic niche." The general principles, however, are extremely important. A fellow well-known hedge fund manager is reputed to have said, "If you don't do macro, macro will do *you!*" Well, *Applied Big History* does macro *and* micro. It zooms elegantly in and out, between the two throughout this engaging book by applying the general principles of acquired scientific and historical knowledge available to us today. As a result, we learn that value and wealth represent not just the flow and accumulation of money, but also stand for the fundamentals of energy, matter, and ingenuity that flow in and out of the economy and the financial system.

These dynamics appear in different ways across individuals, private organizations and businesses, and government institutions. *Applied Big History* essentially argues that the fundamental scientific and social structures of economies and financial markets impact business and investor behaviors, and business and investor behaviors impact those structures. Consequently, *Applied Big History,* as the subtitle implies, may well be a crucial addition to Munger's "latticework of mental models" for investors, business leaders and entrepreneurs, policy makers and regulators, and beyond.

It is well worth finding out.

Mitch Julis
Canyon Partners

And the things best to know are first principles and causes. For through them and from them all other things may be known but not they through the things covered by them. . . . But these things, the most universal, are perhaps the most difficult things for men to grasp, for they are farthest removed from the senses.

— Aristotle
Metaphysics
Book I
350 B.C.E.

Chapter 1:
Thriving in a Complex World

This book is written as a guide for doing good and doing well in a fast-changing world. It is intended for all living things, but especially for entrepreneurs and investors. The ambitious goal of this book is to show how economics, business, and finance can be better understood through the lens of "Big History"—a metanarrative that captures the 13.8-billion-year journey of our universe, the 4.5-billion-year evolution of our planet, the million-year rise of our species, and the 10,000-year accelerating drama of human civilization. Understanding this epic of evolution from multiple perspectives gives investors, entrepreneurs, and other living things a competitive edge today in a world of uncertainties. Through the lens of Big History, we will build what the famed investor Charlie Munger called "a latticework of mental models" that will help you to understand "the big ideas from all the big disciplines."[1]

Big History is the term de jure. During my graduate studies in the early 1990s we used terms like "the epic of evolution," "the new cosmology," "the journey of the universe," "the history of nature," "the great story," or simply, "the cosmos." By whatever name, it is all the same story with different titles, and told with different emphases and interpretations. The whole story of the whole cosmos involves astronomy, physics, chemistry, geology, biology, anthropology, history, psychology, technology, economics, and more. I like to call it "our common story," because for the first time we have an origins story that transcends ethnic, political, religious, and linguistics differences.

This book is written for people who have forgotten or who never properly learned basic science, or for that matter, economics and finance. And if you're of a certain age, your exposure to the sciences in high school or college is partly out-of-date. What we remember and what we forget are determined by whether or not we use that knowledge. You won't find many physicians, for instance, who remember much of undergraduate calculus, physics, or organic

---

[1] Charles Munger, "Usc Law School Commencement Address, May 1, 2007," Genius.com, http://genius.com/Charlie-munger-usc-law-commencement-speech-annotated.

chemistry, though once they excelled in those subjects. Science is not like riding a bicycle, which, once learned, stays with you all your life. If you don't use it, you quickly lose whatever knowledge you've acquired. This is particularly the case when the knowledge is fragmented and compartmentalized out of context. Science is complicated, changing, and burdened with too much technical jargon. Most people consult science on an as-need basis and otherwise stay clear of it. Science may seem irrelevant to their lives. And the gap between the specialized knowledge of the few and the general knowledge of the many continues to grow.

This book is not about specialization, but rather about learning how to weave all the specializations together in a useful framework that you can use every day in your work and in your life. My goal in this book is to acquaint you with basic science in a fun and memorable manner through the lens of Big History and to show how this new understanding of the universe and its evolution can inform business and investing in particular and life in general.

Among the many big ideas to be discussed is the history of the great acceleration in human population and consumption patterns during the twentieth century. How did our species come to grow exponentially, cheating the logic of Darwin and Malthus? How does the $117 trillion global economy of over seven billion people function? What might cause it to dysfunction? And how might our species, and your business, continue to prosper in the future?

The evolution of money and its recent exponential growth is astounding. Our global economy is quantitatively and qualitatively different from anything in the past. Ecologists and geologists now refer to our era as the Anthropocene—the age of humans. It is certainly the end of the Holocene, which comprises the ten thousand years since the retreat of the last ice age. We will explore what Big History might mean for economics, finance, and the evolution of our species and the planet. We will learn about complex adaptive systems, collective learning, and how to calculate value based on the evolutionary formula of energy, matter, and ingenuity.

Applying Big History to understanding business and finance will inform economic trends, niche opportunities, and endogenous dangers in the economic landscape of the twenty-first century. We will gain new perspectives on how to create and capture value in physics and biology and in business and finance. By studying the epic of evolution,

2

we will come to understand emergent complexity, creative destruction, and micro-macro dynamics in nature and society.

I take investing to also be a metaphor for life. I take the challenges of managing a portfolio to be a proxy for also managing a business and a career. We invest in education. We invest much of our waking hours at work. We invest in our homes, family, and friends. We invest time, energy, and attention in all manner of endeavors, hopefully growing in riches broadly defined and difficult to measure. Big History is therefore relevant not only to managing your portfolio and business, but also to managing your life. By focusing finance, instead of the diverse landscape of companies, we gain useful macro-perspectives. In discussing investments, portfolios, and markets below, feel free to substitute terms that might better capture the dynamics within your profession, company, cooperators, and competitors.

Outperforming the Market

The investment landscape provides an overview of the ecological contexts in which businesses cooperate and compete to provide goods and services to consumers in a now global market. To be sustainable, businesses must profit in particular niches. While entrepreneurship is the engine of capitalism, focusing on finance provides an important insight into the evolution of wealth creation in history and economics.

Beating the market—in other words, outperforming the index funds like the S&P 500—is not an easy undertaking. The consensus of the market at any one time dictates that most fund managers will not beat the averages in the competition of buying low and selling high.

In an efficient market, as idealized by traditional economics, it would not be possible to beat the averages. If everyone was perfectly rational with perfect information, there would be no disagreement on price, or so the theory goes. Of course, markets, like people, are not perfect. Inefficient markets seethe with disagreements and passions, booms and busts. This gives rise to the possibility of being lucky, even dumb lucky. But luck is hardly a sustainable investment strategy.

Another way to beat the market is to cheat or steal. One can acquire insider information. One can bribe, coerce, and collude. This can be done in both illegal and legal ways, depending on the context. One can also "make a market" or "front run" transactions. In a market without rules, where anything goes, relative power determines the winners and losers. That's another way to outperform the market.

Day traders sometimes beat the market. Pattern seeking in the daily flux of stocks, however, has evolved into high-frequency trading. The new day traders use computer algorithms to buy and sell securities in microseconds. Of the trades made every day on Wall Street, 50 to 80 percent are high-frequency trades exploiting the inherent chaos and complexity of markets.[2] This has been an extremely successful strategy for some with the requisite mathematical expertise and powerful, high-speed computer resources, but as we will see, complexity theory in economics suggests that high-speed trading by computer algorithm may actually create more chaos in the end.

Another way to beat the market is through value investing, as advocated by Benjamin Graham and practiced by Warren Buffet, Charlie Munger, John Templeton, and others. Value investing seeks to buy undervalued stocks in well-managed companies with long-term prospects for growth. Value investors are looking for long-term growth, not a get-rich-quick scheme. Benjamin Graham, the grandfather of value investing, understood that "Mister Market" had bipolar disorder, oscillating between manic highs and low depressions.[3] Graham's recipe for successful value investing involved a rigorous assessment of the fundamentals of a company (price, earnings, balance sheet, prospects, management, market sector), acquiring ownership below the "real" value of the company so as to provide a safety cushion from normal price fluctuations, and a long-term commitment to the company. Value investors tend to buy, diversify, and hold.

In a complex world with complex markets, governed by rules restricting our vices and follies, there are opportunities to beat the market, even if the law of averages is against you. One can craft superior long-term and short-term strategies. One can identify and exploit structural changes better and earlier than others, and recognize and exploit instabilities. And one can arbitrage widespread errors of collective inference and pricing. In short, complexity economics provides lots of opportunities for growing income and wealth. Of course, this includes the possibility of losing income and wealth. As the saying goes, luck favors the prepared mind. This book is an exercise in preparing your mind.

---

[2] Seth Shobhit, "The World of High Frequency Algorithmic Trading," Investopedia, https://www.investopedia.com/articles/investing/091615/world-high-frequency-algorithmic-trading.asp.

[3] Benjamin Graham, *The Intelligent Investor* (New York: Harper, 1949).

To understand energy, technology, food, population, politics, religion, and other global challenges, you need to understand Big History. It is essential to understand how the world came to be the way it is and why people are the way they are. The major problems in the world today look different from the perspective of Big History, and the solutions to those problems become clearer. This is why I am so passionate about Big History and hope to persuade you to be as well.

Caveat Emptor

I, William Grassie, your humble guide, have spent the last forty years studying global trends and contemporary science. I began my journey as a star-struck boy in the 1960s contemplating the night sky, the Apollo space program, Carl Sagan's *Cosmos*, and the voyages of the Starship Enterprise. It continued through my many years of schooling and travel. This included an undergraduate degree in political science and international relations and a doctorate in comparative religion. My doctoral dissertation explored what it would mean to treat the modern scientific cosmology as a mythopoetic creation story.[4] And I fell down this rabbit hole.

I don't have a CFA or an MBA. I am not an economist by training. I have never worked in finance. I don't trade stocks and bonds. Nor am I formally trained as a scientist. It is not necessarily clear how a doctorate in religious studies qualifies me to authoritatively discuss economics and finance, let alone physics and biology.

Philosophical hermeneutics and therefore also philosophy of science, were a big part of my graduate training. Hermeneutics is the theory of interpretation and first arises in the disciplines of interpreting sacred texts, historical events, and jurisprudence. As I learned writing my dissertation many years ago, the interpretation of the epic of evolution is hardly straight forward.

The term *hermeneutics* invokes the Greek god Hermes, who was a messenger between the gods of Olympus, the gods of the Hades, and mortal humans. Hermeneutics is thus the "craft of Hermes." Renamed Mercury in the Roman tradition, Hermes was unique in the ancient pantheon as the singular translator between worlds. He was also

---

[4] William J. Grassie, *Reinventing Nature: Science Narratives as Myths for an Endangered Planet* (Philadelphia: doctoral dissertation, Temple University Department of Religion, 1994).

something of a trickster. Interpretation turns out to be remarkably complicated and can make fools of us all.

I imagine that there are at least six possible "big" interpretations of Big History:

1. Stoic, existentialist, atheist[5]
2. Evolutionary spiritual, theist[6]
3. Techno-utopic[7]
4. Eco-romantic[8]
5. Free market, libertarian[9]
6. Socialist-Communitarian[10]

This book is not about exploring or resolving those big debates about Big History. Indeed, I do not think these six interpretations are necessarily mutually exclusive and are in any case context-dependent and involve emplotments and predictions about a future which may or may not come to pass based on the "correct" ideology-interpretation. Rather, it is my more limited goal to apply insights from the sciences to better understand business, economics, and finance. This will involve "a close reading of the text," in this case the new book of nature and humans as understood by contemporary science.

The Latin root of the word *religion* is verb *religare*, meaning "to tie together." In this larger sense, a doctorate in religious studies is actually an excellent preparation for this endeavor. And religions, as we understand the term today, are at the very least a complex manifestation of human nature, utilizing symbolic systems of value that radically change the world—not unlike money. Of course, religion and

---

[5] See for instance, Richard Dawkins, *The Blind Watchmaker: Why the Evidence of Evolution Reveals a Universe without Design* (New York: Norton, 1986); *The God Delusion* (New York: Houghton Mifflin, 2006); Daniel C. Dennett, *Darwin's Dangerous Idea: Evolution and the Meaning of Life* (New York: Simon & Schuster, 1995); *Breaking the Spell: Religion as a Natural Phenomenon* (New York: Viking, 2006).

[6] Ian Barbour, *Religion in an Age of Science: The Gifford Lectures 1989-1991*, vol. Volume One (San Francisco: Harper, 1990); Holmes Rolston, *Genes, Genesis, and God: Values and Their Origins in Natural and Human History* (New York: Cambridge University Press, 1998); John Haught, *God after Darwin: A Theology of Evolution* (Boulder, CO: Westview, 2000).

[7] Ray Kurzweil, *The Singularity Is Near: When Humans Transcend Biology* (New York: Penguin Books, 2005).

[8] Thomas Berry and Brian Swimme, *Universe Story, The: From the Primordial Flaring Forth to the Ecozoic Era* (San Francisco, CA: Harper, 1992).

[9] Matt Ridley, *The Evolution of Everything: How New Ideas Emerge* (New York: HarperCollins, 2015).

[10] John B. Cobb Jr. and Herman Daly, *For the Common Good: Redirecting the Economy toward Community, the Environment, and a Sustainable Future* (Boston: Beacon Press, 1989).

commerce are not really the same, but money certainly is a symbolic system of value, more powerful and more universal than any religion today. Whether in metal, paper, or digital form, money is always virtual—a useful social fiction—that dramatically changes the facts of life. Or so we will learn. I hope to surprise you with orthogonal and sometimes contrarian insights. *Applied Big History* builds a common foundation across disciplines, helping to unify knowledge and know-how currently fragmented in specialized guilds and trades, of which finance is one.

For decades now, through my career, curiosities, and concerns, I have been professionally involved in addressing big questions and big problems, in and out of higher education, philanthropy, research, writing, and social entrepreneurship. I have been blessed with opportunities to learn from great scientists, philosophers, theologians, entrepreneurs, and investors. Many of whom are cited in these pages. We have wrestled with great debates in philosophy, anthropology, psychology, evolution, economics, technology, conflict, and social change. I especially follow the new discoveries about our common origins, our evolved human natures, and the accelerating drama of our global civilization. Charlie Munger, the famed partner at Berkshire Hathaway I cited earlier, is a fan of multidisciplinary techniques. Munger recounts:

> So I went through life constantly practicing this . . . approach. Well I can't tell you what that's done for me, it's made life more fun, it's made me more constructive, it's made me more helpful to others, it's made me enormously rich . . . [11]

While not formally trained in economics and finance, I have been fortunate to find many mentors and guides, so I can say with confidence that we have important things to explore and debate together. I bring to this endeavor a large bibliography accumulated over several decades of study. For the last few years, I have religiously read *The Economist*, the *Financial Times*, and *Barron's*. My approach is partly that of an anthropologist in a distant land, trying to translate the practices, culture, and languages of tribal groups that trade in securities and by extension the vagaries of businesses in a complex economic ecology.

---

[11] UCLA Law School Munger, "Usc Law School Commencement Address, May 1, 2007".

Applied Big History

It is extraordinary how much humanity has come to know. Collective learning has allowed our species to exponentially accumulate knowledge and know-how. Indeed, most of what we now know about Big History in detail, we learned in the last fifty years.

It turns out that the universe and the economy can be understood as complex thermodynamic flows of energy, matter, and ingenuity. Both nature and markets manifest common dynamics as sometimes chaotic systems, in which we discover thresholds, tipping points, Goldilocks parameters, feedback loops, nonlinear dynamics, scaling effects, deterministic chaos, and patterns of emergent and truly elegant complexity. Nature, appropriately interpreted, can and should inform investment and business decisions.

Applied Big History helps investors and entrepreneurs learn how to zoom into the details and zoom out to the big picture, back and forth, taking multiple viewpoints on decision across time frames and scales. In so doing, the investor and entrepreneurs learns analytic, associative, and inductive thought processes essential to success. *Applied Big History* provides an essential framework for successful capital managers and business leaders by uniting microeconomic and macroeconomic perspectives, anticipating market instabilities, and building resilient businesses and portfolios.

These insights and habits of mind are not just relevant to investors and entrepreneurs. The applied part of Big History impacts how we conceive every career and industry, every academic discipline and vocation, every problem and opportunity. Every aspect of your career and life can be reframed as a "little Big History"—a story that you will be equipped to narrate by the end of this book.

Big History is not simply an esoteric scholastic endeavor. Indeed, many global thought leaders recognize Big History as a powerful pedagogical tool for promoting general literacy in the twenty-first century. The narrative approach—from the Big Bang to the twenty-first century—provides a mnemonic to help students understand and remember the many details of science and history. It provides a framework for understanding, debating, and solving the great challenges of our time. It provides an ennobling perspective on our lives, generating wonder, awe, amazement, and gratitude. Bill Gates was inspired to create the Big History Project, a free, online curriculum for high school students now used in about three thousand classrooms around the world.[12]

Numerous books have been written about Big History. David Christian, Fred Spier, Eric Chaisson, Yuval Hariri, Sean Carol, and others have penned excellent books that use this approach to explain the many insights offered by contemporary science.[13] Dorling Kindersley Books (DK) recently published a 400-hundred-page textbook on Big History with spectacular illustrations and content. This twenty-first century version of an illuminated manuscript might well be your best Bible to Big History.[14] It also makes a great gift to growing minds.

My book is not another chronological retelling of Big History. Nor do I offer much background information about the history of various scientific discoveries—how we came to know what is presented here as factual. When appropriate I will point out where there are evolving debates within scientific disciplines. This book gives you some sense of the chronology of Big History. Important thresholds in the rise of complexity, including our human complexity, will be noted. It is my intention, however, to jump around from the micro- to the macro- to the meso-levels and back again. The ability to adopt multiple perspectives will help you to better understand the creation and capture of value and wealth. Feel free to skim and jump around. For instance, you might not need a refresher on fundamental science or cell biology in the next two chapters, but you might want to pay attention to how and why I frame emergent complexity.

This book will not help you pass the CFA exams. Nor is it likely to help you obtain an MBA or any other professional certification. It will give you a larger macro perspective for understanding the predictions and choices that make up portfolio and business management. As hedge fund manager Daniel Och said, "If you don't do macro, macro will do you." Big History is as macro as we can get.

One of the things we learn from studying Big History is how incredibly lucky we are to live at this moment in the natural history of

[12] Bill Gates et al., "The Big History Project," http://www.bighistoryproject.com.

[13] David Christian, *Maps of Time: An Introduction to Big History* (Berkeley, CA: University of California Press, 2004, 2011); Fred Spier, *Big History and the Future of Humanity* (New York: Wiley-Blackwell, 2011); Eric Chaisson, *Epic of Evolution: Seven Ages of the Cosmos* (New York: Columbia University Press, 2006); Yuval Noah Harari, *Sapiens: A Brief History of Humankind*, Kindle ed. (New York: HarperCollins, 2015); Sean Carroll, *The Big Picture* (New York: Dutton, 2017).

[14] Elise Bohan et al., *Big History* (New York: DK, 2016).

our planet and the cultural evolution of our species. Pharaoh and Caesar would trade places with any of us to have the same opportunities for health and wealth, travel and education, entertainment and food. It helps to have this larger perspective on our lives to weather the daily onslaught of bad news, as well as the ups and downs of the market. It puts our immediate worries in perspective.

Still, past performance is no guarantee of future success, as they say in finance. This is true for us individually, for your managed funds, for your business, and for our global civilization. Humanity faces some grave challenges with which we are ill equipped to deal, but understanding Big History can significantly shift the odds in our favor.

Throughout the book I use the word "grok" to describe the desired outcome. The verb "grok" was coined by Robert Heinlein in his 1961 science fiction novel *Stranger in a Strange Land*. The word has now entered the English language. The Oxford English Dictionary defines "grok" as "to understand intuitively or by empathy, to establish rapport with" and "to empathize or communicate sympathetically (with); also, to experience enjoyment." Bill Gates groks Big History. He writes:

> Today, whenever I learn something new about biology or history or just about any other subject, I try to fit it into the framework I got from Big History. No other course has had as big an impact on how I think about the world.[15]

My hope is that you, too, will internalize Big History in your life so that it becomes implicit knowledge always at the ready. My hope is that you will see old things with new eyes. May you come to also grok Big History!

Wikipedia

This book is dedicated to Wikipedia, and not just because it is a constant companion in my research and writing. Wikipedia is an icon for collective learning—the process by which knowledge and know-how accumulates in human networks spanning generations and geographies. Founded in 2001, today Wikipedia is the tenth most-visited website in the world. There are editions of Wikipedia in 295 languages. Half the traffic is on the English-language edition, which

---

[15] Ibid.

contains 5.4 million articles.[16] Scientific and technical entries are particularly reliable and up-to-date. This is not always the case with highly politicized or obscure topics, but for the most part, Wikipedia is a place to find facts—a good place to get a reality check on a wide variety of topics. Wikipedia receives hundreds of millions of visitors and many billions of pageviews every month. And it's free!

Collective learning is also largely free—a rare example of positive economic externality. It is the foundation of our evolutionary and economic success story. Knowledge and know-how are passed on and accumulated exponentially. Proficiencies, however, are hard to acquire. Decades of rigorous training are often required to master a technical profession. Moreover, every generation must be taught anew, lest what we have so recently learned be forgotten. If our descendants are going to succeed, come what may on our restless planet, they must never forget what our generation has been so fortunate to recently learn—a new, practical, evolving, and inspirational story of the universe and ourselves. It is our duty to ensure that what we have received and recently learned not be forgotten but only added to and improved upon. This is how our species has and will continue to succeed. From this vantage point, we come to understand education in all its forms as a sacred intergenerational duty; but first I need to show you how Big History gives you an edge when facing the challenges of business, economics, and finance. Here begins a 13.8-billion-year journey into territory and topics rarely discussed in classrooms, let alone in boardrooms or on trading floors.

---

[16] "Wikipedia," Wikipedia Foundation, https://en.wikipedia.org/wiki/Wikipedia.

Chapter 2:
The Great Matrix of Being

Learning "the big ideas of all the big disciplines," as famed investor Charlie Munger suggested earlier, is not really all that hard. Indeed, he claims it is both fun and profitable. He recommends building "a latticework of mental modules."[17]

Another word for lattice is "matrix." A matrix is a structure, medium, or environment in which something develops. Matrices can be physical, biological, social, or mathematical. They can be a mold that shapes organisms, such as the intercellular matrices in our body. In mathematical usage, a matrix is like a spreadsheet—a grid of quantities and formulas, charts and comparisons, statistics and accounts, or, more abstractly, geometric possibility spaces. The etymology of the word matrix is from the Latin for "womb" or "mother." We might also title this chapter "the Great Womb of All Beings."

In all of these senses, including that of the creative maternal, we begin by considering the "Great Matrix" as discovered and elucidated by science. I find this metaphor and mnemonic a useful way to navigate a lot of science in diverse disciplines. Everything that exists in the universe, every process that science has discovered, every power of nature, everything that constitutes our human bodies and brains, our histories and cultures—all this and more—can be located within a number of hierarchies and scales involving size, time, matter, energetics, electromagnetism, sound, information-ingenuity, sentience-consciousness, culturally constructed hierarchies, all resulting in emergent complexity. There are other scales and hierarchies, to be sure, but these ten natural scales are the warp and woof of the universe upon which all complexity is woven. Recognizing this is the first step toward applying Big History to understanding "all the big ideas of all the big disciplines."

---

[17] Munger, "Usc Law School Commencement Address, May 1, 2007".

Size

It takes some effort to grok the scales of size from the macrocosm to the microcosm as discovered by science. How can we internalize the new scales of science that extend far beyond our direct sense perceptions? Most of science is by definition counter-intuitive. You can't see much of what science is about—it's too large or too small, too fast or too slow. The existentialist in you may stay awake at night pondering how big the universe is, but it is perhaps more instructive to pay attention to how small entities can be. The known universe is as many orders of magnitude smaller than us as it is larger.

The smallest units in particle physics are the Planck units. Beyond the Planck scale, the concepts of size and distance break down and quantum indeterminacy becomes absolute—whatever that means. You need to find a particle physicist to make more sense of these subatomic realms in which matter turns into miniscule fields and forces.

From the Planck scale we jump about twenty-four orders of magnitude in size past the scale of the subatomic particle to the scale of simple atoms. The diameter of a single hydrogen atom—one proton, one electron, and a lot of empty space—is approximately 0.1 nm (nanometers). Just to be clear, one nanometer (10^{-9} m) is a billion times smaller than one meter.

Amino acids—small molecules essential to cell chemistry and varying in atomic composition—are approximately 0.8 nm in size. The DNA (deoxyribonucleic acid) molecule is about 2 nanometers wide but varies dramatically in length. DNA has an aperiodic property that allows it to encode information for cell construction and replication. The longest human DNA is found in chromosome 1 and consists of 220 million base pairs. When stretched out it would be about 85 millimeters long and very, very thin. In terms of length, human genome has some 3 billion DNA base pairs, but that's nothing compared to the marbled lungfish genome, which clocks in at 133 billion base pairs. At the other end of the DNA spectrum is the diminutive bacteria *Carsonella ruddii* with the smallest-known genome containing 159,662 base pairs.

Prokaryotes—single-cell bacteria and archaea—are the smallest and ur-units of life. A teaspoon of ocean water contains a million prokaryotes and ten times as many viruses.[18] The smallest bacteria are about 150–250 nm long. The bacterium *E. coli*, part of your large

---

[18] Edward De Long, "Deciphering the Ocean's Microbiome," (Simons Foundation 2017).

intestinal microbiome, measures approximately 2 μm (micrometers, or microns). Here, we have moved up in the scale a thousand-fold, from nanos to microns, from 10^{-9} m to 10^{-6} m.

It takes imagination to grasp these jumps in orders of magnitude. At the other end of the size spectrum, we measure in light-years, which in spite of its name is a measurement of distance, not time. One light-year is the distance that a photon travels in one Earth year—9.4 trillion kilometers, in case you were wondering. The most distant entity known observationally in the universe is the background radiation from the Big Bang, which can be found 13.8 billion light-years away from Earth. If you multiply 9.4 trillion kilometers by 13.8 billion, you get a really big number and an incomprehensible distance to grasp.

To get a feel for the relative size and scale of the universe, imagine holding a big beach ball 1 meter in diameter. It is summer and you're vacationing on Cape Cod, Massachusetts. If this beach ball were the size of the sun, then the next closest star, Proxima Centauri, would be another beach ball 6609 km away—the flight distance from Boston to Rome (the actual distance is 4.2 light-years).

On the other hand, if your 1-meter-diameter beach ball were the size of our Milky Way galaxy, then the next closest galaxy—the Andromeda galaxy—would be another beach ball 25-meters away (the actual distance is 2.5 million light-years). Indeed, at the scale of the galaxies, everywhere you looked on the beach that day, above, below, and all around, you would see beach ball galaxies in all directions—a hundred billion of them. In scale, galaxies are quite close to each other and gravitationally bound in a vast moving web, while the distance between stars within the galaxies is enormous and for the most part gravitationally not interactive with neighboring stars. When galaxies collide, as Andromeda and the Milky Way some day will, they pass through each other and nary a star will collide. The universe is a web of a hundred billion galaxies held together in a dynamic gravitational embrace.

The tendency is to focus on how puny we are in the scale of hundreds of billions of galaxies spanning billions of light-years, but we should also remember how enormous we are when compared with cells, molecules, atoms, and subatomic particles. Humans exist at scales measured in millimeters, centimeters, meters, and kilometers, which turns out to be about halfway between the very small and the very large. Given the building blocks of atoms, molecules, and cells, the human scale is also the only scale where certain types of complexity can exist.

The Cosmic Uroboros is a graphic representation of the hierarchy of size. The image of a snake eating its own tail is a symbol appearing in ancient Egyptian, Greek, Norse, and Indian art. The symbol is thought to represent self-reflectivity and self-regeneration. In a rendering of the Uroboros by cosmologist Joel Primack and co-author Nancy Abrams, the hierarchy of size is plotted in powers of ten along the circle.[19] The universe is swallowing its own tail, because the very large scale of the universe loops back on the very small scale of subatomic particles. The particle accelerator at CERN recreates the intense energy of the early universe in order to study the constituents of matter. The sought-after "Grand Unified Theory" of fundamental physics would unite the four fundamental forces—gravity, electromagnetism, and the strong and weak atomic forces—connecting the subatomic and the cosmic dimensions, much as uroboros swallows its tail.

The first axis in the Great Matrix of all beings is size. Note again the curious fact, and perhaps necessity, that life exists halfway between the largest and smallest entities known to science. And take a moment also to cogitate and meditate on how your own being is built and functions bottom-up from small to ever-larger combinatorials of atoms, molecules, and cells.

Time

The time scales of the universe are measured today in billions of years down to the nanosecond vibrations of cesium in atomic clocks. We have discovered a progressively true account of the 13.8-billion-year history of the universe, the 4.5-billion-year evolution of our planet, the 300,000-year rise of our species, and the 10,000-year accelerating drama of human civilization. These chronologies represent how Big History is generally approached in books and curricula, telling the story as an integrated narrative of complexity thresholds from the Big Bang to the twenty-first century.[20]

In brief, our omnicentric universe began infinitesimally small some 13.8 billion years ago as something like infinite heat, infinite

---

[19] Joel R. Primack and Nancy Ellen Abrams, *The View from the Center of the Universe: Discovering Our Extraordinary Place in the Cosmos* (New York: Riverhead, 2006).
[20] See Christian, *Maps of Time: An Introduction to Big History*.

density, and total symmetry. This universe expanded, cooled, and evolved into more differentiated and complex structures—forces, quarks, hydrogen, helium, stars, galaxies, heavier elements, complex chemistry, and planetary systems.

Some 4 billion years ago, in a small second- or third-generation solar system, the intricate biophysical processes of life began on at least one small planet circling a diminutive, slow-burning star. Animate energy-matter on Earth was a marvelous new intensification of the creative dynamic at work in the universe. Life adapted, evolved, and became more complex. Fueled by the power of the sun, Earth became a jewel of a planet with ever more complex forms and relations giving rise to the wonders of the natural world.

Then, some 7 million years ago, proto-humans emerged on the savanna of Africa. By a million years ago, they mastered fire and made simple tools. About 80,000 years ago, a small band of *Homo sapiens* wandered out of Africa. With their tools, fire mastery, language, and collective learning, our ancestors spread across the planet. We are the only large mammals to inhabit so many diverse bioregions.

For most of our prehistory, our common ancestors were hunter-gatherers, living in small tribes, each one comprising probably not more than 150 individuals.[21] Our brains, instincts, emotions, and behavioral tendencies evolved to promote survival and reproduction in these small social groups in diverse environments. Then, 10,000 years ago, agriculture began, and with it came growing populations of humans living in ever-larger and more complex societies, accumulating knowledge and know-how, trading in genes, crops, animals, diseases, technologies, and ideas. The fossil fuel revolution began about 200 years ago, ushering in amazing growth in wealth and productivity. This unfolding leads us all the way to today, with over 7 billion of us collectively transforming the planet and ourselves. The wonder of it all is that each of us is also a collection of transient atoms—recycled stardust become conscious beings—engaged in this global conversation brought to you by ephemeral electrons and photons cascading through the Internet and bouncing off of satellites.

---

[21] Robin Dunbar, *Grooming, Gossip and the Evolution of Language* (Cambridge: Harvard University Press, 1996).

That is Big History, in about 300 words and with a little poetic license. The story is generally understood in thresholds of emergent complexity—the early universe gives rise to stars and galaxies, the stars give rise to the periodic tables of elements and complex chemistry, the chemistry gives rise to simple bacteria, the bacteria give rise to eukaryotic cells, eukaryotic cells give rise to the evolution of organisms, the plants and animals give rise to complex ecosystems with ever more sentient organisms, and sentience gave rise to human consciousness, tool-making, language, fire mastery, collective learning, agriculture, and the modern revolution. Throughout the chronology, increased complexity is hierarchical, built from the bottom up. Each threshold realizes new emergent properties and creates new possibility spaces that previously did not exist.

Einstein's theory of relativity, of course, links space and time in a continuum, so separating chronology and size scale is technically an artifact of our minds and not fundamental physics. Moreover, many of the equations of fundamental physics work forward or backward irrespective of time. And when we use terms such as "very fast," "ultra dense," "super hot," or "extreme cold," the concepts of space and time can become elastic, but in between these extremes, time matters. For all practical purposes—such as practicing applied science and managing your portfolio—it is necessary to keep space and time separate. Together, space and time provide the first two dimensions in the Great Matrix.

Matter

Technically, matter is solidified energy, as reflected in the iconic equation $E = mc^2$—energy equals matter times the speed of light squared. However, just as with space and time, matter and energy may reliably be understood as distinct, at least in the context of the Great Matrix that matters most to us here on Earth.

The stuff of the world around us—matter—has a scale and structure that extends from the Periodic Table of Elements down into the subatomic realm in the standard model of particle physics. The latter—particle physics—is beyond my ken and still the subject of ongoing research and debate. The scale of atomic elements, however, is well established and central to all chemistry.

Matter turns out to be a scarce commodity in the universe. The universe is composed of about 70 percent cold dark energy. Another 25

18

percent consists of cold dark matter. Cosmologists don't really know what these are—ergo, cold and dark—but infer their existence from the behavior of the web of galaxies in an expanding universe. Hydrogen and helium, the atoms that fuel the stars, constitute about 0.5 percent of the universe. All the other atoms in the Periodic Table of Elements constitute less than 0.01 percent of the universe. Fortunately, we live in a chemically rich solar system on a special planet. We are made of these remarkable and rare elements born of stars in this vast universe.

The character of elements is determined by the number of protons in their nucleus, along with variations in the number of neutrons and electrons bound to that nucleus (i.e., isotopes of elements). The discovery of periodicity and groupings of elements based on shared properties is one of the most remarkable achievements of science, leading to all manner of new discoveries in physics and biology, not to mention in engineering and technology. Chemistry may not have the same academic sex appeal as physics and biology, but it is the foundation upon which evolutionary and economic complexity builds.

Energetics

The intensity of energy flow is another axis in the Great Matrix. We can metaphorically equate energy with money. Energy does for nature what currencies do for human production and trade. And like all metaphors, it is literally not true. When Shakespeare calls time a beggar, he reminds us of our human finitude, but time is not literally a beggar. Metaphors are also important to science. Terms from computer science, for instance, are helpful in thinking about genetics, the neuroscience, and other fields.

Energetics is the currency of the Universal Central Bank, as guaranteed by the Laws of Thermodynamics. All of the regional banks—astronomy, chemistry, biology, technology, economics, culture—can create their own energy currencies and markets because of this omnipotent guarantee. The Universal Central Bank does not offer fixed rates of return, but rather variable rates of losses in a predictable flux that impacts every domain at every scale. Energy dissipates. Entropy grows. That's not a problem; that's the singular opportunity.

The First Law of Thermodynamics observes that energy can be transferred and transformed, but not created or destroyed. At the first instance of the Big Bang, the universe received its lifetime allotment of energy-matter. That energy allowance is still present, just redistributed and less concentrated as the universe expands.

Physicists calculate the energy of the universe at the moment of the Big Bang as 10^{19} GeV (billion electron volts). At the opposite end is absolute zero or minus 273.15 degrees Celsius (minus 459.67 degrees Fahrenheit).

The Second Law of Thermodynamics states that in a closed system, energy always dissipates from hot to cold, from order to disorder, from concentrations to entropy. What concerns us is not energy per se, but the flow of energy and the work that is done along the way.

Energy is the ability to transform a system—to do work. The Standard International (SI) unit of energy is the joule—defined as the energy required to lift a 100-gram object 1 meter vertically from the Earth's surface (i.e., against a gravitational force of 1 Newton). Lifting the object is mechanical work that creates a kinetic potential energy within a gravitational field of falling back down.

Physics distinguishes energy and power. Power is energy used over time. The SI unit of power is the Watt, defined as 1 Joule per second. That 100-watt light bulb is consuming 100 Joules per second, about the same amount of energy that your body is consuming, albeit in a different form. And that's where energetics gets complicated.

Electromagnetic, chemical, caloric, thermal, kinetic, electrical, nuclear, gravitational—energy comes in different forms that are qualitatively different. There is no standard currency for energy in nature and society, though there are lots of standard equations for converting one energy form into the equivalent of another energy form.

For instance, we can convert the combustion of gasoline into the equivalent of human labor—one gallon of gasoline is the equivalent of 11.6 days of labor. These calculations require multiple energy conversion, turning BTUs (British Thermal Units) into kilowatts into 2,500 food calories per day. We cannot, however, digest gasoline. It is a poison. The energy content of a single gallon of gasoline is equivalent to 28,977 food calories of energy, or fifty-one Big Mac hamburgers, to be precise.[22]

---

[22] One gallon of gasoline = 33.70 kWh = 28,977 kcal.
28,977 kcal @2500 kcal per day = food for 11.6 days of human labor.
28,977 kcal = 51 Big Macs @ 563 Kcal per hamburger.

These kinds of conversions neglect important qualitative differences in energy types, but are nevertheless informative. The energy contained in gasoline or the hamburgers themselves is not the same as energy flow (i.e., power)—it is stored, potential chemical energy. Energy flow is the controlled burning of hydrocarbons by a machine or the body. A gallon of gasoline has a lot more potential chemical energy than a gallon of you (which is mostly water), but the whole of you is able to harness the BTUs, kilowatts, and calories to amazing effects.

Humans are the only entity that we know of that *constructs* complexity outside of our bodies in built devices *using* external energy sources. It goes all the way back to the controlled use of fire. The Prometheus myth got it right. Fire mastery is a god-like gift that separates us from all other animals.

All complex phenomena in the universe can be characterized by a flux of energy from hot to cold, from order to disorder, as required by the Second Law of Thermodynamics. Living organisms excel at capturing energy to drive their creative processes.

One of the most counter-intuitive insights of modern science is the scale of energy flows. Astronomer Eric Chaisson is credited with these calculations and insights. He normalizes for the mass and time frame of each energetic system (ergs per second per gram) in order to estimate the energy density flow of different entities. It turns out that a single-cell eukaryote has an energy density flow 500 times that of our sun. A photosynthesizing plant has about 5,000 times the energy density flow of the sun. A mammalian body has about 20,000 times the energy density flow of the sun. The human brain, comprising about 2 percent of our body weight but consuming about 20 percent of our food energy, has an energy density flow about 75,000 times greater than that of the sun.

Of course, the sun is enormous, and the flow of energy from the sun to the cold of outer space—3.86×10^{26} watts—far exceeds that of our human bodies, consuming the equivalent of a 100-watt light bulb. Remember that we are normalizing for the mass of the system and its time scale. What this means is that if you could expand the mass of the human body—on average, 70 kilograms—to the mass of the sun—1.9×10^{30} kilograms—then it would be 20,000 times more energetic (assuming you could feed it enough hamburgers).

And if we include all of the energy consumed outside of our bodies in our global civilization, then humans today achieve energy density flows that average 250,000 times that of the sun. The privileged few of us who fly around the world—the energy rich—achieve energy density flows millions of times that of the sun. As we will explore in chapter five, this exponential growth in energy density flow extends to the evolution of life and our technology. Humans and our advanced machines may well achieve the greatest sustained energy density flows in the entire universe.[23]

Remember that there are three ways to increase energy density flow: (1) by consuming more energy (or more efficiently); (2) by compressing the time scale of the system; and (3) by decreasing the mass of the system. With too little energy (e.g., starvation) the system will collapse. With too much energy flow, the system will crash and burn. Each complex adaptive system has a range of optimal energy flows that are often limited within a narrow bandwidth, a kind of Goldilocks parameter.

There have been tremendous and accelerating increases in efficiency of our machines and technologies over the last 200 years. Much of this efficiency gain has been accomplished by reducing the mass of the system with new materials and technologies, as in the miniaturization that has occurred in electronics and computers, as well as the invention of more effective combustion processes that waste less heat.

The increases in efficiency over the last one hundred years are stunning. And yet, the overall consumption of energy continues to increase even as the technologies become more efficient. Our car engines are more efficient, but more of us drive more miles. Our planes are more efficient, but more of us fly more miles. Our furnaces and air conditioners are more efficient, but we have bigger houses. These gains in efficiency mean increases in energy density flow. Energy efficiency is as important today as energy production, or, for that matter, labor productivity, because the reduced input can now be deployed elsewhere in creating additional economic growth and prosperity. For now, we welcome energy density flow as the fourth axis in the Great Matrix.

The other scales discussed below—light, sound, information-ingenuity, sentience-consciousness, evolved cultural hierarchies, and emergent complexity—are themselves forms of energy flow, a subset

---

[23] Eric Chaisson, *Cosmic Evolution: The Rise of Complexity in Nature* (Cambridge, MA: Harvard University Press, 2001); *Epic of Evolution: Seven Ages of the Cosmos*; "Energy Rate Density as a Complexity Metric and Evolutionary Driver," *Complexity* 16, no. 3 (2011); "Energy Rate Density. Ii. Probing Further a New Complexity Metric," *Complexity* 17, no. 1 (2011).

of energetics, each with unique properties essential to the evolution of complexity in nature and economics.

Electromagnetism

Electromagnetism is one of the four fundamental forces in physics about which there is an active search for a Grand Unified Theory (GUT) that would combine these four forces in a single equation. Here, we are going to set aside gravity and the two nuclear forces, because electromagnetism governs almost all of the phenomena that we encounter in daily life here on Earth.

Normal chemistry is all about the affinities of electrons. In normal chemistry, as opposed to nuclear chemistry, the elements of the Periodic Table are indestructible. Negatively charged electrons are bound by electromagnetic attraction in orbitals around positively charged atomic nuclei. Atoms combine into complex molecules through electromagnetic preferences and geometries. All chemistry, and therefore all biology, is governed by electromagnetic force. The adenosine triphosphate (ATP) molecules in your cells, the neurons in your brain, the gasoline burning in your car, the food you eat, and all the electronic devices in your life—from the light bulb to the Internet—utilize electromagnetic properties.

Electromagnetic radiation has three properties—frequency, wavelength, and photon-energy. Frequency is measured in Hertz (Hz) in a range of 10^4 to 10^{30} oscillations per second. Wavelength is measured in meters in a range of 10^{-12} to 10^6. Energy is measured in electronvolts (eV) in a range of 10^6 to 10^{-15}. The entire spectrum of electromagnetic radiation spans from long, low-frequency radio waves at one end to short, high-frequency gamma radiation at the other end.

N.B.: Photons (i.e., light) and electrons are different but related phenomena. Photons have no mass, electrons do, but they share similar properties. Moreover, photons interact energetically with electrons in atoms. At different energy states, atoms emit photons. In photosynthesis and solar cells, photon energy creates free electrons. Electrons can "create" photons. Photons can change electron states.

While the electromagnetic spectrum is a single, continuous physical phenomenon, our human eyes have evolved to perceive only a small range of visible light. We can feel infrared radiation on our skin, but the rest of the electromagnetic spectrum is invisible to our direct senses.

The entire spectrum is divided into ionizing and non-ionizing electromagnetic radiation (EMR). Short-fast EMR interacts energetically with atoms and molecules to break and remake chemical bonds. Long-slow EMR reacts minimally with most matter. The break between ionizing and non-ionizing EMR has to do with the size of atoms and the wavelength of the photons. Ultraviolet EMR gives us sunburn. We use short. high-frequency EMR to heat our food (microwave), look through our bodies (x-rays, magnetic imaging), and kill cells (Gamma ray).

Visible light is tucked in a sweet spot just below the range of the ionizing radiation. A prism famously splits white light into its constituent rainbow colors, each with their own specific range of wavelengths and frequency. Beyond purple we move into ultraviolet radiation (<380 nm, <400 terahertz). As the wavelengths get shorter, the frequencies get faster. Beyond red on our rainbow, we move into the infrared (>760 nm, >790 terahertz). As the wavelengths get longer, the frequency gets slower.

Very high frequency (VHF) radio waves—used in television, radios, and other communication devices—range from 1 to 10 meters in wavelength and vibrate at a rate of 30 to 300 megahertz (MHz) (millions of oscillations per second). Electromagnetic radiation in the VHF band is long and interacts minimally with the atoms in the walls of your building or the cells in your body. It takes a special machine— your smartphone or radio—to tune into specific channels, to decode the broadcast woven in airwaves, and to convert that signal into sound or image for your enjoyment and edification.

Your eyes are basically a radio receiver at a different bandwidth. The photoreceptor cells in your eyes tune into specific ranges of electromagnetic radiation. Like the cells themselves, visible light is necessarily in the nanometer range in order to interact with nanometer-sized light-sensing organelles in the cells.

Electromagnetic radiation is central to all of the prosthetic "seeing" devices of science and technology — from radio telescopes to electron microscopes, from smartphones to global communications. These tools extend our vision, our abilities to see, hear, touch, taste, smell, and understand. What we know and know how to do goes far beyond our five natural senses. All of the prosthetic devices that extend human perception utilize the electromagnetic effect. All of the machines and motors that allow us to cross continents and move mountains utilize the electromagnetic effect.

Electromagnetic radiation, as recently harnessed by humans, is magical in how it has transformed our lives and our understanding of the universe. It is a continuous spectrum of wavelengths and frequencies, though divided into qualitatively different segments—radio waves, microwaves, infrared, visible light, ultraviolet, x-ray, and gamma ray. The spectrum of electromagnetic radiation is the fourth axis in the Great Matrix of being—a form of energy flow and a critical subset of all energetics.

Sound

Sound is a vibration that propagates in a medium—gas, liquid, solid, or plasma. Unlike light, sound cannot travel through a vacuum; but like light, it has wavelength-frequency, directionality, intensity, and its own distinct speeds. Sound travels at the rate of 343 meters per second in dry air at 20°C. Sound vibrations jostle molecules in a wave of kinetic energy, much like ripples on still water. Sound, like light, is also a subset of energetics.

An evolving capacity to sense pressure vibrations in the environment certainly has adaptive value for evolving organisms. Rudimentary "hearing" allowed organisms to receive directional information at a distance, thus improving survival and reproduction, while eventually leading also to forms of animal communications.

Curiously, the continuum of sound audible to humans ranges from 20 Hz to 20,000 Hz (17 mm to 17 m), in contrast to the narrow range of visible light, which has no leaps in order of magnitude (790 terahertz to 400 terahertz—760 nm to 380 nm). Humans have much greater "depth" of sound perception than we have "depth" of light perception.

In any case, sound is a physical property of the universe, it has a hierarchical scale, and thus it provides yet another axis in the Great Matrix. Sound may not travel through outer space, but it is an essential component of evolution. And for humans, in particular, sound is central to our perception, communication, cooperation, enjoyment, survival, and reproduction.

Information-Ingenuity

We might postulate a scale of information-ingenuity in the Great Matrix, even though we don't have a universal metric or even proper definition of information-ingenuity that is applicable to all scientific disciplines. Information—seemingly immaterial and ephemeral—can be a slippery metaphysical concept. In the broadest, most abstract sense, however, information is simply physical order in a universe that marches to the tune of disorder.

Out-of-equilibrium energetic systems spontaneously create physical order.[24] This is how the weather—a global system for dissipating the heat from the sun—works, and it works most dramatically and efficiently through hurricanes and tornados. The out-of-equilibrium physical order of the storm is information in the service of entropy. In gases and fluids, however, the spontaneous physical order is fleeting. It arises. It disappears. The weather is always changing. As Heraclitus observed 2,500 years ago, you can't step into the same river twice.

Solid matter, however, can store information, at least for some time. Solid matter has memory. Its physical order can persist in ways that fluids and gas cannot. Solid matter, moreover, can also process that information to rearrange matter, energy, and information to make other stuff. In his book *Why Information Grows*, Cesar Hidalgo writes:

> Information is not tangible; it is not a solid or a fluid. It does not have its own particle either, but it is as physical as movement and temperature, which also do not have particles of their own. Information is incorporeal, but it is always physically embodied. Information is not a thing; rather, it is the arrangement of physical things. It is physical order, like what distinguishes different shuffles of a deck of cards.[25]

If physical order is information, and if it takes energy to transform matter, and if it takes information to specify particular ordered states, then it takes energy to make and translate that information in, out, and back into matter. Hidalgo calls the ability of matter to compute "one of the most amazing facts of the universe."[26] Encoding and reading information in and out of matter is thus also a subset of energetics, and

---

[24] Ilya Prigogine was awarded the 1977 Nobel Prize in Chemistry "for his contributions to non-equilibrium thermodynamics, particularly the theory of dissipative structures." Ilya Prigogine and Gregoire Nicolas, eds., *Self-Organization in Nonequilibrium Systems: From Dissipative Structures to Order through Fluctuations* (New York: Wiley, 1977); I. Prigogine and Isabelle Stengers, *Order out of Chaos : Man's New Dialogue with Nature* (New York, N.Y.: Bantam Books, 1984).
[25] Cesar Hidalgo, *Why Information Grows: The Evolution of Order, from Atoms to Economies* (New York: Basic Books, 2015), 147.
[26] Ibid., Kindle 2477.

is governed by the Laws of Thermodynamics. Information-ingenuity is not free, but it can be cheap. With information-ingenuity, evolution can minimize entropy and maximize creativity. Evolution offers the possibility of doing more with less by coding and processing more efficiently.

DNA is a paradigmatic case of how matter encodes and computes information. In his famous 1944 Dublin lectures and book *What Is Life?* the physicist Edwin Schrödinger postulated that the code of life inside the cell needed to be an aperiodic crystal. Most crystals are periodic, meaning that they form highly ordered microscopic structures. The molecules self-organize, based on their electromagnetic affinities, as they transition from liquid to solid in a tightly packed geometric lattice. These microscopic patterns then grow into macroscopic structures—diamonds, snowflakes, table salt, and metals of all kinds.

In an aperiodic crystal, however, variations in the molecular structure provide the possibility of coding information. Such is the molecule DNA, which consists of two strands of long molecules—polynucleotides—connected by variable bonds of adenine (A) to thymine (T) and cytosine (C) to guanine (G). The DNA molecule does not care about the actual order of these chemical bonds, only that A binds with T and C binds with G along the backbone of the two molecular strands. The pattern of these base pairs—A-T and C-G bonds—is the template upon which DNA codes RNA and RNA codes proteins inside the cell. In cell division, the DNA replicates itself. Solid matter can encode information-ingenuity and then compute that information-ingenuity into living, reproducing, and evolving organisms.

In nature, DNA is always in solution inside the cytoplasm of cells. In a laboratory, however, biologists can separate and concentrate the DNA and then watch as the DNA molecules self-organize into solid crystalline forms. Because DNA is aperiodic, the crystals vary greatly, creating a profusion of psychedelic patterns under the microscope.

As scientists have developed techniques for manipulating DNA molecules, they have successfully used DNA to encode and decode digital information. It is slow and expensive work, but the potential is enormous. DNA can store orders of magnitude more data by volume than current computer hard drives with less energy, and potentially over much longer time frames. A cubic millimeter of DNA can contain 5.5

petabits (10^{15}). As of 2016, a single kilo of DNA would be sufficient to store all of the world's digital data.[27]

In this technological feat—copying digital information in and out of the DNA molecule—we encounter the dual nature of information that causes a lot of confusion. On the one hand, there is information as code. On the other hand, there is information as message. The code has no meaning in itself; it is merely an "arbitrary" vehicle for transmission. Information as message, however, is all about some meaning. Life uses strings of A-T and C-G bonds in DNA to construct protein out of specified sequences of amino acids. Computer scientists can now also use strings of A-T and C-G bonds in DNA as binary code for storing the digital contents of computers. DNA is the code in which the different messages and meanings are embedded. Human languages are also codes in which different messages and meanings can be transmitted (and also translated). So we have two distinct definitions of information to keep separate, but they are also always connected. To avoid confusion, I use the hyphenation—information-ingenuity—and sometimes simply ingenuity.

In both senses—information as code and information as meaning—we might well imagine a scale in which information grows exponentially. Information measured as DNA base pairs, for instance, grows by orders of magnitude in the evolution from prokaryotes to eukaryotes. Information grows again through multicellular organisms and with the evolution of the five senses—touch, taste, smell, sight, and sound: new codes conveying new meanings. And with the rise of symbolic language—spoken and later written—information as code and information as meaning continue to grow exponentially. All the while, information is specifying and computing physical and social order, generating a continuous flux of creativity through our bodies, brains, and global civilization.

Ingenuity is simply information that does something creative, innovative, useful, and intelligent. The Latin root of the word "ingenuity" means "inborn," as in "inborn genius." Indeed, the natural world is full of inborn genius. The inborn intelligibility-intelligence of nature is the precondition for scientific discovery and human technologies. We are surrounded by what philosopher Daniel Dennett refers to as "competence without

---

[27] Andy Extance, "How DNA Could Store All the World's Data," Nature, http://www.nature.com/news/how-dna-could-store-all-the-world-s-data-1.20496.

comprehension."[28] Most of our biological functions, including mental functions, occur without comprehension. Human consciousness is a recent development in evolutionary history. Human comprehension is a rapidly evolving flood of new knowledge in the many domains of science. We have only recently begun to comprehend our true place in the universe.

In computer science the smallest unit of information is a bit—0 or 1. Technically, random garbage on your hard disk contains more "information" than your photos, music, documents, and applications. The latter are encoded in more compact algorithms. No such luck with random 1s and 0s. By the information-as-code definition, disorder contains more "information" than order.

This seemingly esoteric discussion of information theory turns out to be central to economics and finance. The rise of complexity in nature and culture concerns us, not simply the amount of code required to describe a particular state of physical order or disorder.

Humans are the most amazing computers of information-ingenuity, but we also encounter limits. Cesar Hidalgo introduces the concept of *personbytes* to represent the maximum amount of knowledge and know-how that an individual can acquire. *Firmbytes* are the maximum amount of knowledge and know-how that a firm can acquire. It takes time and effort to acquire expertise and skill. There is a limit to how much knowledge and know-how one individual or one firm can acquire. And to accomplish complicated manufacturing or provide complicated services requires a lot of personbytes and firmbytes in collaboration. These limits are why complex economic activity requires networks of firms working in tandem with complex supply lines. Acquiring information-ingenuity is hard work, but it plays a central role in economics, finance, and investing. Humans have taken the computing of energy, matter, and ingenuity to a whole new level.

Money, of course, is also a code, a symbolic language used exclusively by humans. The message money conveys is price. It is also a symbolic store of value. And in the last century we have experienced an exponential growth in money and a flood of information about the many meanings of money. Investors live in a deluge of information and are faced with the challenges of finding order in the flood, restricted as we are by personbyte and firmbyte limitations.

---

[28] Daniel C. Dennett, *From Bacteria to Bach and Back* (New York: W.W. Norton, 2017).

So we imagine inductively another scale in the Great Matrix—a scale of information-ingenuity—the code and the meaning—that also grows exponentially. In evolution, it grows both as the quantity of DNA code, but also as the diversity of ingenious life forms. In human culture, it grows both as the quantity of code—spoken, printed, broadcast, and digital code—and as the quality of ingenuity—knowledge and know-how that accumulate through collective learning across generations and across geographies.

Sentience-Consciousness

We might postulate yet another axis in the Great Matrix: a hierarchy of sentience leading to consciousness. The membranes of microbes already have rudimentary sentience, in so far as they seek out food sources and flee harm. The immune system is also sentient, goal directed in response to its environment. The evolution of the central nervous system and the five senses further increased sentience. Animals have developed feeling and emotions in an amazing intensification of sentience. With the advent of symbolic language and collective learning, another exponential leap in the scale of sentience-consciousness has occurred among humans, with the emergence of intense first-person subjectivity and social intersubjectivity. Moreover, humans have remarkable agency, that is, self-creative capacities to evaluate future options and direct their behavior to pursue alternate goals. "Free will" is probably not the right term for this impressive attribute. Instead, we have "constrained choice," but the ability to evaluate-and-choose several orders of magnitude beyond any of our animal kin.

Across the variety of animal species, brain-mind is an emergent phenomenon and is potentially scalable. While there is no numeric scale that measures feeling and perception, sentience and consciousness, we can identify the ability of single cells to "sense" the presence of food or predators in the environment as perhaps the low end of the sentience spectrum in its most rudimentary form. A roundworm in a neuroscience lab has only a few hundred nerve cells, while a human brain has billions of nerve cells. Surely, there are objective differences in body-brain-mind complexity between roundworms and humans. Perhaps someday we will have such a scale throughout the animal kingdom.

Counting nerve cells alone does not really give us an adequate measure of brain-minds. Our human brain-minds require bodies and metabolism, vocal chords and oppositional thumbs, and an enriching social and natural environment, in order to realize their potentials.

While closely related to information-ingenuity, I treat sentience-consciousness as separate phenomenon dealing primarily with the subjectivity, behavior, and agency of creatures. Human subjectivity and consciousness are on a continuum throughout an evolutionary hierarchy. Sentience-consciousness is a subset of energetics; and like our other scales in the Great Matrix, I imagine exponential leaps occurring throughout the drama of Big History.

Perhaps someday we may have a robust measure of sentience-consciousness that will allow us to compare dogs with cuttlefish, elephants with birds, and smartphones with smart people.

Culturally Constructed Hierarchies

Humans construct social and cultural hierarchies and scales that exist nowhere else in nature. These hierarchies have structured societies for good and ill throughout history. Some of these are evolved dispositions that we share with other animal species. Primate dominance hierarchy behavior may be deep in our genes, for instance, but the organizational flow charts at your company are not. All complex societies and institutions have social hierarchies reflected in their customs and laws, in their mating and childrearing practices, in and their occupations and role models. The alpha male—and sometimes alpha female—is such an archetype, one partially grounded in our evolved human nature, but also constructed by societies.

Applied mathematics also involves human constructed scales and hierarchies. While mathematics is also somehow discovered, humans have used these insights to construct new scales and hierarchies. In his famous 1960 paper physicist Eugene Wigner pondered "the unreasonable effectiveness of mathematics in the natural sciences."[29] Indeed, mathematics is essential to understanding all of the scales and hierarchies of the Great Matrix. Mathematics has a miraculous ability to describe reality in new and profound ways. Mathematics, however, is not simply discovered "out there" in the universe; mathematics is also

---

[29] Eugene Wigner, "The Unreasonable Effectiveness of Mathematics in the Natural Sciences," *Communications in Pure and Applied Mathematics* 13, no. 1 (1960).

evolved and invented. And once mathematics is discovered-invented, it can become completely self-referential. It need not play with any reality except itself in a Neoplatonic universe of ideas.

Economics and finance, of course, use a lot of mathematics. Much of this is arithmetic—measuring and counting. Complex modeling, however, requires the rocket scientists. And here, as we will explore in chapter four, economic models begin to up run up against complexity and chaos theory. It is important to remember that the mathematics of finance and economics is not real. It need not refer to anything real in the way that the laws of physics do. The unit of measurement—currency—is a socially constructed fiction. No other species exchanges goods and services based on a symbolic system of value. Much like advanced mathematics, the measurements and models in economics and finance can be self-referential with no basis in reality. Still, there is an "unreasonable effectiveness" of mathematics in our economic evolution. Indeed, mathematics first took hold in human brains with the growth of trade in early agricultural civilizations.

The accelerating drama of human evolution required us to create all kinds of social and cultural hierarchies, in order to scale human cooperation from intimate hunter-gatherer tribes to millions living in mega-cities around the world.

Emergent Complexity

Taken together, size, time, matter, energy, and all the rest bring us to the final scale in the Great Matrix of all beings—the scale of emergent complexity. Science has no numeric scale for complexity. Here, too, we need to appeal to informed intuition and induction, rather than to some discrete, measurable qualia in nature. The emergence of complexity, however, is certainly one of the key features of Big History, with important implications for economics and finance. Emergence is a bottom-up process by means of which energy, matter, and information create top-down constraints on lower-level processes. Humans in general, and scientists in particular, are extreme examples of the top-down capacities to constrain, collect, and transform energy, matter, and information in our built physical and cultural environments.

Big History traces eight or more thresholds of emergent complexity in the evolutionary narrative from the Big Bang to the twenty-first century to create a pedagogically powerful narrative that enhances understanding, retention, excitement, and relevance. For instance, the creation of the heavy elements in the stellar foundries from which we derive the elements of the Periodic Table was a threshold of emergent complexity necessary for complex chemistry to later evolve. When complex chemistry catalyzed life, we saw again something new and different. And when the evolution of plants and animals gave rise to species with a central nervous system, complex brains, oppositional thumbs, vocal chords, symbolic language, tool-making, fire mastery, and collective learning, something new emerged again in the universe, at least on one small planet.

It is important to emphasize that emergent complexity requires lower levels of complexity to exist and function. Higher orders of complexity are built from the bottom up, though emergent properties cannot be fully explained from below. With thresholds of emergent complexity, the Great Matrix is not simply a coordinate system of reality, but now also an epic narrative of becoming.

We can distinguish between four different kinds of emergent complexity in the new epic narrative of evolution:

1) Evolutionary Emergence: The grand arc of Big History is the story of the universe, Earth, and humanity. In the beginning, there were no stars, no galaxies, no periodic table of elements, no planets, no water, no complex chemistry, no life, and no intelligence. These emerged in a sequence—through thresholds of emergent complexity—over a timescale measured in billions and millions of years.

2) Developmental Emergence: Each of us begins our journey as a single cell in our mother's womb. Over nine months, that cell replicates and differentiates into a few hundred tissue-types of our bodies. The development continues through childhood, into adult bodies composed of some 40 trillion cells. In this example, developmental emergence occurs over a timescale measured in months, years, and decades.

3) Functional Emergence: Protons, neutrons, and electrons form atoms; atoms join together to form molecules; molecules attach to form more complex chemistry. The inner life of a cell is a dense and intense collection of millions of molecular machines undergoing trillions of mind-boggling chemical cascades per second. The atoms and the molecules are not alive, but when functioning together, they can form a living cell, organ, and organism. Functional emergence in our bodies occurs over a timescale measured in nanoseconds and hours.

4) <u>Intelligence Emergence</u>: With the advent of symbolic language and collective learning, we see the accelerating emergence of intelligence in humans. Science, technology, engineering, math, and medicine are the most obvious examples, as new insights and discoveries are built upon the successes of the past in a progressive and self-transcending learning process. This kind of emergence also occurs in the arts and humanities. The emergence of intelligence is a complex distributed phenomenon and is evolutionary (over the course of human history), developmental (over the course of an individual's lifetime), and functional (necessary for the workings of increasingly complex societies).[30]

While evolutionary emergence is the grand narrative of Big History, coming to recognize and understand developmental emergence, functional emergence, and intelligence emergence is no less important. The emergence of complexity is an ongoing process. Indeed, we can further apply these concepts to understanding economic markets. The business of finance emerges through historical, developmental, functional, and intelligent processes.

To truly appreciate Big History, we must count in billions of light-years and take into account the amazing nanoscale functions and developments manifested by quadrillions of atoms dancing in and out of our bodies. We must also appreciate the history of knowledge, creativity, and discovery that characterizes the recent, dramatic, and accelerating successes of our species.

With these different concepts of emergence in hand, we can now begin to understand how the academic disciplines and departments of the modern university map onto the structure of the universe itself. From the bottom up, we begin with fundamental theory, particle physics, nuclear physics, solid-state physics, and chemistry. The disciplines then split into inanimate and animate tracks. Inanimate matter goes from physical chemistry to material sciences, earth sciences, space sciences, astronomy, and cosmology. Cosmology, it should be noted, also takes us back to fundamental theory and particle physics, so the top and bottom are connected in the disciplines of physics and astronomy. Life, animate matter, leads to the many divisions of biology all the way to the human sciences, and indeed also

---

[30] I am in debt to George Ellis for many of these insights. See George F.R. Ellis, *How Can Physics Underlie the Mind? Top-Down Causation in the Human Context* (New York: Springer, 2016).

to all the humanities. Throughout our review of specialization and division of labor in universities, we also encounter applied sciences—for instance, engineering, medicine, and economics. The distinction between science and applied science is not easy to maintain.

A Multi-Dimensional Matrix

The ten dimensions of the Great Matrix give us ten ways to measure reality—by time, size, matter, energetics, electromagnetism, sound, information-ingenuity, sentience-consciousness, culture, and the end product—emergent complexity. Some of these are inductive scales that cannot be measured in numeric units. We might measure information, as bits for instance, but we cannot enumerate the ingenuity embedded in the code. We don't have a consciousness meter that we can put on your head. And beyond the crude measure of energy-density-flow, we don't have a scale for emergent complexity. It is a triumph in intellectual history that we have come to understand the scales of time, size, matter, and the varieties of energetics. These are reliably real and profoundly practical insights about how our universe and our economy function.

All phenomena, all academic disciplines, and all economic activity can be located in reference to these hierarchical scales. It is this Great Matrix of bottom-up and top-down causality that allows complexity to grow.

Medieval Europeans once understood the universe to be a Great Chain of Being. All the entities of the world—animal, vegetable, mineral—were hierarchically organized. At the bottom were metals, precious metals, and precious stones. Then came plants and trees, followed by wild animals and domesticated animals. Humans were also hierarchically ordered from children to women to men and further into the different ranks of commoners, nobility, princes, and kings. The Great Chain of Being continued up into the celestial realm—moon, stars, angels, and archangels—to the very top where God presides over the entire creation. This *scala naturae* provided humans with a natural order, which they also understood to be a natural human order that structured their societies.

Science, or so the story goes, disrupted this view of the universe and of ourselves. Copernicus, Galileo, and Kepler broke the crystalline spheres of Ptolemy and demoted Earth from the center of the universe to an insignificant periphery. Darwin understood plants and animals, including the human animal, to be evolving from common ancestors all the way back into the proverbial primordial slime. Freud showed that rational man was really an unconscious mess and hardly aware of, let alone in control of, his own thoughts and passions.

The Great Chain of Being was rendered a tangled web of happenstance in an enormous universe devoid of transcendence and meaning. God was rendered an unnecessary or incompetent creator. The new existentialists and Stoics argued that the universe was indifferent, that humans were insignificant, that our consciousness was epiphenomenal, and that our evolution was merely accidental. Note that while there is no Great Chain of Being as the medieval Europeans understood, there is a great deal of order in the universe as discovered by contemporary science. There is a Great Matrix to which all beings belong that extends far beyond our direct senses and perception.

Humans are not at the top of the scales of size and time, but somewhere in the middle. On the energetics, information-ingenuity, sentience-consciousness, and emergent complexity scales, however, humans are at the extremes. The human niche is particularly favored in the matrix for the time being—each of us is a nexus of causal relationships (physical, biological, social, economic, psychological, mental), realizing extraordinary flows of energy and ingenuity, intensities of subjective experience, and accelerating transformations in the modern period.

In our drive toward specialization and divisions of labor, we rarely reflect on these hierarchies and what they might mean for our understanding of science, self, and society. "The ongoing fragmentation of knowledge and resulting chaos are not reflections of the real world but artifacts of scholarship," writes Harvard biologist E. O. Wilson in his book *Consilience: The Unity of Knowledge*.[31] Vartan Gregorian, president of the Carnegie Corporation, similarly observes:

> The fundamental problem underlying the disjointed curriculum is the fragmentation of knowledge itself. Higher education has atomized knowledge by dividing it into disciplines, subdisciplines, and sub-subdisciplines—breaking it up into smaller and smaller unconnected fragments of academic specialization, even as the world looks to colleges for help in integrating and synthesizing the exponential increases in information brought about by

---

[31] Edward O. Wilson, *Consilience: The Unity of Knowledge* (New York: Knopf, 1998).

technological advances. The trend has serious ramifications. Understanding the nature of knowledge, its unity, its varieties, its limitations, and its uses and abuses is necessary for the success of democracy . . . We must reform higher education to reconstruct the unity and value of knowledge.[32]

This is not a problem restricted to the ivory towers of universities. It is an acute problem for investors as well, who have personbyte and firmbyte limits, but who also need to understand a world that is rapidly changing due to science, technology, and globalization.

This book is an attempt to construct a common framework for knowledge and know-how, so that we might better capture and create more value—measured as money, perhaps, but actually reflecting real energy, matter, and ingenuity. Understanding how the Great Matrix actually works on different scales is an exercise in changing perspectives. Investors need to be able to zoom in and zoom out, to understand the emergent complexity from physics to chemistry, from cell biology to human brains, from individual producer-consumers to global markets. We need to take account of the energy that flows through our daily lives and our business opportunities. This book proposes that such knowledge and awareness will also give you an edge in the buying and selling of stocks, bonds, and other financial instruments.

We are never outside the bio-social-physical matrix, but in this scientific and philosophical exercise we seem to stand away, looking down on the matrix from above. As far as we know, no other entity in the universe has achieved this capacity, and it is in this domain that humans are no longer middling creatures of the matrix. Our self-transcendence, realized especially through the progress in science, economics, art, and culture, is a super and completely natural emergent phenomenon. We come to understand the matrix from the inside out, though the matrix knows nothing of us.

It is awe-inspiring to grok any or all of these natural scales and hierarchies. Simply appreciating the scales of size and time is awesome, but try also to analyze the flows of energy embodied in the objects and activities in your immediate environment. A process analysis of energy in our built environment gives us a new

---

[32] Vartan Gregorian, "Colleges Must Reconstruct the Unity of Knowledge," *Chronicle of Higher Education* 50, no. 39 (2004).

understanding of the economic world. Training your eyes to "see" the energy flows embedded in the world around you is sure to wake you up in the morning. I look at my library and recall that a ton of paper embodies on average about 35 gigajoules (GJ). This is about as much energy as is needed to manufacture a ton of good-quality steel, to say nothing of the human labor that went into writing these books. I walk through my home and recollect that the average three-bedroom, wood-framed house in North America embodies about 500 GJ of energy in its construction, which is equivalent to 4,157 gallons of gasoline (or something like 48,183 days of human labor).[33] I get into my car and consider that a midsized passenger car requires about 110 GJ to build and might consume about 50 GJ of fuel annually. Over ten years, the energy cost of that car would total about 680 GJ—more than that of the average three-bedroom house mentioned above.[34]

It doesn't stop there. If your eyes could detect the radio waves around you, the empty space of your room would be filled with an altogether different kind of rainbow—the chaotic patterns of dozens of overlapping VHF broadcasts would be evident all around you. If your skin could feel these electromagnetic waves, your entire body would be vibrating and tingling at different frequencies. Indeed, some of the airwaves entering through the window right now have traveled 13.8 billion years from the background radiation of the Big Bang to be with you today. Or if you prefer the wave function of quantum phenomena, consider yourself connected across space and time in a very immediate sense to the distant reaches of the universe. Understanding the Great Matrix provides a kind of instant mystical experience in which you can deconstruct and reconstruct your sense of self and world within these multidimensional scales and hierarchies.

Science offers a sixth sense—a way of seeing beyond the walls of Plato's cave into the realm of what is real. It isn't rocket science to sort-of-know how things actually work, how the pieces form an entire puzzle. Of course, god and the devil are both in the details, but it sure helps to have the picture on the puzzle box when trying to fit the pieces together.

---

[33] One gallon of gasoline = 33.70 kWh = 28,977 kcal. 4157 gallons x 28,977 kcal = 120,457,390 kcal @2500 kcal per day = 48,183 days of human labor

[34] Vaclav Smil, *Energy in Nature and Society* (Cambridge, MA: MIT Press, 2007), 288-89.

Chapter 3:
The Economy of a Single Cell

In this chapter we will explore cell biology using economic metaphors, and in return cell biology will teach us some first principles in economics. In short, markets and cells are bottom-up, disturbed processes, involving countless agents, products, services, and technologies, all utilizing energy, matter, and ingenuity flows to maintain and grow complexity. Markets and cells are all about process and change. And like economic markets, cell biology is stunning to behold—trillions of atoms organizing themselves into dynamic and self-replicating flows of energy, matter, and information.

Cells are really small. You will recall that the diameter of a single hydrogen atom is approximately 0.1 nm (nanometers—a billion times smaller than one meter). The smallest bacteria are about 150–250 nm in diameter. The bacterium *E. coli*, part of your intestinal microbiome, measures up at approximately 2 μm (micrometers or microns). Here we have moved up in the scale a thousand-fold, from nanos to microns, from 10^{-9} m to 10^{-6} m.

To grok these jumps in orders of magnitude is no minor matter. Think of one nanometer as somehow equivalent to $1 USD. Our hydrogen atom would cost about ten cents at the local supermarket. Fortunately, there is an abundance of hydrogen and it doesn't take up a lot of shelf space. A single bacterium, the aforementioned *E. coli* at 2 micrometers, is available for a cool $2,000. Your gut contains trillions of such cells, so stock up. At the millimeter scale, we can actually see what we're buying, if we look carefully. The price of a *C. elegans,* a 1-mm transparent roundworm used widely in genetic and neuroscience research, is going to cost you $1,000,000. A shopping cart full of food would cost you trillions of dollars.

Of course, this analogy is technically misleading—meters and dollars are not equivalent. The analogy, however, illuminates more than just the scale of size from nanometers to meters. It also reminds us that there is always an energetic cost in growing complexity. Bigger entities really are more expensive. Evolving complex cells require orders of magnitude more atoms, and orders of magnitude more energy, to create, maintain, grow, reproduce, and evolve. As we will explore below, there is always a cost.

The Central Bank of Chemistry

We begin with a review of some basic chemistry. Atoms—composed in the first order of protons, neutrons, and electrons—are the building blocks of chemistry. Most of the atoms in the Periodic Table of Elements were created by stellar fusion in giant, fast-burning stars. When these massive stars exhausted their fuel, they collapsed and blew up in supernovae. The remains of these supernovae then gave rise to new star systems containing the possibilities of complex chemistry. Our solar system is such a place—the material remains of a colossal star that died in a dramatic explosion over 8 billion years ago.

It took a lot of energy to fuse simple atoms—hydrogen and helium—into heavier atoms. The sun converts 4 million tons of matter into energy every second through fusion reactions that turn hydrogen into helium. The conversion of matter into energy is expressed in the iconic equation $E = mc^2$.[35] Converting a whole lot of energy into a wee bit of matter is how particle physicists interrogate the subatomic realm of matter at CERN and other particle accelerators around the world.

Chemistry follows different rules than nuclear physics. In normal chemistry, elements in the Periodic Table are indestructible. Atoms can and do join together to form molecules. Molecules can and do fall apart, but the atoms that constitute the molecule retain their basic identity before, during, and after these transformations. That identity—hydrogen, helium, oxygen, carbon, iron, and all the rest—is determined by the numbers of positively charged protons in the atomic nucleus along with an assortment of neutrally charged neutrons.

Chemistry is mostly about the affinities of electrons. As described by quantum mechanics, electrons exist in clouds of "probability space," albeit in distinct orbitals, around a positively charged nucleus. Standing between the nucleus and the electrons is a whole lot of empty space and powerful magnetic fields.

Imagine a simple hydrogen atom—one proton and one electron—as a major league baseball stadium. Think of the proton as a baseball on the pitcher's mound. The electron would be something smaller than a flea somewhere at the furthest reaches of the stadium; and this flea is moving at extraordinary speeds. The electron of a hydrogen atom covers about 2,200 kilometers per second in its frenetic orbit around the

---

[35] Bohan et al., *Big History*, 58.

single proton nucleus of hydrogen.[36] It helps to be really small if you want to travel at these speeds.

Look around at your immediate surroundings—books, chairs, tables, walls, floors, windows, computers, and your hand. Lots of reliably solid objects. Don't think of matter that way. Instead, try to grok the magnetism of ecstatic electrons vibrating with their nuclei. It is this electromagnetism that gives us the illusion of a world of solid objects, when those objects around you are actually mostly empty space. Even when packed tightly in objects like rocks, atoms are always busy. While not alive, atoms are certainly animate, if that makes sense. On the atomic scale, nothing is inert and unmoving. Everything vibrates with intense activity.

There is a kind of electron law of supply and demand. Following their affinities, busy electrons are promiscuously exchanged and shared between atoms, joining together elements into new compounds. The electrons are looking for a place to rest that is not as frantic as where they just were. The logic of the outer electron orbitals determines if, whether, and how atoms combine into molecules and alternately, how molecules fall apart. Poor helium is inert, so stable, that nobody bonds with it. The rest of the Periodic Table, however, is capable of joining into molecules. It's in the nature of the atoms of the right kind in the right conditions to form molecules.

When an electron leaps to another atom, the donor atom's electromagnetic charge is reduced—making it more positive—while the recipient's negative charge is increased. The participants in this electron exchange may be strangers passing in the night. As often as not, though, their newly found positive and negative valences create an instant bond between the two—opposites attract in an ionic bond. Electron transfer is one of the ways that atoms turn into molecules.

Sodium chloride (i.e., table salt) is the textbook example of such a molecule. The sodium atom (Na) loses an electron to chlorine (Cl). Na is now positively charged. Cl is now negatively charged. The two elements are bound together by their positive and negative attraction—an ionic bond.

$$Na + Cl \rightarrow Na^+ + Cl^- \rightarrow NaCl$$

---

[36] Carl Zorn, *Jefferson Lab* (2018), https://education.jlab.org/qa/electron_01.html.

Electrons can also be shared between atoms. This is called a covalent bond. The textbook example is water (H_2O). In water the electrons from the two hydrogen (H) atoms come to orbit around the nuclei of both the oxygen and hydrogen atoms.

$$H_2 + O \rightarrow H_2O$$

Sharing electrons creates a stronger and more enduring bond than the positive and negative attractions of ionic bonding. Complex molecules typically employ both kinds of bonds. The economies of chemistry are a series of limited partnerships (covalent bonding) and merger acquisitions (ionic bonding).

Some atoms, carbon for instance, are especially good at forming covalent bonds with other atoms. Life harnesses the chemical properties of the carbon atom to construct complex molecules. The formula for methane is one carbon atom bound to four hydrogen atoms (CH_4). Having filled its outer orbital with the shared electrons from the hydrogen atoms, the carbon and hydrogen atoms are more stable and less reactive in the new molecular form.

Oxygen, on the other hand, is reactive by its nature. Oxygen is always out to dump an electron or two on its neighbors. When it can, oxygen is said to "oxidize" other atoms and molecules. This combustion can happen fast or slowly, spontaneously or induced. The mere presence of oxygen causes iron (Fe) to slowly rust.

$$2\ Fe + 3\ 0 \rightarrow Fe_2O_3$$

A candle, on the other hand, must be induced to burn with a match. The rapid oxidization of the wax generates heat and light. Both reactions are examples of combustion, though the oxidizing of iron is much slower. It is the same basic chemical process in all living cells, though not necessarily with oxygen as the reactive element. Other elements can also do duty. A key oxidation reaction process inside of complex cells is respiration. All chemical reactions export heat energy to the surrounding environment.

When oxygen reacts with methane, the methane is oxidized, forming carbon dioxide and water. This reaction gives off heat. It is exothermic.

$$CH_4 + 2\ O_2 \rightarrow CO_2 + 2\ H_20 + Energy$$

Molecules greatly complicate the affinities and possibilities of electrons and their atoms. For instance, there are twenty different amino acids with a mean of 19.2 atoms per molecule.[37] Amino acids combine by the hundreds to form proteins. A midsized protein might contain some 400 amino acids. This single protein molecule thus contains 8,000 atoms plus or minus—hence the nomenclature "macromolecule." The elements involved are primarily carbon, hydrogen, oxygen, and nitrogen—held together by both covalent and ionic bonds. The geometry and intensity of these affinities determine how proteins fold into particular shapes that perform specialized cellular functions. Even the smallest single-cell economies contain many millions of proteins inside their cytoplasm.[38]

This trade in electrons drives the economies of chemistry. Unlike human currency, the medium of exchange has intrinsic value. The Central Bank of Chemistry is backed by the Laws of Thermodynamics. Suffice it to say that some chemical reactions release energy to the environment—these are called "exothermic" reactions. And other chemical reactions consume energy from the environment—these are called "endothermic" reactions. Many do both, up and down energetic scales and embodied complexities. It takes a match to start a campfire (an endothermic reaction). The sustained combustion of the wood, however, is a net exothermic chemical process dissipating heat, light, and gases into the environment. If we include the entire energy life cycle of the tree from which the wood came, then we have a net endothermic event. It took orders of magnitude more solar energy to grow a bundle of firewood than the energy that is released in the fire itself.

Chemical complexity requires two things. First, it requires a source of energy in order to arrange atoms into molecules. Having created more complex molecules, it can also require energy to break them down. Second, it requires a heat sink, a place to discard disorder, a garage dump to dissipate energy. On the planetary scale, the cold of outer space is the Earth's heat sink, even as the sun is our primary heat source. On the chemical scale, the local environment of the system will do just fine. Both the energy sources and the energy sinks are found in

---

37 Marie-Paule Lefranc and et.al., "Amino Acids," *International Immunogenetics Information System* (2015), http://www.imgt.org/IMGTeducation/Aide-memoire/_UK/aminoacids/abbreviation.html.

[38] Ron Milo and Rob Phillips, 2015, http://book.bionumbers.org/how-many-proteins-are-in-a-cell/.

the surrounding environment of all complex systems. In all cases, energy is consumed from and released to the environment in order to create, maintain, rearrange, and break down molecules.

Electromagnetism is what holds the world together, at least the scales that matter most to humans. Technically, there are four fundamental nuclear forces—electromagnetism, gravity, strong nuclear force, and weak nuclear force—but at our biological scale electromagnetism does the work of normal chemistry. The electromagnetism of chemistry drives the energetic flux that animates life and the growth of complexity in the world around us.

The Central Bank of Chemistry is always depreciating its energy reserves, a fact that, on the macro-level of Big History, we can happily ignore for a couple billion years. We live on a tiny thermodynamic eddy in a universe where free energy is plentiful and complexity has the possibility of running up hill. The monetary policies of our planet are based on the sun, the deep cold of space, and the fundamental laws of physics. Investors can count on these as a reliable partner in terrestrial markets for at least a billion years.

The Currency of Life

The currency of cell biology is the ATP (adenosine triphosphate) molecule. ATP is an energy delivery system, each molecule a little packet of energy to be put to use in the continuous construction of the cell. Like money, ATP circulates throughout the economy of the cell. Unlike money, it needs to be reminted after each transaction. The molecular remains of spent ATP are quickly recycled to make more ATP. All forms of life—from bacteria to blue whales—use ATP to energize their creative dynamic.

Joining amino acids together to make a protein takes about five ATP molecules for each bond. Constructing a modest-sized protein of 400 amino acids would consume about 2,000 ATP molecules. From there the numbers quickly become astronomical. Protein construction occurs at a frantic pace inside a cell. When we add all the molecular activities going on inside a simple cell, we're looking at hundreds of thousands or even millions of ATP molecules consumed per second. A human typically consumes about its weight in ATP molecules every day, but at any given moment, there are only about 250 grams of ATP in the human body.[39] ATP is continuously consumed and recycled inside the economy of a single cell at a rate that dwarfs daily foreign currency transactions in our human economy (ca. $4 trillion per day is exchanged via the international SWIFT system).

The continuous minting of ATP requires chemical energy—as mandated by the Universal Central Bank (see energetics in chapter 2). Cells take in food from the environment and then break down this food into smaller usable molecules. Electron transfer reactions then turn these small molecules, primarily glucose, into energy for cell construction.

Cells, moreover, have figured out how to store electrical energy by turning membrane barriers into batteries. In order to transport food energy in and waste out, cell membranes need to also be selectively permeable. This is achieved by protein structures embedded in the otherwise impermeable lipid membrane. One such structure oxidizes hydrogen atoms, removing the electron and using the energy therefrom to pump the remaining proton across the membrane.

Normal chemistry, we observed, was about the affinities of electrons. You don't find unattached protons floating around on Earth, as they would immediately grab an electron from its neighbor and revert into a hydrogen atom. But in cell biology protons are the key to storing and utilizing potential chemical energy. If you collect enough protons on one side of the membrane, you've got a battery.

The positive valences of the protons on one side of a membrane create a powerful electromagnetic field that drives the ATP synthesis and other cellular functions. How strong? The electromagnetic valence across a mitochondrion membrane would scale to 30 million volts per meter, equivalent to a lightning strike.[40] Fortunately, this occurs not at the scale of meters and megavolts, but at the scale of nanometers and millivolts. This is the vital force that drives ATP production and the prodigious biochemistry of all life. The molecular machines that drive this process are not found anywhere in inanimate nature, except as mimicked in human technology and engineering.

The Business Models of Life

---

[39] "Adenosine Triphosphate," *Wikipedia* (2018), https://en.wikipedia.org/wiki/Adenosine_triphosphate.
[40] Nick Lane, *The Vital Question: Energy, Evolution, and the Origins of Complex Life* (New York: W.W. Norton & Company, 2015), Kindle 1104.

Life excels at capturing and concentrating energy, harnessing the chemicals in its environment to grow and reproduce. It does so both by evolving new efficiencies, like enzymes that speed up and channel chemical reactions, and by increasing overall energy intake.

Life began about 4 billion years ago as single-cell prokaryotes, which come in two families, bacteria and archaea, distinguished by their membranes and other features. Prokaryotes share many biochemical pathways, including the use of ATP and DNA. Prokaryotes have no nucleus or other membrane-bound organelles. Eukaryote cells, on the other hand, have a nucleus and organelles and are usually much larger and morphologically more complex than prokaryotes. All plants and animals are eukaryotes.

Life probably first got hold in alkaline hydrothermal vents on the ocean floor, an environment rich in energy and chemical possibilities. Somehow this chemical cauldron boot-strapped itself into life, mastering metabolism, membranes, and memory. Early prokaryotes reproduced, evolved, and spread around the planet, developing enormous genetic diversity. Along the way the bacteria and archaea developed all the major chemical metabolic pathways. Their biochemical ingenuity allowed them to harvest more energy and matter from increasingly diverse biomes on our restless planet.

Genes are the architectural plans for cell construction and replication. Without genes, life has no memory of itself and no capacity to "compute" more life. Prokaryotes divide into clones, but they also exchange genes through lateral transfer with their neighbors. Genes can be exchanged through viral transfer or simply proximity as prokaryotes give away and pick up DNA segments. The bacterium *E. coli*, for instance, has only about 4,000 genes. The metagenome of all *E. coli* bacteria, however, may contain 18,000 genes.[41] Indeed, the prokaryotes need not be of the same species to share genes. Keeping a lot of useless genes around is expensive, so bacteria are quick to discard unused genes and to try out new genes that might be useful. The genomic situation between prokaryotes is so confused that some biologists think of all prokaryotes as a single species. "Simple" bacteria and archaea created the world's first global economy of staggering complexity with its own world wide web of information sharing.

---

[41] Ibid., Kindle 2869.

The First Agricultural Revolution

Human agriculture is all about harvesting energy from the sun through domesticated plants and animals. Bacteria figured out how to do this some 3.5 billion years ago when they invented photosynthesis. This ability to tickle a photon from the sun and turn it into food allowed an exponential growth in life beyond the finite chemical and thermal potential energy of our young planet. In the process, bacteria sculpted rocks, laid down huge sedimentary deposits, changed the oceans, and transformed the environment. Photosynthesis enables plants to breathe in carbon dioxide, soak up water, and exhale oxygen in order to create carbohydrate food molecules to fuel cell growth.

Carbon dioxide is one of the greenhouse gases implicated today in anthropogenic global warming. Two billion years ago, the reduction of carbon dioxide in the atmosphere presented a different dilemma. A billion years after photosynthesis began, oxygen levels began to rise in the atmosphere. A reduction in carbon dioxide levels and an increase in oxygen levels in the atmosphere resulted in global cooling. The Earth was soon covered with ice—like a giant snowball—in what is referred to as the Great Oxidation Event.

Those prokaryotes that could not adapt to the new oxygen-rich environment retreated into the anaerobic muck. Others evolved membranes that could resist oxygen and later harness its power through respiration, greatly magnifying the energy production power of the cell. It is not clear whether any lineage of prokaryotes ever actually went extinct, though the environments in which anaerobic prokaryotes can thrive changed dramatically as oxygen became more abundant. With photosynthesis and later respiration, single-cell life had a new and practically unlimited source of energy fueling a Great Radiation of life in the terrestrial oceans.

Photosynthesis is the miracle machine that energizes all life. It didn't start out that way, but in the ensuing eons, the baroque varieties and abundance of life were and still are founded on this molecular legerdemain. Many prokaryotes still make their living by harvesting chemical energy in their environment, as all prokaryotes did before photosynthesis, but they are a small part of the Gross Primary Productivity (GPP) of our planet's annual biomass today. At the bottom of the food chain and the energy economy of our planet is photosynthesis—a process of transforming carbon, water, and sunlight into life more abundant.[42]

Prokaryotes still reign today. Their biomass probably exceeds that of all eukaryotic life. Prokaryotes have an incredible capacity to set up shop inside and on top of every surface, climate, geography, and creature on this planet. We are here today as their descendants, guests, and servants; but we—the royal eukaryote "we" including all plants, animals, and fungi—are also singularly different from the prokaryotes.

The First Industrial Revolution

Eukaryotes appeared about 2 billion years ago. Unlike prokaryotes, they have a differentiated, membrane-bound nucleus and specialized organelles—mitochondria, chloroplast, Golgi apparatus, endoplasmic reticulum, a complex cytoskeleton, and more. Eukaryotes mostly engage in sexual reproduction. And while prokaryotes need not die—their daughter cells continue as clones—most eukaryotes have preprogrammed senescence built into their DNA. Eukaryotes are usually orders of magnitude larger than prokaryotes.

The story of the first eukaryotes—the lineage we share with all fungi, plants, and animals—is astounding science, the stuff of fairy tales, really. It is a story told in bioinformatics and the comparative analysis of genomes in the last few decades. Once upon a time—long, long ago—some microbes made their living by eating other microbes, which turns out to be very nutritious. This was, and still is, pretty normal for microbes and other living things. The technical term for this phenomenon is "heterotrophy"—which means "other feeder"—in contrast to the autotrophy of photosynthesis. Every day we eat other living things—three meals a day perhaps and a few snacks in between. One day, though, something strange happened that apparently only successfully happened once or twice in the history of the planet. A single-cell archeon swallowed some bacteria for breakfast, but the breakfast didn't digest.

Normally, enzymes break down the captured microbe into byte-sized food molecules. Not this time. Instead, breakfast decided that the cytoplasm of the predator cell was a good place to live and start a family. As kids, we feared that a swallowed watermelon seed might

---

[42] Net Primary Production (NPP) is defined as the Gross Primary Production (i.e., all photosynthesis) minus the water content. Smil, *Energy in Nature and Society*, 69.

grow into a new watermelon inside our stomachs. This is kind of what actually happened 2 billion years ago in the great microbial leap forward.

The initial acquisition and merger between the archeon and the bacterium created deadly competition inside the cell. Presumably this has been tried and failed a multitude of times, leaving no geological trace or contemporary intermediaries. The successful merger of two microbes— endosymbiosis—was something quite singular in evolution. It only successfully happened once, maybe twice, in the history of our planet. The ur-eukaryote—the grandmother cell of all fungi, plants, and animals—somehow developed a complex cell with differentiated organelles. The ur-eukaryote acquired and domesticated a parasite, resulting in an exponential evolutionary jump in the flux of energy, matter, and ingenuity.

Breakfast turned into a houseguest that wouldn't leave and kept getting more plentiful as it reproduced. To keep up with its own reproduction, as well as the parasites reproducing in its cytoplasm, the competition had to turn into cooperation and mutual benefit. A house divided cannot stand. Over time, the sons and daughters of the ur-eukaryote figured out how to turn competition into cooperation and then reproduce that know-how. The parasites—powered by photosynthesis and chemistry—began to share ATP with the host cell. Breakfast turned into a parasite, which then turned into a symbiont living inside the cell.

Over time, the newcomers evolved into organelles—mitochondria and chloroplasts. The endobionts started getting rid of excess DNA, keeping only genes necessary for their own reproduction inside the host's cytoplasm. Some of these discarded genes were picked up by the host cell and kept inside its newly formed nucleus. Sexual reproduction mixed things up more.

The new lineage of eukaryotes evolved into new morphologies and possibility spaces. With the radiation of eukaryotes, the quantity of organized information—in the size and varieties of proteins and in the number of DNA base pairs inside cells—begins to grow exponentially. The average size of proteins increases dramatically as we move from archaea and bacteria to eukaryotes. Eukaryotic complexity can also be crudely measured in the amount of DNA that rapidly accumulated inside the nucleus of cells at the time of the Great Radiation of eukaryotic life 2 billion years ago.

The exponential growth in information-ingenuity in the Great Radiation of eukaryotic life required an exponential increase in the flux of energy-matter. Sexual reproduction was one of the technological innovations that helped solve this problem. Sex is how eukaryotes explored adjacent morphological possibilities in the environment. The chloroplast and mitochondria organelles inside the eukaryote cells became the energy engine of evolution. The Central Bank of Chemistry was able to dramatically grow the supply of ATP in the economy of cells, energizing the great microbial leap forward.[43]

At first, the new lineage of eukaryotic microbes was made up of single-cell creatures known as protists. They come in plant-like, animal-like, fungus-like, and mixed-up varieties. *Chlamydomonas reinhardtii*, for instance, is a single-cell alga that reproduces both sexually and asexually, has motility and heterotrophy, and behaves like an animal but is also capable of photosynthesis like a plant. Most protists vary in size from 10 to 100 μm (i.e., thousands of times larger than the average prokaryote).

Unlike prokaryotes, which are biochemically complex but morphologically simple, the newly incorporated eukaryotes grew in size and morphological complexity. Sexual reproduction within distinct lineages of eukaryotes and the inevitability of death gave rise to a dramatic evolutionary radiation of diverse kinds in the history of our planet. Eukaryotes took cooperation-competition to new levels by forming multicellular organisms with specialization and divisions of labor.

The diminutive, ever-adaptive prokaryotes in the environment, of course, went along for the evolutionary ride with the big, new eukaryotic creatures. Bacteria and archaea are an essential component of our environment, development, and health, and we contain multitudes in our bodies. Sometimes, of course, bacteria cause disease and death, but we are learning that early and frequent exposure to the bacteria in the environment is essential to developing a healthy immune system. We did not evolve to grow up in an antiseptic environment.[44]

Eukaryotes evolved through natural selection into the marvelously diverse and complex fauna and flora that amaze us in nature today.[45] And it apparently had a singular origin in the early history of life.

---

[43] Olivia Judson, "The Energy Expansion of Evolution," *Natue Ecology & Evolution* 1 (2017).
[44] Ed Yong, *I Contain Multitudes: The Microbes within Us and a Grander View of Life* (New York: HarperCollins, 2016).
[45] Ibid.

The Whole Economy of Nature

In *On the Origin of Species*, Charles Darwin wrote of "the whole economy of nature." We have extended the metaphor of "economy" to the level of single-cellular life. Economics and biology have come a long way since Darwin first used this analogy. Single-cell prokaryotes and eukaryotes have their own laws of supply and demand involving electron markets and the currency of ATP. Specialization and the division of labor were already nascent in the biochemistry of hunter-gatherer prokaryotes. The invention of photosynthesis was a kind of agricultural revolution, dramatically increasing the energy that could be harnessed to support the growing economies of life. The microscopic prokaryotes also created a global trade in DNA fragments, which continues to this day, aided now in their spread by human trade and travel. Specialization and division of labor took a giant leap forward in the industrial revolution of eukaryote lineages. Multicellular organisms took this profligacy to new heights.

Cells—big or small—maintain their identity through inconceivably frenetic activity. Trillions of chemical cascades occur every second inside each cell. Even the smallest bacteria contain many thousand different types of protein molecules. To maintain such complexity, cells need to take in matter and energy and dispose of waste. Cells needs to defend themselves from predation and harm, while seeking out new sources of energy and matter from their environment so they can exist, grow, reproduce, and complexify. This is how human economies also function at a much grander scale.

There are about 37 trillion cells in a 70-kilo human body (and approximately an equal number of prokaryotes—weighing about 3 kilos).[46] And though you may experience yourself to be unified and coherent, at times even calm and relaxed, the incomprehensible frenzy of each cell in your body continues throughout the nights and days of your life.

Life is an energy-matter and information-ingenuity processing system. The flux of energy-matter is guided by information-ingenuity.

---

[46] Eva Bianconi, Allison Piovesan, and et al., "An Estimation of the Number of Cells in the Human Body," *Annals of Human Biology* 40, no. 6 (2013). Ron Sender, Shai Fuchs, and Ron Milo, "Revised Estimates of the Number of Human and Bacteria Cells in the Body," *PLOS Biology* (2016).

Life has a built-in telos—which is to survive, grow, and reproduce life that is more abundant, more diverse, more extravagant. Information is passed on to descendants in the code of DNA, which is then read into protein structures that function within this vast biochemical cauldron. The code choreographs the marvelous dance of energy, matter, and ingenuity in the great flux of emergent complexity called life.

It begins and ends with energy density flows. Cells achieve a temporary homeostasis inside their membranes through a dynamic chemical-energetic disequilibrium with the outside environment. If you don't understand bioenergetics and bioinformatics, you don't really understand the economy of a cell, let alone the whole economy of nature. If you don't understand energetics and informatics, you also don't understand human economies. As we will explore in upcoming chapters, the universal formula for wealth creation is energy, matter, and ingenuity.

By changing scale, we can shift from inside a single cell to the economy of many individual cells interacting. The latter—individuals interacting—occurs in the form of microbial ecosystems and is also manifested in the rise of multicellular organisms. At this point I don't know how the economic metaphor best applies. In the context of cell biology, what counts as an individual or a corporation? Where should we draw the line between microeconomics and macroeconomics? I don't know. But certainly, like economic markets, cell biology and cell ecologies are emergent phenomena. Many actors buying and selling make the market. One cannot predict market trends based on a single corporation or individual. Similarly, one cannot really understand the behavior of a single cell by studying a single protein, let alone a single atom. Multicellular organisms and microbial ecosystems add orders of magnitude more complexity to the level of analysis.

Cell biology and economic markets are examples of complex adaptive systems. The economy of cells, however, is more than just a metaphor for economics. Complexity theory—and its cousin, chaos theory—allows us to discover common patterns in disparate natural phenomena. Star formation, cell biology, genomics, ecology, earthquakes, floods, neuroscience, and economic markets turn out to share common patterns. This book is an attempt to build those connections between domains and disciplines—in this case, to learn how the physical and biological patterns appear also in economics and finance.

Chapter 4:
Complexity Economics

In chapter 2, we began by laying out a matrix of scales and hierarchies—size, time, matter, energetics, electromagnetism, sound, information-ingenuity, sentience-consciousness, cultural constructs, and the end product—emergent complexity. This Great Matrix helps us to understand and interpret all phenomena as understood by contemporary science. These scales are reflected in the distributions of specialized knowledge and know-how in universities, industries, and government. In chapter 3, we then went on to use economic metaphors to explain chemistry, cell biology, and evolution. We underscored the role of energy, matter, and information-ingenuity in creating, sustaining, and growing complexity in nature and society.

Big History is a story of emergent complexity. And like the stock market, it hasn't all been uphill. There have been mass extinctions and there will be again. Evolution is a story of punctuated equilibrium and creative destruction in the service of emergent complexity meandering from atoms to cells to organisms to us. Complexity is a bottom-up process that creates top-down constraints on the flows of energy, matter, and ingenuity. On the billion-year scale of the universe, the Earth has surely become more complex and intense, more beautiful and valuable.

Given a sufficient flux of energy in the medium of matter, information will emerge and grow. In our little thermodynamic eddy in the universe, complexity has acquired a telos— to survive, grow, reproduce, and adapt, and to make life more abundant and more extravagant. The history of economics is a continuation of this drama, so let's explore how human economies manifests this fundamental evolutionary drive.

"All Hell Broke Loose"

Economics—which describes the behavior of billions of human agents around the globe—may be the most complex of all empirical phenomena. Indeed, this is why economics has always been a troubled science. Economists in the last century caught a bad case of physics envy, which led them partly astray. It is great to be precisely mathematical, descriptive, and predictive, but physics largely deals with rather simple and idealized systems. Humans are neither simple nor ideal. Studying humans is singularly hard. Doing so in the aggregate on a global scale is harder still.

Traditional neoclassical economic theory in the twentieth century was inspired by the equilibrium mathematics of nineteenth-century physics. Economic theorists came up with many elegant equations and insights to describe idealized macro- and microeconomic behavior. The laws of supply and demand call for a self-seeking balance in pricing. Government monetary policies seek to manage the money supply in hopes of cultivating stable, inflation-free growth. The goal has been to dampen and flatten the business cycle, minimize and mitigate macroeconomic crises, and find some kind of happy equilibrium.[47] The assumptions of symmetry are already embedded in the use of double-entry bookkeeping. Every credit is always offset by a debit. Income minus expense equals net profit or loss.

In his 1202 book *Liber Abaci*, Leonardo Fibonacci changed world history by teaching Europeans how to count. Roman numerals were replaced by the simple and superior Indo-Arabic notation system (try balancing your checkbook with Roman numerals!). Fibonacci taught his readers how to handle fractions. The decimal system made basic reckoning easier. He introduced double-entry bookkeeping. He explained the mathematics of currency conversions and compounded interest. He applied these mathematical techniques to the making of money, to commercial bookkeeping, to commodities, and to lending. All this he learned from the Muslims in North Africa. Within a century, northern Italian bankers would use these new mathematical tools to revolutionize trade and finance throughout Europe. The publication of *Liber Abaci* in 1202 is a critical conceptual watershed in the history of economics and indeed human history. The revolution in finance that followed helped to precipitate the Industrial Revolution.[48]

Economics must also be about the study of human history, including its own history as a discipline. Economic theories that deals

---

[47] Eric D. Beinhocker, *The Origin of Wealth: Evolution, Complexity, and the Radical Remaking of Economics* (Cambridge Harvard Business Press, 2006); David Warsh, *Knowledge and the Wealth of Nations: A Story of Economic Discovery* (New York: Norton, 2006).

[48] See Jack Weatherford, *The History of Money: From Sandstone to Cyberspace*, Kindle ed. (New York: Crown Publishing Group, 2009); Niall Ferguson, *The Ascent of Money: A Financial History of the World*, Kindle ed. (New York: Penguin Press, 2008).

only in present-tense, short-term prediction and analysis is missing the big story.

Economic history is not about equilibrium, rather it is all about process, change, instability, adaptation, and evolution. Complexity economics takes disequilibrium and transformations to be the norm. Economic complexity is dynamic. It is adaptive. It is accelerating. In his book *The Origin of Wealth*, Eric Beinhocker summarizes 2.5 million years of economic history thus: "For a very, very, very long time not much happened; then all of a sudden, all hell broke loose."[49]

The guiding assumptions of traditional economics are often wrong. Humans are not rational actors with access to perfect information engaged in frictionless, auction-like economic transactions with the purpose of maximizing their self-interest. Richard Thaler, a recent Nobel laureate in economics, notes that "[t]he purely economic man is indeed close to being a social moron. Economic theory has been much preoccupied with this rational fool."[50] In the words of UCLA economist Axel Leijonhufvud, humans are not "incredibly smart people in unbelievably simple situations," as traditional economic theory would assume, but rather "believably simple people [coping] with incredibly complex situations."[51] Or to paraphrase Harvard biologist E. O. Wilson, we humans have hunter-gatherer brains, medieval mythologies, and twenty-first-century technologies.[52] As we will explore later in this book, Big History is an opportunity to get to know our Paleolithic emotions and cognition—something that investors ignore at their own peril.

The equilibrium models borrowed from nineteenth-century physics turned out to be a dead end. Beinhocker writes:

> The models of Walras, Jevons, and Pareto began with the assumptions that an economy already exists, producers have resources, and consumers own various commodities. The models thus view the problem as how to allocate the existing finite wealth

---

[49] Beinhocker, *The Origin of Wealth: Evolution, Complexity, and the Radical Remaking of Economics*, 11.

[50] Richard Thaler, *Misbehaving: The Making of Behavioral Economics* (New York: W.W. Norton, 2015).

[51] Beinhocker, *The Origin of Wealth: Evolution, Complexity, and the Radical Remaking of Economics*, 52.

[52] Edward O. Wilson, *The Social Conquest of Earth* (New York, NY: Liveright, 2012).

of the economy in a way that provides the maximum benefits for everyone. An important reason for this focus on allocation of finite resources was that the mathematical equations of equilibrium imported from physics were ideal for answering the allocation question, but it was more difficult to apply them to growth. Equilibrium systems by definition are in a state of rest, while growth implies change and dynamism.[53]

Complexity economics begins with dynamic, out-of-equilibrium models. It includes agents—individuals, corporations, governments, investors—who are far- from-perfect maximizers of self-interest and who change behavior and adapt over time to new circumstances. These agents interact through networks that also change over time. Macroeconomic patterns emerge bottom up from the microeconomic behaviors of countless differentiated and asymmetrical actors. And this panoply of dynamism, agents, networks, and emergence gives rise to novelty, growth, increased complexity, and endogenous turbulence in markets.

Economic value is created, much like biological complexity, out of energy, matter, and ingenuity. Moreover, economic value is a mash-up of objective needs and perceived goods. To survive, we need food, water, shelter, and sociality, but once we get beyond the bare necessities of life, our perceptions of economic value become all important. The market equates value with price, but humans are much more complicated, divergent, and conflicted about values, economic or otherwise.

Beinhocker doesn't get around to defining wealth until over 300 pages into *The Origin of Wealth*:

> Economic wealth and biological wealth are thermodynamically the same sort of phenomena, and not just metaphorically. Both are systems of locally low entropy, patterns of order that evolved over time under the constraint of fitness functions. Both are forms of fit order . . .

---

[53] Beinhocker, *The Origin of Wealth: Evolution, Complexity, and the Radical Remaking of Economics*, 39.

The economy is like ecologies of bacteria and eukaryotes that we discussed in chapter 3. Energy flows are an essential component of wealth creation in nature and in economics:

> If wealth is indeed fit order, then we can use another more familiar word to describe it. In physics, order is the same thing as information, and thus we can also think of wealth as fit information; in other words, *knowledge* . . . The origin of wealth is knowledge. Yet rather than treating knowledge as an assumption, an exogenous input, a mysterious process outside the bounds of economics, the Complexity-based view I have outlined puts the creation of knowledge at the endogenous heart of the economy.[54]

Beinhocker is not the first person to make these observations. There have been many heterodox economists over the decades who have advanced ecological, energetic, evolutionary, and knowledge-based models of economic progress as dynamic, complex, and chaotic systems. Joseph Schumpeter (1883–1950) understood economics to be driven by innovation and entrepreneurship leading to a "gale of creative destruction." Friedrich Hayek (1899–1992) understood economics to be a bottom-up, evolutionary process that creates spontaneous order. For Hayek, the pricing mechanism in markets was a way of transmitting information between economic agents.[55] Nicholas Georgescu-Roegen (1906–1994) and others have applied the laws of thermodynamics to understanding economics.[56] More recently, Paul Romer (b. 1955) and Cesar Hidalgo (b. 1979) have also shown that technological innovation—knowledge and know-how—is the key to increased productivity and economic growth.[57]

In the history of economics from the Paleolithic period to today, technology has played a critical role in our evolution and development. From fire mastery and prehistoric tools to fossil fuels and computers, technological innovations have had a huge impact on the depth and breadth of human life. The geological deposits of concentrated

---

[54] Ibid., 317.

[55] Friedrich Hayek wrote, "In a system in which the knowledge of the relevant facts is dispersed among many people, prices can act to coordinate the separate actions of different people"(quoted by Hidalgo, *Why Information Grows: The Evolution of Order, from Atoms to Economies*, 137.

[56] Nicholas Georgescu-Roegen, *The Entropy Law and the Economic Process* (Cambridge, MA: Harvard University Press, 1971).

[57] Warsh, *Knowledge and the Wealth of Nations: A Story of Economic Discovery*; Hidalgo, *Why Information Grows: The Evolution of Order, from Atoms to Economies*.

hydrocarbons—oil, gas, coal—have been around for hundreds of millions of years, but humans have only recently learned how to divert this chemical potential energy to our own purposes. Electromagnetism has existed since the earliest moments of the universe, but humans have only recently learned how to harness and shape it to our purposes.

Beinhocker labels these "Physical Technologies," which he distinguishes from "Social Technologies." The evolution of physical technologies is perhaps obvious to readers, but let's reflect on what is meant by "Social Technologies."

Human language—spoken and later written—is the most important social technology. Symbolic language allows for coordination of activities, teaching and learning, and the accumulation of knowledge and know-how across generations and geographies. Moreover, human language also allows for the creation of social fictions that bind communities together in ever-larger and more productive networks of cooperation and competition.

"Social Technologies," writes Beinhocker, "are methods and designs for organizing people in pursuit of a goal or goals."[58] In the history of economics, social technologies include the use of money, family networks, property rights, double-entry accounting, limited liability joint stock corporations, the rule of law, effective banking systems, economic transparency, lack of corruption, social capital, trust, and reputation. All of these play a profound role in determining economic outcomes in communities and nations throughout human history. Social technologies and physical technologies are necessary for unleashing productivity growth through which new wealth is created to the mutual advantage of many. Here, too, we see a biological analog in the evolved divisions of labor and mutualism inside and between cells and organisms.

It is a marvel that 7.3 billion people today participate in a $119 trillion global economy. No one oversees it. No one designed it. No one can control it. Economic complexity emerges from the bottom up. How has this marvelous self-organized system evolved? What is economic growth and how is it created? Beyond mere money, what is income really? What is wealth? How can individuals, business, and societies get more of it?

---

[58] Beinhocker, *The Origin of Wealth: Evolution, Complexity, and the Radical Remaking of Economics*, 262.

Big Money

Money, we should always remind ourselves, is a human construct—a social technology—that has radically changed human history, but is in itself not "real." Money does not exist in non-human nature. No other species exchanges energy, matter, and ingenuity by way of an abstraction. Symbolic thinking and symbolic calculating are probably uniquely human. Money is merely a symbolic system of value. It is really distributed trust. In principle, it does not matter whether the symbol is metal, paper, or digital. It is all virtual. Money is therefore an extremely practical fiction that has become a critical fact of social life.

The use of money enabled a remarkable transition in early agricultural societies. It solved the problem of how to conduct exchanges between strangers in ever-larger, more complex societies, across ever-greater distances. The use of money meant that people could cooperate more effectively and at greater scales. Money further transformed the traditional bonds of family and tribe. Written languages, we should remind ourselves, evolved first in human history to facilitate accounting and trade, not works of poetry, scripture, literature, history, or science.[59]

Money, by definition, promotes trade. The two terms are really synonymous, because without a transaction, money has no purpose. Money allows the exchange of unlike things via a generalized abstraction—apples and iPhones for strings of numbers on a bankcard linked to a network of ledgers. It does this across space and time. The "value" of money can be stored and accumulated on the promise of future exchanges at distant times and places for different utility functions. In the course of human history, trade promoted specialized services, products, and skill sets, as in "the trades," as well as travel and exchange across greater distances and terrains.

Trade and travel then created a positive feedback loop in the history of collective learning, as ideas, technologies, and products quickly dispersed around the globe. We have tools and opportunities that would seem like magic to our ancestors even a hundred years ago. Money turns out to be a medium not just for exchanging goods and services, but also for facilitating the flow of information-ingenuity.

---

[59] John Kenneth Galbraith, *Money: Whence It Came, Where It Went* (New York: Houghton Mifflin, 1975, 1995); Ferguson, *The Ascent of Money: A Financial History of the World*; Weatherford, *The History of Money: From Sandstone to Cyberspace.*

In the great economic acceleration of the past century, money has become ever more abstracted and more powerful. The idea of redeemable paper for gold and silver bullion now seems quaint and has been replaced with electronic money traveling at the speed of light. While there is more paper money and coinage in circulation now than at any other time in human history, this cash-on-hand accounts for less than 10 percent of the total money in the world.

In 1934, Simon Kuznets invented the concept of Gross Domestic Product (GDP) in a report to Congress. He calculated the US GDP at $66 billion, which, when adjusted for inflation, would be $862 billion in constant 2014 US dollars. By way of comparison, in 2014 the US GDP was $17,419 billion—a twentyfold increase. In 1934, the population of the United States was 126 million. By 2014, the US population had increased to 318 million. So over the eighty years between 1934 and 2014, the US population almost tripled, while economic activity increased twentyfold.[60]

GDP, however, is "gross" in both senses of the word. GDP is an ugly aggregate, a calculation full of biases and distortions, so we need to examine its uses and abuses carefully.[61] And yet, the consistent use of a flawed yardstick can provide some interesting insights. GDP helps us better grok the unprecedented growth in scales and intensities of economic activity on the planet even as it ignores many other quantitative and qualitative factors in accounting for human well-being.

Most money is merely numbers on someone's ledger stored digitally in a vast, free-floating cyberspace of overlapping and interconnected electronic ledgers. The symbols on the ledgers can be moved instantaneously in any amount anywhere in the world. Today, we might talk about Big Money, because the money supply in the world today, like everything else, has grown exponentially in the last century. Big Money is quantitatively and qualitatively different.[62] Let's get some perspective using economic statistics from 2014. All of these numbers are moving targets. All are open to interpretation and dispute:

---

[60] Bureau of Economic Analysis, "U.S. Gdp by Year," (Washington, D.C.: U.S. Department of Commerce, 2017); Max Roser, "Gdp Growth over the Last Centuries," University of Oxford, https://ourworldindata.org/gdp-growth-over-the-last-centuries/.
[61] Herman E. Daly and Joshua Farley, *Ecological Economics: Principles and Applications*, Second ed. (Washington: Island Press, 2011); "The Trouble with Gdp," *The Economist* 2016.
[62] See also Roser, "Gdp Growth over the Last Centuries".

- The median US household income was $54,000.

- The top 1 percent of people in the United States earned $430,000 per year or more (8 times the median income).

- The world's richest person, Bill Gates, was worth about $79.2 billion.

- Apple had a market capitalization worth $616 billion, the world's largest.

- The Federal Reserve balance sheet was $4.5 trillion (up from $1 trillion in 2008).

- All coins and paper currency circulated globally were roughly equivalent to $5 trillion.

- Commercial real estate, a small portion of the entire real estate market, had an estimated value of $7.6 trillion globally.

- Gold—183,600 tons above ground at a $1,200 spot price—was worth $7.8 trillion.

- Narrow Money—coins, banknotes, and checking deposits—was roughly $28.6 trillion.

- The value of all stock markets in the world was roughly $70 trillion (52 percent of which is American based).

- Broad Money—coins, banknotes, money markets, savings, checking, and time deposits—was roughly $80.9 trillion globally.

- Global annual GDP was estimated at $107.5 trillion (in purchasing power parity).

- All global debt was roughly $199 trillion (up by 29 percent since the 2008 financial crisis). This includes $59.7 trillion in sovereign national debt, of which about 29 percent was owed by the US government.

- Foreign exchange markets averaged currency trades totaling $4 trillion per day for a staggering annual flow of $1,400 trillion.[63]

- The SWIFT system processed over 15 million transactions per day, transmitting funds between over 10,000 financial institutions in over 200 countries.[64]

- The notional value of derivatives—over 20 billion such contracts per year now—were estimated at the low-end around $630 trillion and at the high-end around $1.2 quadrillion.[65]

Big Money is unprecedented in human history. It has grown exponentially. It is moved around the globe in enormous quantities measured in trillions and with accelerating speeds now measured in nanoseconds.

The mere presence of these symbols in a room—dollars, euros, yens, roubles—has powerful, unconscious effects on our behavior. Indeed, most people are literalists, fetishizing the printed pieces of paper and coins, when the real money supply is mostly credit extended to borrowers by private lenders, not the government's fiat currency. Money is better understood as debt owed.

Debt and derivatives are controversial, and rightly so. One school of thought sees careful debt issuance as the royal road to prosperity; another sees it as the road to certain ruin. One school of thought sees derivatives as zero-sum trades that promote market efficiency. The other sees derivatives as inherently dangerous. Warren Buffet famously wrote:

The derivatives genie is now well out of the bottle, and these

---

[63] "Otc Derivatives Statistics at End of 2014," (2014), http://www.bis.org/publ/otchy1405.pdf.
[64] "Society for Worldwide Interbank Financial Telecommunication (Swift)," Wikipedia, http://en.wikipedia.org/wiki/Society_for_Worldwide_Interbank_Financial_Telecommunication.
[65] "The Money Project," Visual Capitalist, http://money.visualcapitalist.com/worlds-money-markets-one-visualization-2017/; "Wfe Annual Statistics," World Federation of Exchanges, https://www.world-exchanges.org/home/index.php/statistics/annual-statistics.

instruments will almost certainly multiply in variety and number until some event makes their toxicity clear. Central banks and governments have so far found no effective way to control, or even monitor, the risk posed by these contracts. In my view, derivatives are financial weapons of mass destruction, carrying dangers that, while now latent, are potentially lethal.[66]

Short- and Long-Term Oscillations

We need to always remind ourselves that the measuring stick—money, GDP, price—is not really real. Money is a convenient and powerful fiction. People disagree about religion and politics, but they all agree about the value of money. And though money is not ontologically real outside of human minds, the supply of money is nevertheless both a dependent and an independent variable in the function and dysfunction of economic markets.

Most of the money supply is debt issued by private lenders, not money issued by government treasuries. Most people, including many policy makers, don't understand this fundamental fact of economics. One entity's credit is another entity's debt, which results in spending toward another entity's income. The principal of the debt is repaid over time with the addition of compounded interest. Whether by individuals, corporations, or governments, debt is generally incurred with an expectation of future growth in income and sometimes also growth in the value of underlying assets. The expectation is that the debt burden will decrease with time. This, of course, is not always the case, as seen in the 2008 collapse in the housing market and ensuing recession.

The standard macroeconomic model envisions a happy balance between inflation and the economy's growing productivity. When there are more goods and services, there needs to be more money. This is good inflation. And it was certainly true during the last century, during which productivity increased by leaps and bounds. Humanity has more money and more goods and services than it had at any other time in human history. That in itself is astounding and difficult to grok.

A more detailed view, however, reveals a lot of instability—a long history of recessions and depressions, booms and busts, bull markets and bear markets. If incomes and asset values don't rise as anticipated,

---

[66] Warren Buffett, "Berkshire Hathaway Annual Report," (Omaha: Berkshire Hathaway, 2002).

compound interest payments can become an exponential burden for individuals, corporations, and nations on the way down. Debtors declare bankruptcy. Assets are devalued and sold in fire sales. Individuals and corporations lose fortunes—often for no fault of their own. The downward spiral becomes contagious. Instabilities ripple through far-flung economic sectors and supply lines across the globe. In the process, some countries are crushed by deflation or inflation, unemployment, and social unrest. All of this is in the nature of credit and debt—borrowing against future income (debt-liability) and counting your chickens before they hatch (credit-assets). The oscillations are endogenous to the economic markets quite independently of the psychology of the market, though the two causal factors inevitably align in boom-bust cycles.

The instability is seen in a short-term debt cycle that churns along as economic actors leverage and deleverage debt. This is an ongoing process that builds into a long-term debt cycle in which the whole economy needs to deleverage. Economists believe that the long-term debt cycle is somewhat periodic and that the subsequent recession and reflation of credit and asset value are also periodic. Investors make big guesses about the timing and severity of these economic downturns. Fortunes are won and lost by riding the growth waves up, exiting at the crest, and reentering the market when asset prices have tanked and growth resumes. Buy low and sell high is the truism, or as John Templeton was fond of saying, "Buy at the point of maximum pessimism."[67]

Ray Dalio, the founder of Bridgewater Associates, the world's largest hedge fund, produced a short video titled "How the Economic Machine Works" accompanied by a lengthy historical research paper.[68] Dalio plots the short- and long-term debt cycle onto a line of steady productivity growth. In the chart below, the straight line is rising productivity growth (per capita) while the oscillating lines represent the short- and long-term debt cycle.

The short and long-term oscillations of the debt cycle are a bottom-up phenomenon—a complex ecology of economic actors including consumers, corporations, employees, producers, supply

---

[67] Lauren Templeton and Scott Philllips, *Investing the Templeton Way: The Market-Beating Strategies of Value Investing's Legendary Bargain Hunter* (New York: McGraw-Hill Education, 2008).

[68] Ray Dalio, *How the Economic Machine Works* (Westport, CT: Bridgewater Associates, 2013).

chains, banks, governments, investors, and others in enormous networks across the globe.

Dalio shows how the central bank tries to moderate the short- and long-term debt cycle from the top down by making credit more or less expensive. The primary mechanism is raising or lowering interest rates. The goal is to avoid too much inflation or deflation, which turns into self-reinforcing, feedback loops. When borrowing goes down, spending goes down. Incomes go down. Taxes go down. It is a viscous spiral that eventually hits bottom like an alcoholic on a bender.

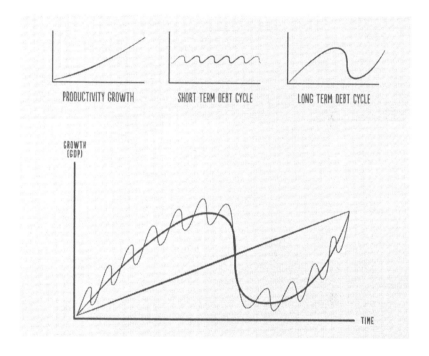

Fig. 4.1 Short and Long-Term Debt Cycle
Source: Ray Dalio, *How the Economic Machine Works*, 2013

There are a number of possible responses to a debt crisis. The central bank can issue more money, eventually devaluing the currency. (This doesn't work, however, if the principal debt is in a foreign currency.) Individuals, corporations, and the government can cut costs. The lenders can restructure debt. The government can increase taxes on the wealthy. And the government can increase deficit spending. If the economy is to grow, credit must be extended again (i.e., new debt issued), so money will flow through the larger economy.

Whatever the mix, the piper must be paid. Deleveraging is painful for individuals, corporations, investors, and nations. Dalio suggests that "a beautiful deleveraging" is possible with the right combination of spending cuts, debt restructuring, wealth redistribution, government stimulus spending, and disciplined monetary policies.

The goal of government tax, monetary, and spending policies in a depression is to prevent a self-reinforcing inflationary or deflationary spiral from causing widespread economic collapse. Depressions and recessions, in this view, are primarily monetary events caused by the debt cycles. Depressed economies generally have plenty of surplus production and lots of people willing, able, and anxious to work, earn, and spend.

Monetary policy is both a dependent and an independent variable in how an economy functions. Bad monetary policy can destroy an otherwise healthy economy. Good monetary policy can restore a sick economy. The intended goal is to increase credit issued and thereby increase spending and consuming, leading to economic growth. These policies, which also guide private investment decisions, may only be loosely connected to the prime economic movers—energy, matter, and ingenuity. Money becomes merely a self-referential numeric concept as investors deploy differential calculus to plot and predict the curves of interconnected market sectors as they ride the short- and long-term debt cycles up and down.

In practice, conservatives and liberals promote deficit spending, whether through tax cuts or increased government spending, in order to stimulate economic growth. Without private or government credit being issued, spending contracts and the economy collapse. The oscillations are an endogenous feature of an economy based on future promises to pay with interest.

If it were not for increasing productivity, the whole credit-debt canard would come tumbling down. Indeed, without a baseline of productivity growth, the credit-debt system is just a giant Ponzi scheme. Productivity growth, the straight line in Dalio's chart, is why income and wealth grow over time. He offers three take-home conclusions:

1. Don't have debt rise faster than income.
2. Don't have income rise faster than productivity.
3. Do all that you can to raise your productivity.

This is sound advice for individuals, corporations, and governments. Growing productivity is critical, but how?

Productivity Growth

"The greatest improvements in the productive power of labour," wrote Adam Smith in *The Wealth of Nations* in 1776, "and the greater part of the skill, dexterity, and judgment with which it is anywhere directed, or applied, seem to have been the effects of the division of labour."[69] Traditional economics, following Smith's lead, has focused on specialization and the division of labor as the key to increasing economic productivity. Indeed, we saw in the last chapter that specialization and the division of labor were also critical to the rise of eukaryotic and multicellular life in the evolutionary narrative.

Imagine, for instance, what would be involved in making your lunch sandwich from scratch. You would need not only to bake the bread, but also cultivate and harvested the wheat. You would not only need to cook and slice the chicken meat, you would also need to raise and slaughter the chicken. Put it altogether with some lettuce and mayo, salt and pepper—which you would also need to source on your own— and you would have to spend the better part of a year and many thousands of dollars to make the $5 deli sandwich for today's lunch.

The focus on specialization and the division of labor as a means to boost economic productivity, however, neglects the more important role of ingenuity in promoting this growth. It is not the division of labor per se that makes the difference, but the innovations that result from the deductive tinkering of specialists in various domains, resulting in the adoption of new physical and social technologies.

Merely surfing the instabilities in the short- and long-term debt cycles to arbitrage the bipolar oscillations in "Mister Market" doesn't produce productivity growth, though it can produce income in the less-than zero-sum markets. We should not assume that growth in productivity is uniform and consistent. Indeed, from the perspective of Big History, "all hell broke loose."

Certainly, productivity has grown exponentially during the last century. It may be, however, that we have reached a kind of productivity plateau. In his book *The Great Stagnation*, economist

---

[69] Adam (1723-1790) Smith, *An Inquiry into the Nature and Causes of the Wealth of Nations* (London: Methuen and Co., 1776).

Tyler Cowen considers the possibility that "we have been living off low-hanging fruit for at least three hundred years" and that we have reached "a technological plateau." Increased productivity may be harder to come by in the future. For the US economy, the low-hanging fruit were free land, technological breakthroughs, and smart kids. The land is no longer free, the revolutionary technological innovations of the past are harder to come by, and educating young people in knowledge and know-how is expensive and arduous. In the case of education, it gets more and more difficult to make up for earlier deficiencies as children age through their schooling. While more young people go to college (incurring more debt to do so), colleges and universities also find themselves providing more remedial education in reading, writing, and simple arithmetic. Moreover, even as enrollments have increased, dropout rates in higher education have also increased. We should not assume that productivity grows at a steady rate, certainly not in all sectors of the economy.[70]

Emerging markets, for instance in Africa, can still achieve significant productivity growth by implementing innovations already deployed in wealthy countries. The developed countries, however, may no longer expect consistent growth in economic productivity. Without this productivity growth, debt spirals into an exponential drag. Moreover, without a growing population, the macroeconomic debt distributed across a society is inherited by an ever-smaller number of economic actors. If and when it happens, the big deleveraging is likely to be a dangerous time. The peasants and the proletariat will rise up with pitchforks and torches, or their more destructive modern equivalents, assault rifles and bombs.

In a second book, *Average Is Over*, Tyler Cowen considers a future in which robots, mechanization, and artificial intelligence will dramatically increase productivity, but also lead to mass unemployment. A small percentage of highly trained workers will add value to new smart machines. Others will provide services to this new technocratic elite, but the majority will be chronically underemployed. Democracies would be untenable with such extremes. Happily, productivity will also increase. Cowen holds out the possibility of universal guaranteed income as the only viable solution. The permanently poor will have basic income and more free education and

---

[70] Tyler Cowen, *The Great Stagnation: How America Ate All the Low-Hanging Fruit of Modern History, Got Sick, and Will (Eventually) Feel Better* (New York: Penguin eSpecial from Dutton, 2011).

free entertainment than they know what to do with. Maybe the leisure of the underclass would be quite pleasant in such a brave new world, where work was optional and, in any case, restricted to the busy and bright few, who would add value to the robots.[71]

Scaling Effects

Scaling effects describe a wide variety of natural and human phenomena in which power law dynamics are manifested at different magnitudes. Entrepreneurs and investors are looking for positive scaling effects in the form of economies of scale and exponential returns-on-investment.

In his book *Scale*, Geoffrey West, physicist and president of the Santa Fe Institute, explores a number of these growth patterns in nature and society. In mammals, the number of heart beats over a lifetime averages out around 1.5 billion for each species. This is true of mice and men—all mammals have approximately the same number of heart beats over their life span. This is an invariable value, as are the size of the capillaries and cells that compose mammalian tissue. Larger mammals, however, are more efficient than smaller mammals. Their hearts beat slower. They live longer. They need less food proportional to their size. Larger mammals achieve "economies of scale" and are more efficient than smaller mammals than one might intuitively expect. West observes:

> These systematic scaling relationships are highly counterintuitive. They show that almost all the physiological characteristics and life-history events of any organism are primarily determined simply by its size. . .

> If you tell me the size of a mammal, I can use the scaling laws to tell you almost everything about the average values of its measurable characteristics: how much food it needs to eat each day, what its heart rate is, how long it will take to mature, the length and radius of its aorta, its life span, how many offspring it will have, and so on. Given the extraordinary complexity and

---

[71] Tyler Cowen, *Average Is Over: Powering America Beyond the Age of the Great Stagnation* (Dutton Adult, 2013).

diversity of life, this is pretty amazing.[72]

What is perhaps more amazing is that these scaling patterns also apply to cities and companies. West and his colleagues have undertaken extensive data analyses and shown that the infrastructure of cities—the total length of roads, electric lines, water pipes, and gas lines—also achieve economies scale with growth in population. The metabolism of big cities is systematically more efficient than smaller cities, at a sublinear rate (0.85) comparable to mammals (0.75).

Larger cities are not just more efficient on per capita basis, socioeconomic quantities grow with size. Thus, the per capita number of professionals, patents, and restaurants, as well as disease and crime, increase at a superlinear rate (1.15). Thus, larger cities are systematically 15 percent richer per capita than smaller cities and 85 percent more efficient per capita. Size matters.

Part of the mystery of these scaling effects have to do with the structure of networks in organisms and cities. The invariable components—the size of cells and capillaries in the case organisms and the size of electric sockets in your home in the case of the electricity—need to be provided by a network—circulator system and the electric grid—which fills the entire space of the organism or city.

Business also display scaling effects. These can be sublinear—what economists call economies of scale— and superlinear—what economists call increasing rates of return. In business, exponential growth can be achieved through the widespread adoption of intellectual property (e.g., pharmaceuticals, computers, entertainment), branding and franchise (e.g., fast food, fashion), exclusive and complex services (professionals, sports, medicine), and network effects that increase the utility of goods and services with growth (e.g., phones, fax, email, social media).

Unfortunately, scaling effects are not all more-for-less-while-getting-bigger good news. The credit-debt cycle is an example of a complex adaptive system that also scales over time. What this means is that market failures are more like earthquakes—frequent small failures and infrequent larger failures that scale exponentially in intensity.

Large earthquakes occur less frequently than small earthquakes. Several hundred thousand earthquakes are detected with current

---

[72] Geoffrey West, *Scale: The Universal Laws of Life, Growth, and Death in Organisms, Cities, and Companies* (New York: Penguin Books, 2017), Kindle 1758.

instruments every year, but most of these are not actually felt by humans on the surface of the Earth. The world averages eighteen major earthquakes and one great earthquake each year, though we have only about a hundred years of measurements to base this pattern on. The longer it has been since an earthquake in some locale, the bigger the next earthquake is likely to be, and with it, greater property damage and loss of life.

What should give us real pause are the inevitable hundred- and thousand-year earthquakes in our future. The logarithmic Richter scale suggests that rare mega-earthquakes will be several orders of magnitude more destructive than anything we have previously experienced in recorded history. The power of the infrequent earthquakes, however, scales exponentially. The implication is that at some point in our economic future, we are due for a rare, but exponentially more powerful, global economic disruption.[73]

Complex Adaptive Systems

In the example of power laws, we see how complexity sciences provide new ways for understanding and modeling natural phenomena. These models are also be applied to understanding and modeling economic activities. The Santa Fe Institute (SFI) was founded in 1984 to pursue interdisciplinary research on complexity and chaos. SFI researchers undertook some of the first studies applying complexity and chaos theory to economics.[74] Today, others have also taken up the challenge, such as the Institute for New Economic Thought and the MIT Center for Mapping Economic Complexity.[75] Academic departments and journals are now also on board. Complexity economics is now widely discussed and debated in academic departments, government agencies, think tanks, financial institutions, and publications.[76]

The most interesting and creative phenomena in the universe are complex adaptive systems. Complexity requires a system composed of many independently interacting parts linked in

---

[73] Mark Buchanan, *Forecasts: What Physics, Meteorology, and the Natural Sciences Can Teach Us About Economics*, Kindle ed. (New York: Bloomsbury USA, 2014).
[74] "Santa Fe Institute," https://www.santafe.edu/.
[75] "Institute for New Economic Thinking," https://www.ineteconomics.org/; "The Observatory of Economic Complexity," MIT, https://atlas.media.mit.edu/en/.
[76] Carlos Gershenson, "Complexity Digest," Complex Systems Society, https://comdig.unam.mx/.

reiterative, mutually constitutive, causal pathways. The inner life of a cell, discussed in the last chapter, was our paradigmatic example. Complexity is a science of evolving processes and relationships. "Complex system" is actually redundant, because "complexity" already presupposes that there is a system involved.

Complexity sciences are interdisciplinary, cutting across many domains. Researchers have discovered many patterns in nature and society that are complex, and where the whole is more than the sum of the changing parts. Scientists observe complex behavior in subatomic particles, collections of molecules, genomic bureaucracies, predator-prey population variations, epidemics, earthquakes, the floods of rivers, the weather on Jupiter, the beating of our hearts, the formation of stars, the gravitation dance of galaxies, the historic price of cotton, and—critically for investors—the endogenous behavior of economic markets.[77] In order to understand an ecosystem or a complex business enterprise, we have to set aside hierarchical and mechanistic models. Complex adaptive systems are decentralized, networked, interactive, emergent, and evolving.

Feedback loops are an essential feature of complex dynamic systems. Instead of a linear causal chain—X affects Y to cause Z—complex phenomena involve feedback— X affects Y to cause a new X, X_1, which is run again in endless reiterations. Minor variable tweaks in feedback loops at the outset can dramatically accelerate or mitigate some processes. The effect is not linear. It involves fluctuations, phase transitions, scaling effects, and disorder. Feedback is an ever-updating variable in an iterative loop that bites its own tail. Feedback is what drives the churning of markets and the morphing of balance sheets over time. The hedge fund titan George Soros calls this "reflexivity"—a circular and bi-directional cause-effect relationship between fundamentals, price, and perception.[78]

Some, but certainly not all, complex phenomena can be approximated mathematically, often with very simple reiterative equations. This was a major discovery facilitated by the new mathematics, fluid dynamics, nonlinear equations, and fractals. [79]

---

[77] James Gleick, *Chaos: Making a New Science* (New York: Penguin, 1987).

[78] George Soros, *The Alchemy of Finance* (New York: Wiley, 2003).

[79] The mathematics of complexity works both ways. For instance, a statistical approach to economic forecasting developed by Clive Granger, for which he won the Nobel Prize in Economics in 2003, is being used by neuroscientists to calculate the probability that activity at one

The power of computers enabled complex phenomena to be iterated as equations at a scale beyond human capacity. Thanks to computers, these kinds of equations gave rise to novel and amazing patterns, self-similar across different-sized scales, somewhere between order and chaos. Without the power of computers, it is difficult to simulate, analyze, or understand complexity in nature and economics.[80] It is worth reminding ourselves what the financial services industry was like a few decades back, before Excel spreadsheets, Bloomberg terminals, Blackberry devices, and so-called rocket scientists came to town.

Complicated and Complex Systems

There is an important distinction between *complicated* systems and *complex* systems. An automobile is an example of a complicated system. It is engineered, constructed, adapted, improved, and reliably used. A traffic jam, however, can be a complex system, arising spontaneously from the dynamic behavior of individual drivers, as small variations in speed reverberate and amplify through a stream of cars on your commute—stop, start, stop again. Short- and long-term debt cycles are more like traffic jams. They arise spontaneously from the dynamics of the economic system.

A bird is a complicated organism—or let us pretend so for a moment. Assume that ornithologists have a completely reductionist understanding of the physiology and behavior of birds. The bird, in this case, is more like a complicated machine. The behavior of a flock of thousands of migrating starlings, however, is a complex phenomenon. Indeed, the flock of birds can be modeled in a computer simulation with a few simple rules. Of course, lots of aspects of avian biology—from bird brains to bird genomes—are not really machinelike at all. Birds are complicated and complex organisms, as are humans.

---

brain location predicts subsequent activity at other brain locations. EurekaAlert, "Pinpointing Where Seizures Are Coming from, by Looking between the Seizures," news release, 2017, https://www.eurekalert.org/pub_releases/2017-05/bch-pws050117.php.

[80] Gleick, *Chaos: Making a New Science*; Kevin Kelly, *Out of Control: The New Biology of Machines, Social Systems, and the Economic World* (New York: Addison-Wesley, 1994), 22-25.

Many complicated phenomena, natural and built, can be reductively understood, engineered, and reengineered from the bottom up. Complex phenomena, on the other hand, can be simple or complicated, but the behavior is an emergent property of an interactive system. Science was traditionally dominated by bottom-up and reductionist understandings of natural phenomena, in which causation was described as linear, predictable, controlled, and repeatable. This methodological reductionism has been incredibly successful in figuring out how things work. Reductionism is an essential component of the scientific method. Reductionist analysis is also an essential component of any successful business or investment strategy. Ironically, though, in science and in finance, the very pursuit of reductionist explanations, along with some unusual mathematics and experiments, has led us down the rabbit hole of complexity and chaos sciences.

Complex adaptive systems evolve over time and in response to changing environments. Like a single-cell organism, complex adaptive systems are self-regulated. They achieve a temporary internal homeostasis within an ever-changing external environment. Complex adaptive systems produce novelties. They can be both incredibly resilient and fragile. Moreover, these systems generally cannot be optimized, cannot be controlled, cannot be predicted, and cannot be understood through linear models of causation, at least not with any predictive certainty.

Complex adaptive systems typically have chaotic attributes. When certain thresholds are crossed—such as when a system becomes too hot or too cold, too fast or too slow—the system can turn chaotic, varying wildly, unpredictably. When certain tipping points are reached, fluctuations, oscillations, turbulence, disorder, and new patterns may result. In biological and economic systems, these tipping points generally lead to systemic collapses (i.e. death and depressions). The effect of multiple feedback loops within any complex adaptive system means that small changes in initial conditions can reverberate through the system, causing chaotic, unintended, unforeseen, and sometimes catastrophic consequences—i.e., the proverbial "butterfly effect."

New mathematics often describes these erratic sides of nature and markets, but it does so without the possibility of prediction and control. The only way to test the mathematical model is to plug in some variables and run the simulation, which can vary dramatically over many runs based on sensitivity to initial conditions. It would be like water turning from solid to liquid to gas and back when the temperature of the phase transition was an inconsistent variable.

Fluid Dynamics of Markets

Fluid dynamics is an example of the mathematics used in studying complex adaptive systems. A few short equations correlate velocity, pressure, density, and viscosity of a gas or fluid in motion. The equations give a pretty good approximation of the behavior of the wind and weather, the turbulence on the wings of an airplane, the propeller of a ship, or the plasma in a fusion reactor. The problem is that the equations are nonlinear, sensitive to initial conditions, and prone to volatility at unknown thresholds. Indeed, this chaotic behavior may be why humans have not, and may never, succeed at attaining the holy grail of harnessing controlled fusion reactions.

If someone ever figures out how to apply the insights of fluid dynamics to the stock market, they would become very rich indeed (at least until the other agents in this complex adaptive system adapt accordingly). No one knows, however, what the appropriate economic analogies are to velocity, pressure, density, and viscosity.

Today, high-frequency trades (HFTs) account for more than 50 percent of the daily trades in stock, bond, commodity, and currency exchanges around the world, so it sure seems like the velocity, pressure, density, and viscosity of economic flux is increasing. Computers, guided by pattern-recognition algorithms, conduct thousands of trades per second—buy, sell, buy, sell—in order to profit through correlations between slight variations in pricing without regard to any fundamentals of the securities involved. It may be that big money, high-frequency trading, derivatives, and all the rest make the market more stable by creating extreme liquidity and therefore more efficiency in the markets-pricing mechanism with ever lower transaction costs. The idealized efficient market models neglect the resulting turbulence precipitated by the increased flow and flux, such as the world witnessed in the 2008 financial crisis and as seen in the flash crashes that are now a regular feature of our computerized exchanges.

In his book *Forecasts*, physicist Mark Buchanan argues that the efficient market hypothesis is a dangerous fantasy, "like weather forecasters who do not understand storms." He continues: "This doesn't mean, of course, that markets aren't useful or don't have interesting properties. It does mean that many economists have perpetrated something like scientific fraud in presenting economic ideas to the public."[81]

It would be better to have the creativity without the destruction. Markets, argues Beinhocker, are great at promoting "deductive tinkering" in the invention of new technologies, products, and services that can harness more energy, matter, and ingenuity to meet various human needs and desires. Markets are not good at promoting equilibrium.

MIT's Cesar Hidalgo similarly defines the economy as "a system that amplifies the practical uses of knowledge and knowhow through the physical embodiment of information and the context-specific properties that this information helps carry . . . Ultimately, the economy is the collective system by which humans make information grow."[82] Every product and every artifact that humans produce is embodied information-ingenuity.

Yes, markets create spontaneous order, magically so like Adam Smith's Invisible Hand, but markets also create spontaneous disorder. Punctuated equilibrium applies to economic history as well as to the evolution of life. There will be calm waters in between the rapids, but fortunes will be won or lost around the disruptive moments when the market turns into a rushing torrent of chaos. Do your due diligence. Timing is everything, but you won't and cannot know the hour, day, month, or year. Investors play both sides of order and disorder, stability and instability, the creative and the destructive sides of economic evolution.

---

[81] Buchanan, *Forecasts: What Physics, Meteorology, and the Natural Sciences Can Teach Us About Economics*, Kindle 275.

[82] Hidalgo, *Why Information Grows: The Evolution of Order, from Atoms to Economies*, Kindle 1112.

Natural and Economic Selection

Complexity economics adopts biological evolution's model of natural selection to understand "economic selection."[83] Darwin's theory is based on a three-step algorithm: inheritable variations > selection > reproduction. This evolutionary algorithm runs on the backdrop of what Darwin called "the high rate at which all organic beings tend to increase," which then leads to "a universal struggle for survival" and, significantly, also a struggle for reproduction. He observed that all species have the capacity to reproduce exponentially over many generations. Darwin writes in *On the Origin of Species*:

> It is the doctrine of Malthus applied with manifold force to the whole animal and vegetable kingdoms; for in this case there can be no artificial increase of food, and no prudential restraint from marriage. Although some species may be now increasing, more or less rapidly, in numbers, all cannot do so, for the world would not hold them.[84]

Referenced by Darwin is the Rev. Thomas Robert Malthus, a Scottish economist who argued in his 1798 book *An Essay on the Principle of Population* that the pattern of exponential growth in human population due to high birthrates would quickly outpace agricultural production, leading to a collapse due to famine, disease, and warfare.[85] Happily, Malthus's dark prognostications were mostly wrong in the ensuing centuries. Since he published his book, the world population has grown sevenfold—from roughly 1 billion people to now over 7 billion.

Malthus, however, is essential to understanding the Darwinian principle of natural selection,[86] so we must ask if and how these

---

[83] Beinhocker, *The Origin of Wealth: Evolution, Complexity, and the Radical Remaking of Economics*; Nick Gogerty, *The Nature of Value: How to Invest in the Adaptive Economy* (New York: Columbia Business School, 2014).

[84] Charles Darwin, *The Origin of Species* (Online, 1859).

[85] Thomas Robert (1766-1834) Malthus, *An Essay on the Principle of Population*, 1798, 18032 1826, 1830 ed. (London: J. Johnson, 1798).

[86] If the aphids on your houseplants were to reproduce unconstrained for a year, "the world would not hold them." It might take the mice a few decades to inherit the entire surface of the Earth. It might take the elephants a few centuries, but "the world would not hold them." Every species has

insights apply to economics and human populations more broadly. Few economists think much of poor Malthus today—the dismal science of economics has now become a cheerful science of abundance—but how have humans cheated the logic of Malthus and Darwin? And how can we continue to do so? To answer that question, we must dig deeper into Big History.

In evolution, selection occurs through death by predation, starvation, disease, exposure, and preprogrammed senescence. How and when an individual organism dies matters greatly. Does the individual have offspring that will carry on its lineage? Will the offspring survive and reproduce? How will this lineage and species fare over many generations in variable future environments? Natural selection is not so much "the survival of the fittest" as it is "the survival of the fitting in." What we fit into are specific niches in particular ecologies. There is no all-purpose, generic evolutionary model for success.

The evolutionary algorithm is complete when we posit a feedback loop by which "positive" variations will tend to be passed on as "adaptations" through the selection process. In other words, those traits that enhance survival and reproduction of the offspring will statistically tend to accumulate in future generations, thus leading to the "improvement" of the lineage in its specific niche. Run the algorithm on repeat over hundreds of millions of years through hundreds of millions of species on a restless planet —variation, selection, reproduction— and voilà, we have humans today streaming Nature channel documentaries on their devices.

Complexity economics posits a similar algorithm on repeat: differentiate > select > amplify. Much like individuals of different species in particular ecosystems, different businesses compete and cooperate for profit in specific market sectors. Businesses and markets go through periods of growth, decline, and death.[87]

There is a great debate within evolutionary biology about the level of selection. Does selection occur only at the level of the genes, or does it occur at the level of the individual organism, a group of individuals, or even entire ecosystems? And how do these disagreements among evolutionary biologists map onto a theory of economic selection? In

---

the potential to grow exponentially, as humans along with our domesticated plants and animals have done over the last century.

[87] Gogerty, *The Nature of Value: How to Invest in the Adaptive Economy*; Beinhocker, *The Origin of Wealth: Evolution, Complexity, and the Radical Remaking of Economics*.

life the environment provides selective pressures and plays a critical role in regulating the gene expression (i.e., epigenetics).[88] Like evolution, microeconomics and macroeconomics are mutually constituted through numerous dynamic feedback loops. Like ecology, the causal vectors in an economic system are bottom up, top down, side-to-side, and dynamic.

In his book *The Nature of Value*, Nick Gogerty develops an evolutionary model of economics based on units of innovation—what he calls an "ino" or "inos" in the plural. And inos are to economics what genes are to evolution. Innovations determine competitiveness and profitability within a "cluster space" of other business providing similar goods and services.

Businesses, much like organisms, arise, thrive, and die in a particular niche within a particular "ecological" space of other businesses in a vast network of goods and services traded around the world. Some of these businesses are symbionts, others competitors, but most cooperate and compete in completely different cluster-spaces. Gogerty writes:

> In economic clusters, competitors battle for the scarce resource of customer value flow. Just as the conditions in the pond determine which frogs will survive, the nature of the cluster determines which organizations can flourish. Clusters thus act as macroprocessing machines, providing selective feedback—choosing which inos are fed resources and amplifying the presence of those inos in the economy.[89]

The secret to productivity growth is inos. We can trace the role of inos in the history of particular industries—agriculture, electricity, car manufacturing, computers, consumer electronics, and so on. For Gogerty, the challenge is understanding the evolution of clusters as much as any particular business within a cluster. As innovations are replicated by other adjacent businesses in the same cluster, competition for customers drives down prices and profit margins. Clusters are like

---

[88] David Sloan Wilson argues persuasively for group selection in the case of human evolution. See David Sloan Wilson, *Darwin's Cathedral: Evolution, Religion, and the Nature of Society* (Chicago: The University of Chicago Press, 2002); *Evolution for Everyone* (New York: Bantam Dell, 2007); Scott F. Gilbert and David Epel, *Ecological Developmental Biology: Integrating Epigenetics, Medicine, and Evolution* (Sunderland, MA: Sinauer Associates, 2009).

[89] Gogerty, *The Nature of Value: How to Invest in the Adaptive Economy*, Kindle 1569-72.

"a selfish superorganism seeking out the best value-creating innovations." Clusters "are mechanisms for transferring ino-enabled capabilities into consumer value," which then undermines the industries' profit-margins. This, then, is "the paradox of innovation." As businesses within a cluster create more innovation, it gets harder for individual firms to capture value in providing goods and services to their customers, unless they have some barrier to entry—a moat that provides them a monopolistic dominance within an economic niche.[90]

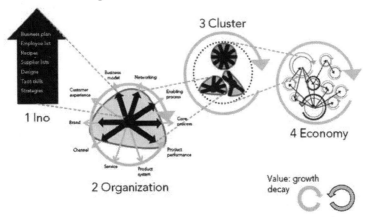

Evolution's Economic Process across Levels. Value flows through the network, adapting as it moves from one level of the panarchy to the next. *Source*: Nick Gogerty, *The Nature of Value*.

Clusters, like businesses, have a life cycle. For investors, the challenge is, first, knowing when to enter and later exit a cluster and, second, knowing which business within a particular cluster is likely to prosper. Gogerty writes:

> It bears repeating—selecting a stable long-lived cluster at the correct development life cycle stage is as important as selecting the correct firm within a cluster. Clusters do not have equilibrium regions, fixed points, or "solutions" as traditional economics crudely implies. Rather, they are bombarded by constant storms of innovation and competition. Like ecological niches, clusters are born, grow, and disappear continuously in evolution's ever-adapting economic network.[91]

---

[90] Ibid., Kindle 1867.
[91] Ibid., Kindle 2532.

Gogerty created the schematic above to illustrate the relationship between innovations, individual businesses, the clusters in which they compete, and the entire economy of many clusters. The causative vectors within clusters and between networks of clusters are bottom up, top down, and side-to side.

Darwin talked about "the whole economy of nature," but now economists are talking about the whole nature of economics.[92] Economics and ecology are often pitted against each other as conceptually incompatible—one seeks continued growth and the other sees limits to growth. Both are mistaken in thinking that some kind of equilibrium could and should be achieved. Big History teaches us that there are pockets of temporary stability, predictability, homeostasis, and control in the universe, in life, and in human affairs. The driving forces, however, are instability, disequilibrium, and increasing entropy. In life, equilibrium equals death.

---

[92] Darwin, *The Origin of Species.*

Chapter 5:
Death and Taxes

The only certainties in life are death and taxes, a truism reportedly first uttered by Benjamin Franklin but recently proven by science. This insight turns out to be a hard-and-fast rule of fundamental physics, as we learn from the Laws of Thermodynamics. All complex adaptive systems require a flow of energy for growth, maintenance, repair, reproduction, innovation, and evolution of the system—this applies to bacteria and businesses. The energy tax must always be paid up until death.

The Second Law of Thermodynamics describes the tendency over time of all isolated physical systems to move toward states of thermodynamic equilibrium. Differences in temperature, pressure, and chemical potential energy, when not acted upon by external forces, invariably move from concentrated to more diffuse states. Entropy is a key principle of fundamental physics. Here are some of the implications:

1. Heat energy always flows spontaneously from hot to cold.
2. Energy always goes from more useful, more concentrated forms (low entropy) to less useful, less concentrated forms (high entropy).
3. The amount of disorder (entropy) in any isolated system increases with time.
4. It is impossible for an engine (or an organism or an economy) to convert energy into an equivalent amount of work (there is always waste, friction, and entropy).
5. Complex adaptive systems are fundamentally disequilibrious (i.e., equilibrium equals death).

The hot cup of coffee left alone reaches room temperature. The heat is conserved (First Law of Thermodynamics), but it is now dispersed throughout the room (Second Law of Thermodynamics). The inevitable dispersal of energy from a more ordered state (the hot coffee) into a less ordered state (the room) is referred to as increased entropy.

The concept of "negentropy" was introduced by the physicist Erwin Schrödinger in his 1944 paper "What is Life" to account for the increase in complexity within thermodynamics systems.[93] Negentropy, or negative entropy, is what you do when you brew the coffee, prepare breakfast, and clean up the dishes afterward. You create order. Negentropy always requires energy, flowing through the coffee machine, your body, and the larger economy. A system that consumes energy to create, maintain, and grow complexity is said to be negentropic. *All negentropic systems also increase entropy in their environment.* Yet while entropy can be indirectly measured as heat loss in some systems, negentropy is more of a hypothetical concept. We can't measure negentropy, in part because we have no quantifiable definition of complexity outside of the crude measure of energy-density flow, which we briefly discussed in previous chapters and will return to again here.

Life is an example of entropy and negentropy. There has to be continuous energy flow from outside some membrane into the cell and self. Humans acquire energy by eating plants and animals. Add water, respiration, some waste disposal, and we have a functioning body. Add science, technology, industry, commerce, communication, and fossil fuels, and we have our 18 terawatts and 7-billion-person global economy.

Nothing violates the letter of the Second Law of Thermodynamics—but Big History seems to violate the spirit of the Second Law. The history of the universe, the evolution of life, and the human drama are events of increasing complexity, what Schrödinger called negentropy. The universe is like a super-hot, super-dense cup of coffee in the morning at an empty construction site that explodes over the course of the day into the completely furnished residence where you're now sitting reading this sentence. An unfathomable amount of energy was lost to entropy during the construction; yet what should bewilder us is also the finished product—the universe and you—on the other end of that explosion.

In the early universe, gravity operated on quantum fluctuations in the hot, dense plasma to gradually pull clouds of gases together. Eventually, hydrogen and helium were packed together so densely and so hot as to ignite stars and sculpt the fantastic web of galaxies we observe today. Thus, within small pockets of the universe, complexity increases, driven by the entropy of stars. These localized energy

---

[93] Erwin Schrödinger and Roger Penrose, *What Is Life? With "Mind and Matter"* (New York: Cambridge University Press, 2003).

gradients have the capacity to run uphill for a long, long time, even as the system as a whole must at some point come tumbling down.

The Earth is such a place, a jewel of a planet where the temperatures are not too hot and not too cold, where the radiation is not too strong and not too weak. Thus, complex chemistry can occur here and—following the bottom-up possibilities of such chemistry—give rise to life and evolution and consciousness. Our Sun will be a reliable partner in sustaining complexity on Earth for at least a billion years to come. Without the energy from the Sun, coming from outside the physical system of our Earth, the concentrated energy flows of life on Earth would quickly become a very cold cup of coffee in a big, mostly dark universe.

There is nothing in the Second Law that specifies how complexity is to emerge and expand, even as there is nothing in the universe that violates the Second Law. We may not be able to measure negentropy, but we see it all around us and in our own being. We must faithfully follow the Second Law, because we have no choice. By paying attention to energy flows, however, we are best positioned to innovate and try to violate the spirit of the Second Law.

Energy Density Flow

As previously discussed, energy flow is one of the axes in the Great Matrix. Tufts-Harvard astronomer Eric Chaisson has done some rough calculations of just how much energy is harnessed by the complex adaptive systems on Earth. He estimates comparative energy density flow in "ergs per second per gram," denoted by the symbol Φ_m. The measurement is thus a mass-normalized energy flow over time, signifying the free energy available in a system to do the thermodynamic work of building structures and creating complexity. What we learn is quite counterintuitive and not widely understood.

Chaisson's rough estimate of the average energy density flow of the entire Milky Way galaxy is 0.5 Φ_m and of our Sun is 2.0 Φ_m. The atmosphere and oceans of the Earth have an energy density flow of 75 Φ_m (35.7 times that of the Sun). A photosynthesizing plant has an energy density flow of 900 Φ_m (450 times that of the Sun). A mammalian body has an energy density flow of 20,000 Φ_m (10,000 times that of the Sun). The human brain, which is about 2 percent of our body weight but uses about 20 percent of our body's food energy, has an average energy density flow of 150,000 Φ_m (75,000 times that of the Sun). If we include the energy that humans now harness outside of our bodies, then humans today average about 500,000 Φ_m (250,000 times that of the Sun). The privileged few of us who fly around the world—the energy rich—achieve energy density flows millions of times that of the Sun.

Chaisson has also calculated an exponential growth in energy density flow in the evolution of engines and computers. The energy density flow of an early steam engine is 10,000 times that of our Sun. The Daimler engine of 1899 was 40,000 times greater. The energy density flow of the Wright brothers' 1903 engine was 1 million times that of the Sun, and the energy density flow of a modern fighter aircraft is 82 million times greater.[94]

The ENIAC computer from the 1940s weighed 8.5 tons and used 50 kW of electricity. Today, a laptop today weighs 2.2 kg and uses 60 W of electricity. Energy density flow in computers has increased from 64,000 times that of the Sun to more than 280,000 times. By these measurements, humans and our advanced machines may well achieve the greatest sustained energy density flows in the entire universe.[95]

This exponential growth in energy density flow is a critical factor in understanding natural and economic complexity. In the calculation of real value in economics—energy, matter, and ingenuity—energy density flow provides at least one numerical scale essential for increased complexity and perhaps also fundamental economic value. Chaisson writes:

> Better metrics than energy rate density may well describe each of the individual systems within the realm of physical, biological, and cultural evolution that combine to create the greater whole of cosmic evolution, but no other single metric seems capable of uniformly describing them all. The significance of plotting "on the same page" a single quantity for such a wide range of systems

[94] Eric Chaisson, "Using Complexity Science to Search for Unity in the Natural Sciences," in *The Self-Organizing Universe: Cosmology, Biology, and the Rise of Complexity*, ed. Lineweaver, Davies, and Michael Ruse (New York: Cambridge University Press, 2012).

[95] Eric Chaisson, *Cosmic Evolution: The Rise of Complexity in Nature*; *Epic of Evolution: Seven Ages of the Cosmos*; "Energy Rate Density as a Complexity Metric and Evolutionary Driver."; "Energy Rate Density. Ii. Probing Further a New Complexity Metric."

observed in Nature should not be overlooked. I am unaware of any other sole quantity that can characterize so extensively a principal system dynamic over >20 orders of magnitude in spatial dimensions and nearly as many in time.[96]

Remember that there are three ways to increase energy density flow: (1) you can increase energy consumption and/or efficiency of combustion; (2) you can decrease the time scale; and (3) you can decrease the mass of the system. Our machines and technologies have exhibited tremendous and accelerating increases in efficiency over the last 200 years. Much of this efficiency gain has been accomplished by reducing the mass of the system with new materials and technologies, as, for instance, in the miniaturization that has occurred in electronics and computers. The development of more effective combustion processes that waste less heat has also contributed to efficiency gains.

Overall, consumption of energy continues to increase, even as the technologies become more efficient. Our cars are more efficient, but more of us drive more miles. Our planes are more efficient, but more of us fly more miles. Our furnaces and air conditioners are more efficient, but we have bigger houses. This is known in economics as the Jevons Paradox. Energy efficiency is as important today to economic growth as energy production, or, for that matter, labor productivity, because the reduced input can now be deployed elsewhere to create additional economic growth and prosperity.

Energy flow is the real currency of evolution and economics—a fact of life poorly reflected in the price of energy today, but critical from the perspective of Big History.[97] If we take evolution as our guide, investors and economists will pay closer attention to the total energy budget of any process across its life cycle. Indeed, we might well predict that further exponential increases in energy density flow are essential for economic growth. This need not entail actually increasing energy production and consumption, if we can gain further efficiencies in combustion and further reductions in mass and time scales of any

---

[96] Chaisson, "Using Complexity Science to Search for Unity in the Natural Sciences."

[97] In 2012, for instance, the overall GDP for the entire United States grew by 2.5%. The fastest-growing states were those that embraced energy industries of mining, drilling, and fracking for fossil fuels — Texas at 3.7%, West Virginia at 5.1%, and North Dakota at 9.7%. By contrast, states that were not in the energy business, like Connecticut and New Mexico, grew by 1–2%. Bureau of Economic Statistics, "Quarterly Gross Domestic Producti by State, 2005-2013," U.S. Department of Commerce, http://blog.bea.gov/category/gdp-by-state/.

given process. We should expect, however, that the overall evolutionary pattern will continue, perhaps at an exponential rate.

Over the deep time of evolution, life tends toward greater and greater complexity. Each new threshold of complexity seems to require greater concentrations of energy flowing through the system. This is an important lesson from Big History: the phenomenon of exponential increases in energy consumption and greater overall efficiencies in energy consumption is consistent with the trajectory of evolution and economic history. Increasing human energy consumption and efficiency may be essential to the future complexification of our species, with an important caveat.

Goldilocks Gradients

Too little energy flowing through a system leads to disintegration and collapse. Too much energy flowing through a system can cause it to crash and burn. Instead, we need to talk about optimal energy flows for different systems. The energy that is most important to our lifestyle today is not the energy that flows through our bodies, but the energy that flows through our economies and cultures. If all that energy were flowing through our bodies instead, we would all be burnt toast.

Creative thermodynamic gradients appear many times and at different scales in Big History, but they seem to always occur within narrow bandwidths of possibilities, what Chaisson calls "optimum energy flow." If temperatures on Earth were continuously below minus 10 degrees Celsius or above 40 degrees Celsius, then life as we know it could not exist. Other optimal bandwidths also exist for stars, planets, rocks, and polymers. These boundary conditions for emergent complexity appear to be fine-tuned and exist throughout the universe, evolution, and human life. The Dutch anthropologist Fred Spier terms this "the Goldilocks Principle," in reference to the familiar fairy tale.[98]

The online Big History Project designed for high school students adopts the Goldilocks terminology in understanding increasing complexity: Ingredients + Goldilocks Condition = New Complexity. The curriculum traces eight major thresholds in the story of the universe (Big Bang, Stars Light Up, New Chemical Elements, Earth

---

[98] Spier, *Big History and the Future of Humanity.*

and Solar System, Life on Earth, Collective Learning, Agriculture, and the Modern Revolution).[99]

Creative Destruction

Alongside creativity, destruction is an essential feature of our cosmic story—a necessary consequence of entropy. During their explosive death, supernovae can radiate in an instance as much energy as our Sun does over its entire lifespan. Out of this destruction, the elements of the Periodic Table arise. Our solar system and our planet are the remnants of such a supernova, and life would not be possible without the complex chemistry created in supernovae. Joni Mitchell captured this truth in her 1969 song: "We are stardust/ Billion-year-old carbon/ We are golden/ Caught in the devil's bargain/ And we've got to get ourselves/ back to the garden."

On the terrestrial scale with which we are more familiar, we also witness incredible destructive events in the form of continental drift, earthquakes, tsunamis, super-volcanoes, impact events, solar flares, and periodic ice ages. These geological events have dramatically reshaped our planet in the past and will again in the future.

To natural destruction, we now add human-caused destruction. Paleolithic humans around the world torched huge swaths of land and apparently hunted hundreds of large mammal species to extinction. Early agriculture and irrigation in Mesopotamia turned once-fertile fields into salinated deserts. Beginning with the Bronze Age, early civilizations deforested much of Eurasia. Humans also unintentionally harm each other through the spread of diseases and ecological blunders.

Of course, humans have a long and dark history of intentionally harming one another through warfare, murder, rape, slavery, theft, and other forms of exploitation and oppression, as extensively detailed in Steven Pinker's book *The Better Angels of Our Nature*.[100] Human violence has a moral character that we would not ascribe to natural events, in part because human evil seems gratuitous and avoidable. We would not, for instance, want to impute "creativity" to horrific human-caused events like the Holocaust because naturalizing evil runs counter to our moral intuitions and instincts. And yet, at every stage of human history and human economics, we see creative destruction as an

---

[99] Gates et al., "The Big History Project". See also Bohan et al., *Big History*.
[100] Steven Pinker, *The Better Angels of Our Nature: Why Violence Has Declined* (New York: Viking, 2011).

integral part of the story. Pinker argues that humans today live much more peaceful lives than our ancestors and that we are much less likely to die a violent death than our ancestors. We will return to this topic in the next chapter.

Energy Regimes

Energy is the engine of evolution and economics. Frank Niele, a researcher at Shell, details six "energy regimes" in the history of the planet.

Life probably began on alkaline thermal vents on the ocean floor by harnessing heat and the chemical potential energy of these unique environments. This was the first energy regime. Life bootstrapped itself by being thermophilic.

The second energy regime is photosynthesis, without which the drama would have long ago plateaued and declined. Photosynthesis is the foundation of evolution, the bottommost rung of the food chain, where sunlight performs magic on hydrogen, carbon, oxygen, and nitrogen to manufacture molecular packets of potential chemical energy.

The third energy regime begins with oxygen-driven respiration. Previously, prokaryotes metabolized carbohydrates through fermentation and anaerobic respiration. Photosynthesis created our oxygen-rich atmosphere and oceans, and then the cells hacked aerobic respiration. Oxygenic respiration enabled life to extract almost twenty times more energy per carbohydrates consumed than anaerobic metabolism previously allowed.[101]

Evolution is thus also an evolution of energy pathways— thermophilic, phototropic, and aerobic. Each level is a leap in energetics.[102] The biochemistry is awesome, much of which we have only recently learned. And for the last two billion years, all evolution until recently was energized by this fundamental biochemistry. The energy pathways that first appeared in single-cell prokaryotes and eukaryotes billions of years ago are still the primary sources of the planet's primary productivity today, except for one important exception, humans.

---

[101] Frank Niele, *Energy: Engine of Evolution* (New York: Elsevier, 2005), 18.
[102] See also Judson, "The Energy Expansion of Evolution."

The mastery of fire—the stuff of great mythologies—is the next great leap in the bioenergetics of evolution. Humans, curiously, are the only species to control fire. This was a seismic shift in bioenergetics for the planet and the cultural evolution of our species. Pyroculture is the beginning of our species' dramatic rise to the top of the food chain.

The next energy regime is agriculture, beginning about 10,000 years ago, followed by the fossil fuel regime beginning in earnest 200 years ago. Agriculture and later fossil fuels enabled exponential leaps in the available energy to support the growth and complexification of human culture.

Frank Niele holds out the possibility and necessity of shifting to a heliocentric regime in which ample solar energy is directly and indirectly captured to power our species future evolution.

Available energy will likely not be the limiting factor in our future evolution. In addition to vast quantities of fossil fuels, there is an enormous amount of renewable energy available on Earth. The total solar energy intercepted by our planet is 174.26 petawatts (10^{15}). Our current global consumption of 18,000 terawatts (10^{12}) is tiny in comparison. The total fossil fuels on the planet may be as large as 200 zettajoules (10^{21}), an enormous number to be sure, but equivalent to only thirteen days of the Earth's supply of solar energy.[103] Of course, burning all that fossil fuel would also have dire consequences for Earth's atmosphere, climates, and biomes. Technologies may soon allow us to further concentrate solar energy in usable forms, and should commercially viable fusion energy ever be available, then humanity would have a virtually unlimited source of "clean"—but not entropy-free—energy. The logic of moving toward a heliocentric energy system is compelling. The technology and infrastructure are rapidly evolving.

The challenge is not energy per se, but the kind of entropy this energy consumption would unleash on the planet in the form of industrial production, waste generated, mountains moved, and ecosystems altered.

While anthropogenic climate change from the burning of fossil fuels is a real danger, we should also anticipate naturally caused climate change as a future inevitability. Our species is well positioned to survive dramatic climate changes, more so than other large mammals, but the short-term results would be widespread devastation and a dramatic devolution in quantity and quality of life, especially

---

[103] Smil, *Energy in Nature and Society*, 29.

human life. We don't really know what the Goldilocks boundary conditions are for the planet, our species, or our global economy.

Energy density flow is indicative of complexity, but by itself, it does not tell us enough about the nature of complexity within any particular domain of the universe. Energetics alone also misses important qualia and differences between emergent natural kinds and the energetic processes that sustain them. A songbird, for instance, has roughly the same energy density flow as a human body. Does this mean that the bird is as complex as a human? Our kidneys consume as much oxygen as our esteemed brains. Does this mean that our kidneys are as complex as our brains?

The environmentalist slogan "reduce, reuse, recycle" is only partly right, because what drives the evolution of increasing complexity on our planet and in the universe is actually "consume more energy-matter-ingenuity in order to be more complex." This is what Bertrand Russell calls "chemical imperialism," in which living things try to transform energy-matter from their environment into their own well-being.[104] A. N. Whitehead similarly referred to life as a form of "coercion" and "robbery," related to the need to always find energy sources to maintain complexity, growth, and reproduction.[105] We could call it the Great Eucharistic Law: "Eat and be eaten." You live, you kill in order to eat, and then you eventually die and become a source of energy-matter for other life. Your atoms will be recycled after death; indeed, your atoms are recycled every day.

The prime directive of evolution and economics might be expressed in the aphorism "Minimize Entropy, Maximize Creativity." Creativity here could mean "value/work/profits." In other words, we should seek the optimal parameters of each system. This doesn't necessarily occur at the level of an individual or even species, but it seems to be how the larger ecosystem functions as a complex adaptive system in which waste becomes an energy source used by other species large and small in a vast, efficiency-maximizing food chain in which microbes still rule. Humanity's opportunity—in the past and in the future—is to build economic systems that minimize energy-matter consumption by maximizing information-ingenuity while increasing human utility functions. This requires more creativity and greater

---

[104] Bertrand Russell, *An Outline of Philosophy* (New York: Routledge, 1993).
[105] Alfred North Whitehead, *Process and Reality* (New York: Free Press, [1929]1978).

efficiencies—in other words, increased productivity and economic growth.

Instability and Resilience

Ours is a restless and creative planet. We wouldn't be here otherwise. We are a restless and creative species. Is it any wonder that economic markets churn and froth, that bubbles grow and burst, and that instability rules? Investors must now embrace this instability and the growing complexity. The economic flux today is like a hurricane compared with anything prior in human history. The great acceleration of the last century and the history of financial crises should give us all pause to reevaluate and reassess.

All living entities must achieve a temporary dynamic stability in the face of turbulence. All living entities have an internal telos—to survive and reproduce through species-specific patterns of behavior that optimize energy-matter-ingenuity flows for that creature. How do living organisms persist and thrive, in spite of entropy's constant pull toward disorder, dissolution, and death? How might the economy, or an investment portfolio, model itself accordingly?

What are the boundary conditions for human life and other species on our planet? What are the limits to humanity's biochemical imperialism over other species? Might human growth and activities set off a destructive cascade of failures and collapses? Might the torrential flows of Big Money contribute to such a collapse? Our species has been on an amazing exponential growth spurt, but at some point, it must end. Will the global economy and humanity have a soft or hard landing?

Chapter 6:
Your Hunter-Gatherer Brain

Big History teaches us many things about how the universe works. We have already discussed cosmology, physics, chemistry, biology, evolution, and the nature of complex adaptive systems. The center of this epic drama, however, is humanity. In the Great Matrix, humans are off the charts when it comes to capturing energy, matter, and ingenuity. We are the discoverers and receivers of an incredible font of knowledge and know-how accumulated and passed on by our ancestors and then added to exponentially by our contemporaries. Humans are the talking animals that have grown by orders of magnitude in the blink of a geological eye. Big History is the story of human origins and the accelerating drama of our species' rise from ecological insignificance to the top of the food chain.

This "new" natural history of humans occasions a new understanding of human nature supported by an enormous amount of empirical and experimental research. In recent decades, we have learned a lot about ourselves with respect to physiology, genetics, development, brains, cognition, emotions, and behaviors. Anthropology, sociology, psychology, primatology, the cognitive neurosciences, behavioral economics, genomics, medicine, archeology, radioactive dating, and related sciences provide significant evidence for a new understanding of our forbearers and how they live on in us today.

This natural history of humanity is the foundation of all of the human sciences. So if you want to understand why people are the way they are, then Big History is a necessary part of your "latticework of mental modules." Scientists have pieced together our evolutionary history in ever-greater detail with new insights into our evolved cognitive biases and behavioral dispositions. For instance, we have come to understand that much of our behavior, emotion, and judgment is governed by the variable flows of powerful endogenous chemicals in our brains and bodies that affect our emotional and social life—testosterone, oxytocin, serotonin, endorphins, adrenalin, estrogen, vasopressin, and more.

And while there is broad consensus supporting this evolutionary account of human origins, there are also important debates within the scientific and philosophical disciplines about how to interpret and interpolate the evidence for our biologically and culturally evolved human natures. To the extent possible, I am ring-fencing the philosophical interpretations. It is important, however, to flag significant scientific debates.

The attributes that helped ensure survival and reproduction in human prehistory, however, do not necessarily prepare one for being a successful investor in the twenty-first century. Our thinking is fast and slow.[106] We are predictably irrational.[107] We are status-conscious and inclined toward team aggression.[108] There are sex-/gender-specific predispositions that cause conflict and confusion.[109] We are innately tribal creatures.[110]

Investors ignore these insights at their own peril. You become a danger to yourself, your firm, and your clients if you don't understand your hunter-gatherer brain and how to effectively compensate. The exigencies of reproduction and survival over hundreds of thousands of years of human evolution have shaped our bodies and brains, our psychology and behavior.[111] All of this turns out to have profound ramifications for investors dealing with their own psychology and behavior, their own bodies and brains, those of their colleagues and families, and, more broadly, the psychology and behavior of markets, corporations, and nation-states.

A Really Great Ape

Our closest living animal relatives are chimpanzees and bonobos with whom we share 98.8 percent of our genes. The common mother of our lineages—chimpanzees, bonobos, and humans—would have lived 6 to 7 million years ago in Africa. Along the way from them to us, from then to now, there were numerous offshoots on our evolutionary family

---

[106] Daniel Kahneman, *Thinking, Fast and Slow* (New York: Farrar, Straus and Giroux, 2011).

[107] Dan Ariely, *Predictably Irrational: The Hidden Forces That Shape Our Decisions* (New York: HarperCollins, 2009).

[108] Pinker, *The Better Angels of Our Nature: Why Violence Has Declined*; Malcom Potts and Thomas Hayden, *Sex and War: How Biology Explains Warfare and Terrorism and Offers a Path to a Safer World*, Kindle ed. (Dallas, TX: BenBella Books 2008).

[109] Helen E. Fisher, *Anatomy of Love: A Natural History of Mating, Marriage, and Why We Stray* (New York: W.W. Norton, 2016).

[110] Jonathan Haidt, *The Righteous Mind: Why Good People Are Divided by Politics and Religion* (New York: Random House, 2012).

[111] Potts and Hayden, *Sex and War: How Biology Explains Warfare and Terrorism and Offers a Path to a Safer World*; Christopher Ryan and Cacilda Jetha, *Sex at Dawn: How We Mate, Why We Stray, and What It Means for Modern Relationships* (New York: Harper Collins, 2012); Fisher, *Anatomy of Love: A Natural History of Mating, Marriage, and Why We Stray*.

tree. Many phenotypes, genotypes, and experiments didn't succeed in the long run, which we deduce from fossil remains of extinct subspecies. Perhaps bonobos and chimpanzees can serve as stand-ins for our last common ancestor. We certainly recognize something of ourselves in their behavior, as well as in our shared genes.

By 2 million years ago, the hominid lineage arose, characterized by phenotypic features we would recognize as more human-like—large brains, upright posture, and the ability to use tools. By 800,000 years ago, and perhaps much earlier, some of these hominid subspecies learned how to use fire, which created an evolutionary feedback loop that changed diets, dentures, range of habitat, and early culture. Homo Erectus, Neanderthal, Denisovan, and other hominids managed to migrate across Eurasia and survive in diverse climates. There is still a lot of work to be done piecing together this family tree. Paleoarcheologists do not all agree about how to interpret the skeletal and genetic remains of early hominids.

The species *Homo sapiens* arose in Africa over 300,000 years ago, one of a number of hominid species at the time. Humans quickly supplanted other hominid species within Africa. A small band of humans wandered out of Africa around 90,000 years ago and supplanted other hominid species throughout Eurasia. We are all descendants of these wanderers, though along the way there was some interbreeding with other hominids. We know this through recent genetic analysis. Many Northern Europeans carry some traces of noncoding genes from Neanderthals. Many Asian carry some Denisovan noncoding genes. Most human racial differences—skin, hair, eye colors, etc. (i.e., coding genes)—are relatively recent developments in our prehistory, the result of founder effects and inbred adaptations to local environmental conditions in the diverse geographies that humans came to inhabit.[112]

We don't really know how or why the other hominid species died out. Some speculate that the Sapiens exterminated their hominid relatives, but there is little archeological evidence to support this theory. Perhaps it was some new disease to which the other hominids had no resistance. It is the case, however, that soon after *Homo sapiens* arrived, the other hominid species in the region disappeared from the archeological record.

---

[112] Ian Tattersall, *Becoming Human: Evolution and Human Uniqueness* (New York: Harcourt Brace, 1998); Harari, *Sapiens: A Brief History of Humankind.*.

It seems safe to assume that much of the migration of humans around Africa and Eurasia occurred along coastlines where seafood would have been plentiful. There may well have been semi-permanent fishing villages in our prehistory. We may never know, because sea levels rose 160 meters since the last ice age receded, beginning about 20,000 years ago. Most of the archeological evidence about early humans is presumably deep underwater.

Before agriculture, and for all of our prehistory, our common ancestors lived in small tribes, probably not larger than 150 individuals.[113] Our brains, instincts, emotions, and behavior evolved to survive and reproduce in these small social groups. The last 10,000 years of human history is a brief chapter in what is really a million-year story of hominid evolution and migrations.[114] Our genes, emotions, and cognition haven't changed as quickly as our culture. We still have hunter-gatherer brains and bodies, though our lifestyles are profoundly different.

The Great Cooperators

Humans cooperate and compete, survive, and reproduce in groups. Humans are a uniquely social species. This "eusociality" is something rare in evolution and has been achieved by only a few other species of ants, termites, bees, wasps, shrimp, and one other mammal—the naked mole rat.

In his controversial book *The Social Conquest of Earth*, E. O. Wilson argues that humans are eusocial. The controversy is partly a matter of definition about the hallmarks of eusociality and mostly a disagreement about multilevel selection theory in evolution. Does natural selection occur at the level of the genes, groups of genes, individual organisms, populations, or even ecosystems? The prokaryotes in your gut would answer "yes" to all of the above.

The distinct lineages of eukaryotes, however, combined with the phenomenon of sexual reproduction, suggests a more reductionist understanding of natural selection. At the level of DNA code, what reproduces is information-ingenuity in the form of genes. At the level of the phenotype, individuals must survive long enough to reproduce and pass on their genes in a particular ecological niche. "The origin of

---

[113] Dunbar, *Grooming, Gossip and the Evolution of Language*.
[114] John Cartwright, *Evolution and Human Behavior: Darwinian Perspectives on Human Nature* (New York: Palgrave, 2000), 28.

eusociality," writes Wilson, "has been rare in the history of life because group selection must be exceptionally powerful to relax the grip of individual selection."[115]

In the standard model of natural selection, what matters most in evolution is passing on genes with mating partners in an unbroken chain of babies. Successful mating is evolution's greatest gift—it's why you have your life in the first place. All plants, animals, and humans are by definition children of survivors who lived long enough to reproduce. In the competition to pass on genes, the logic of natural selection suggests that individuals matter much more than groups ever could. And though many species live in groups—herds, flocks, pods, packs, folds, schools, societies—they are also always competing with other members of their group. Sometimes the competition is for food and safety, but always it is also for a mate. The reproductive competition can be fought between individuals—usually males competing for females. The battles, however, can also be outwardly peaceful. In nonexclusive mating, females have many male partners, and the evolutionary competition occurs at the level of the sperms entering the cervix. As we will explore below, the "theory of sperm competition" has implications for our understanding of human nature.

Eusociality, at least in ants and termites, involves cooperative care of broods, overlapping generations within a colony, a common nest to construct and defend, and a division of labor into reproductive and nonreproductive groups. Species that cooperate can accomplish more than species that always compete. This "superpower" is reflected in the comparative biomass of eusocial species in the world today.

Estimates of the number of insect and arthropod species vary from 1 million to 10 million. There are 2,600 taxonomical families of insects and arthropods. Only fifteen of these families have given rise to eusocial species. Researchers have actually weighed all of the animals in a single hectare of Amazonian rainforest, even though these animals are difficult to measure. Ants and termites made up almost two-thirds of the weight of all insects. The ants alone weighed four times than all the mammals, birds, reptiles, and amphibians.[116] Wilson crudely estimates 10,000 trillion ants (10^{16}) on the planet with a combined weight comparable to the 7 billion humans (10^9).[117]

---

[115] Wilson, *The Social Conquest of Earth*, 55.

[116] Ibid., 113.

[117] Ibid., 117.

The "superpower" of eusociality is also seen in the relative biomass of humans and our domesticated plants and animals. Wilson argues that humans in the past crossed a threshold into true eusociality. We share shelter, childcare, and food. We have multigenerational social groups and division of labor. The scientific controversy about eusociality revolves around whether and to what extent group selection operates in human evolution. Critics of multilevel selection theory argue that reciprocal altruism and kin selection are adequate explanations of individuals coming together as functional group-cooperators.

What We Don't Know

Paleoarcheologists and anthropologists debate the extent to which early human tribal groups competed with each other and the extent to which they were monogamous in mating and child rearing. In these disputes some of the evidence for or against comes from European encounters with hunter-gatherer tribal groups in North America and Australia in the eighteenth and nineteenth centuries, as well as surviving hunter-gatherers in remote parts of the Amazon, Africa, Siberia, and other regions of the world.

Let's look at both of these questions in turn, because they will inform and provide nuance to our understanding of the "new" human nature. Did prehistoric human groups compete violently with each other, and did prehistoric humans practice monogamy? In other words, how did they survive, how did they reproduce, and how might that still be relevant to understanding our behavior today?

Survival

In evolution, what doesn't survive long enough to reproduce won't make it into the future population's gene pool. Human survival requires food, safety, and shelter. This is true in different ways for all species. The difference, in the case of humans, is our groupishness. Survival is as much about our social environment as it is about our natural environments. Human survival is also a matter of competition and cooperation with our fellow humans. Humans literally need other humans in their lives in order to survive and thrive. To be shunned and excluded from the tribe would be a death sentence. Even today, social isolation is highly correlated with a decline in mental and physical health—a kind of a slow death sentence for many lonely souls. So strong is our need for friends, family, intimate relations, and physical contact with other humans that the absence thereof gives rise to mental and physical illness. Indeed, a human infant tragically deprived of social interaction will grow sickly and stunted in body and mind.

Our emotions and behaviors have been shaped over the eons by living around a common hearth. Maintaining a common hearth required cooperative skills and is already indicative of the cognitive revolution that transformed humans and the planet. Firewood needed to be collected and stored. The fire needed to be tended day and night. This required planning, taking turns, and divisions of labor. Fire mastery, however, also united the band—men and women, young and old— around a common source for cooking, heat, light, protection, and cultural formation. The Prometheus myth gets it right—fire is a godlike gift that uniquely distinguishes humans from all other animals. Fire mastery allowed humans to settle in climates and regions where they otherwise could not survive. There is something primordial in our attraction to fire. Fire mastery is archetypally human.

Hunting large game with spears also required cooperative skills. And the fossil record indicates that wherever humans went—Australia, Siberia, North America, South America, Madagascar, New Zealand— they hunted large game to extinction. Hundreds of large mammalian species disappeared from the geological record around the world soon after the humans arrived.

There seems to be a primal and optimal size for intense human collaboration of between six to twelve men. The primal hunting team functions as a synchronized unit, instinctively cooperating as if with one mind and body to achieve shared goals. Teams also give rise to altruistic bonds. Even today this is the "natural" unit—ten plus or minus—for modern armies, effective business units, and all team sports. Women may have participated in these hunting teams, but a woman with one or more infants would be uniquely burdened. Women certainly form teams, perhaps more naturally then men do. Men, however, are more predisposed to violent behavior.

Hunting large game and avoiding predators required the ability to run. Distance running allowed early humans to chase down wounded animals. Humans are unique among mammals in this ability to run long distances. Other mammals overheat and collapse. Humans have an extreme capacity to regulate our body temperature during intense and prolonged exercise. No other mammal runs twenty-six-mile marathons.

We don't really know the extent of Malthusian limits and intergroup competition between early hunter-gatherers.[118] There is no question, however, that much of human history since the advent of agriculture and recorded history has involved high rates of interhuman violence. Warfare, genocide, enslavement, rape, theft, patriarchy, and primogeniture are prominent features of all agricultural civilizations.[119]

It is also clear that the vast majority of violence through recorded history and in the world today is perpetrated by young men between puberty and the age of forty. Interpersonal violence within a group must be distinguished from intergroup violence. Violence between individuals (interpersonal violence) mostly arises when a man's self-esteem is threatened and not typically for utilitarian reasons or sadistic motivations.[120] These are crimes of passion, not premeditation. Marriage and children greatly diminish a man's willingness to engage in risky and life-threatening behavior. Testosterone goes down in new fathers. Oxytocin goes up. Pair bonding seems to have a "humanizing" effect on men.[121]

Intergroup violence, however, has a different rationale than interpersonal violence. In their book *Sex and War*, Malcolm Potts and Thomas Hayden argue that the cooperative skills needed for hunting large game in our past are easily transferred to attacking other humans.[122] When occasion arose, hunter-gatherers might well have engaged in offensive or defensive warfare.

In agricultural societies, moreover, there is a logic to violent group competition that may not have been a prominent factor for hunter-gatherers. In agricultural societies, wealth could be accumulated and stored, measured in land, labor, grain, and livestock. Because productivity was basically flat over many centuries, the only way to get rich quick in agricultural societies was to steal your neighbors' land, grain, and livestock, while capturing and enslaving your unlucky neighbors (or, alternately, to defend your own group from such threats). Much of recorded history is about just such conflicts.

Hunter-gatherers, on the other hand, would not have been able to accumulate and store wealth. Nor is it clear that hunter-gatherers faced

---

[118] Ryan and Jetha, *Sex at Dawn: How We Mate, Why We Stray, and What It Means for Modern Relationships*.

[119] Gwynne Dyer, *War: The Lethal Custom* (New York: Carroll & Graf, 1985, 2004).

[120] Roy Baumeister, *Evil: Inside Human Creulty and Aggression* (New York: Macmillan, 1996).

[121] Potts and Hayden, *Sex and War: How Biology Explains Warfare and Terrorism and Offers a Path to a Safer World*.

[122] Ibid.

a lot of resource competition. They were few in number and spread across a vast world. Flight through migration would presumably be a better option than fight in those cases where intergroup conflict arose. Encountering other tribal groups might well have been rare and welcome occasions, rather than occasions for deadly competition. And as long as there was big game to be hunted or plentiful seafood to be had, there would also have been lots of surplus food to share. And food sharing is certainly archetypally human behavior.

We do know, however, that tribalism, team identity, and team aggression are deeply rooted in our evolved nature. The camaraderie experienced by soldiers in their "band of brothers" is a universal human phenomenon. The male warrior culture almost always included prostitutes and frequently also organized rape supported by a male "locker-room" culture of sexism and vulgarities. It is the same camaraderie within the gangs of Los Angeles, the football hooligans in Europe, Ivy League sport rivalries, military combat units, and terrorist cells. Today, the big business of regional and national team sports— soccer, football, baseball, basketball, ice hockey, cricket, rugby—is evidence enough of our innate tribalism. To this we can add ideological movements, religious fundamentalism, extreme nationalism, ethnic chauvinism, culture wars, and clashing civilizations. The tribe is also archetypally human.

Historically, women didn't go out and fight wars. In many cultures and moments in recorded history, women may have applauded and goaded men as they went off to fight. Women were often victims of war, including experiencing rape, enslavement, and slaughter. A woman with an infant child is uniquely vulnerable. Until recently, women have not been warriors. It will be interesting to see whether a new military culture evolves in the United States and elsewhere as a result of the inclusion of women in the armed forces. The increased participation of women in team sports in the United States following Title IX may have a similar effect. Of course, women today are also pursuing careers in business and finance, professions that until recently were also exclusively male.

How far back does our competitive and violent nature go? Surveys of skeletal remains of pre-agricultural societies are inconclusive. Archeological remains in Portugal and Israel are suggestive of largely peaceful pre-agricultural societies, while remains in the Danube and

Sudan are suggestive of high rates of violent deaths.[123] Certainly by the time agriculture appears in the late Neolithic, we see intergroup violent competition as a regular feature of human civilization. As we will explore in more detail below, humans cooperate to compete and compete to cooperate. These dynamics affect every business enterprise and every team endeavor. This, too, is part of our hunter-gatherer brains and our recent social conquest of the planet.

Survival of the fittest is really about fitting into a particular niche. Fitness is measured by particular ways of living and reproducing within an ecological context. Sometimes evolution is a Darwinian jungle, red in tooth and claw; and sometimes evolution is just a White Elephant Sale, a big mishmash of complexity coexisting in an enormous variety of forms. Energy, matter, and ingenuity need not be limiting factors in many ecological niches and certainly not for the Earth as a whole. The Sun provides a superabundance of energy for evolution to grow in diversity, density, and complexity of life forms. Cultural evolution was a giant leap for the White Elephant Sale version of evolution. There are a lot of different ways for humans to fit into societies today. There are many different pathways and niches for humans to realize fitness, survival, and reproduction in the twenty-first century.

Reproduction

Reproduction is the other essential ingredient of evolution, including human evolution. We all begin first as children of genetic parents. Our parents may have been good or bad, absent or involved, alive or dead during our childhood, but we carry their genes. Our parents imprint themselves on us before we were born. Our genetic pathways and possibilities begin with the endowments we received from our parents and those before them. Studies suggest that personality traits, types, and attributes are deeply tied to genetic predispositions. We must survive, but we must also reproduce in order to pass on genes and culture to the future. Human and animal reproductive behaviors have been extensively studied over the past few

---

[123] One study concludes that "the levels of violence was much higher than in modern state societies and in the world today" but the data does not extend beyond 12,000 years ago. See Max Roser, "Ethnographic and Archaeological Evidence on Violent Deaths," OurWorldinData.org, https://ourworldindata.org/ethnographic-and-archaeological-evidence-on-violent-deaths/.

decades. Sex and gender are critical components of understanding our hunter-gatherer instincts and behavior.

In her book *The Anatomy of Love*, anthropologist Helen Fisher discusses three different biological systems—lust, romance, and attachment—at play in human mating and reproduction. Sexual attraction is driven by testosterone in men and women. The infatuation of romantic love activates serotonin and endorphins in the brain. The romantic obsession typically lasts months or perhaps a year. When romantic love is reciprocated, it is literally a drug high. When romantic love is not reciprocated, it is like a drug withdrawal.[124] The third mating system is attachment, driven primarily by oxytocin. The attachment bond between mother and child is preprogrammed in our biology. Men also generate oxytocin, though less than women. Long-term pair bonding between partners is driven by this so-called snuggle drug.[125]

Lust, romance, and attachment need not coincide in any given mating relationship. Indeed, Fisher argues that there is a "four-year itch," associated with the time at which hunter-gatherer partners often had a single child old enough to become part of the tribal playgroup. At this stage, men and women might often change partners. Fisher argues that serial monogamy with clandestine affairs is the "natural" reproductive strategy for both men and women.[126]

In their book *Sex at Dawn*, Christopher Ryan and Cacilda Jetha present evidence to suggest that the mating norm of Pleistocene humans would have been promiscuous sex within the tribal group and confused paternity. They criticize "the standard narrative" in evolutionary psychology, which understands male parental investment through monogamy as an adaptation in which the female trades sex with a single male for food and protection for her children and herself. The woman, in this view, exchanges erotic pleasure for access to the man's wealth and security. By this account, note the authors, "your mother is a whore."[127]

Ryan and Jetha argue that monogamy is not really "in our nature," but rather a recent artifact of agricultural societies and private property. Hunter-gatherer groups were egalitarian, characterized by shared food

---

[124] Fisher, *Anatomy of Love: A Natural History of Mating, Marriage, and Why We Stray.*

[125] Robert M. Sapolsky, *Behave: The Biology of Humans at Our Best and Worst* (New York: Penguin, 2017).

[126] Fisher, *Anatomy of Love: A Natural History of Mating, Marriage, and Why We Stray.*

[127] Ryan and Jetha, *Sex at Dawn: How We Mate, Why We Stray, and What It Means for Modern Relationships*, 50.

and shelter, little privacy, and no private property. Promiscuous sex and shared paternity within the tribal group would have provided many evolutionary advantages in raising children. Moreover, sexual jealousies would have threatened the cohesiveness and survival fitness of the tribe. The technical term for this is "polygynandry." It is what chimpanzees and bonobos do. Remember, also, that there was a very limited number of mate choices in small hunter-gatherer tribes, and exogamy—mating with outside groups—might also have been common.

Some of the most compelling evidence for promiscuous mating in our prehistoric past comes from physical anthropology and the theory of sperm competition. Primates provide a telling example, though the theory applies to other mammals, birds, and reptiles. The theory is built upon a number of physiological comparisons between different species and their reproductive behavior:

- Male/female body-size dimorphism (average weight).
- Ratio of testicular volume to body mass.
- Whether testicles inside body or in external scrotum.
- Comparative penis length (erect).
- The coronal ridge and glans that appear only on human penis.
- Seminal volume and sperm concentration per ejaculation.
- Swelling of female genitalia during primate ovulation (estrus) versus the concealed ovulation and continuous sexual receptivity in human females.
- Evolution of pendulous breasts in human females.
- Coitus typically face-to-face versus rear entry for other primates.
- The structure of the cervix as a barrier to insemination and the interaction of bodily excretions inside the vagina that inhibit insemination.
- Female vocalizations during intercourse in both humans and chimps.
- The frequency of intercourse per pregnancy.[128]

128 Ibid., 224.

Perhaps that's too much information—TMI, as they say—but taken together it provides important clues into Pleistocene sex, gender, and behavior. Gorillas and chimps provide clues.

Gorillas have a harem-based mating system. Individual males fight it out to control the harem. As a result, the male evolved to be twice the size of the female, while his gonads devolved to the size of kidney beans. His erect penis is only 3 cm. Gorilla intercourse takes about 60 seconds, with less than 20 copulations per pregnancy.[129]

Bonobos and chimpanzees, on the other hand, have promiscuous sex. A female in heat advertises her fertility with swelling in her genitals. She will mate during estrus many times with most of the males in the band. As a result, male chimps and bonobos have larger erect penises and especially large testes producing a lot of semen and sperm. Scaled to the size of a human male, the testes of chimps would be the equivalent of a man with a pair of grapefruits between his legs. It is an evolutionary arms race to get genes into the next generation, one that is fought between gonads, not individuals.

In terms of their physiology, human testes can be seen as half-full and half-empty, suggesting that our "natural" reproductive strategies are somewhere between that of gorillas and chimps. Human male-female body dimorphism is comparable to that of chimps and bonobos. Human testes are thankfully not scaled to grapefruit size, but they still produce an enormous amount of sperm per ejaculation. The erect human penis is enormous in comparison to chimps and unique also in having a coronal ridge (the supposed evolutionary function of which we need not discuss in polite company). And unlike all the other primates, human females have concealed ovulation. They don't advertise their fertility. Our evolutionary history is built into our reproductive organs, even if our cultural practices today are very different.

Much of evolutionary psychology is founded on the belief in an intrinsic war between the sexes. Ryan and Jetha argue that this is a mistaken belief, an artifact of agriculture and patriarchy. Ryan and Jetha colorfully summarize the theory of sperm competition in comparative evolution thus:

If a species has *cojones grandes*, you can bet that males have frequent ejaculations with females who sleep around. Where the

---

[129] Ibid., 230.

females save it for Mr. Right, the males have smaller testes, relative to their overall body mass. The correlation of slutty females with big-balled males appears to apply not only to humans and other primates, but to many mammals, as well as to birds, butterflies, reptiles, and fish.[130]

They continue:

So the game's still the same—getting one's genes into the future—but the field of play is different. With harem-based polygynous systems like the gorilla's, individual males fight it out before any sex takes place. In sperm competition, the cells fight in there so males don't have to fight out here. Instead, males can relax around one another, allowing larger group sizes, enhancing cooperation, and avoiding disruption to the social dynamic.[131]

In his book *Sapiens*, Yuval Harari agrees. "Nuclear families and monogamous relationships are incompatible with our biological software," writes Harari.[132] But he urges caution. The diversity of primal cultures globally during the Pleistocene is probably reflected in the diversity of aboriginal cultures in the Australian subcontinent. For instance, prior to the British conquest, Australia had 200 to 600 distinct hunter-gatherer tribes living in multiple bands. Harari writes:

Each tribe had its own language, religion, norms and customs. Living around what is now Adelaide in southern Australia were several patrilineal clans that reckoned descent from the father's side. These clans bonded together into tribes on a strictly territorial basis. In contrast, some tribes in northern Australia gave more importance to a person's maternal ancestry, and a person's tribal identity depended on his or her totem rather than his territory.[133]

Harari emphasizes the sheer variety of cultures among ancient hunter-gatherers. On the eve of the agricultural revolution, there were 5 million to 8 million humans spread across vast territories divided into

---

[130] Ibid., 222.
[131] Ibid., 223.
[132] Harari, *Sapiens: A Brief History of Humankind*, Kindle 700.
[133] Ibid., Kindle 744.

many thousands of different languages and cultures.[134] People lived intimately in small groups and may have had few occasions to interact with outsiders given their dispersal across vast regions.

Forager tribes had no private property to speak of, as they could "own" only what they could carry with them during seasonal and geographic migrations. As already mentioned, permanent fishing villages, like those among the indigenous peoples of the Pacific Northwest, may have been widespread, but the archeological remains are now underwater, as sea levels have risen some 160 meters since the last glacial maximum 20,000 years ago.[135] So we just don't know and may never know how our ancestors lived and thrived over hundreds of thousands of years. Moreover, we may be misled in drawing implications from surviving primal societies in the modern world, as they have all been influenced by neighboring societies, have tended to survive in harsh environments, and are quite different from one another.

Whatever our prehistoric past practices might have been, we do know that agriculture domesticated us as much as we domesticated plants and animals. The changes brought about by agricultural evolved slowly and were not uniformly beneficial. Anthropologist Jared Diamond calls agriculture "the worst mistake humans made." Skeleton remains indicate that early agriculturalists were more likely to suffer from malnutrition, disease, and starvation than their foraging neighbors. Domesticated animals brought new infectious diseases. Agriculture involved backbreaking work.[136]

Permanent agricultural settlements led to private property, patriarchy, and hierarchical social structures. As villages grew into towns and towns grew into cities and cities grew into civilizations, small groups of elites were able to capture surplus production and labor from peasants in order to build monumental architecture and create standing armies. The history of agricultural civilizations is certainly dominated by organized violence. Tribute-taking rulers used coercion.[137]

---

[134] Ibid., Kindle 747.

[135] Vivien Gorntz, "Sea Level Rise, after the Ice Melted and Today," *Goddard Institute for Space Studies* (2007), http://www.giss.nasa.gov/research/briefs/gornitz_09/.

[136] Jared Diamond, "The Worst Mistake in the History of the Human Race," *Discover Magazine*1999.

Much has changed in the last few centuries. Economic production grew exponentially in recent history, even as human numbers exploded. Humans got rich quickly, not through conquest, but through ever more cooperation to harness more energy, matter, and ingenuity. Indeed, warfare today has evolved from win-lose competition to lose-lose disaster for all sides. And contrary to what the news media reports, there has been a remarkable decrease in both interpersonal and organized violence in recent history. We will further explore this counter-intuitive insight below.

Sex-Gender Differences

The sciences have come a long way in understanding evolved sex and gender differences in human cognition and behavior. There is substantial cross-cultural empirical research that supports the view that there are innate differences between men and women, as well as significant cultural variation and individual differences. On average, women are more verbal than men. This has been linked to the estrogen cycle, as well as structures of the female brain. On average, men excel in spatial reasoning, puzzle solving, map reading, and abstract mathematics. This, too, has been linked to brain differences. Women are more dexterous with their hands, and men tend to have better large motor skills. Anthropologist Helen Fisher speculates about the evolutionary basis for these differences:

> Moreover, these gender differences make evolutionary sense. As ancestral males began to scout, track, and surround animals more than two million of years ago, those males who were good at maps and mazes would have disproportionately survived. Ancestral females needed to locate vegetable foods within an elaborate grassy landscape. So those who could remember where these resources were located would have also lived another day— passing on this female spatial skill. Moreover, superior verbal aptitudes must have been critical tools to ancestral women as they soothed, scolded, educated, and played with their growing young.[138]

---

[138] Fisher, *Anatomy of Love: A Natural History of Mating, Marriage, and Why We Stray*, Kindle 3341.

110

Women are also more empathetic than men. This is linked to oxytocin and other hormones, as well as the structure of the neuronal connectome between left and right hemispheres and between the front and back of the brain. Elevated empathy in women also makes evolutionary sense given women's role in rearing infants. Women are less aggressive than men, as their reproductive strategy is less competitive. Women have higher pain tolerance and are better at delayed gratification than men. Autism Spectrum Disorder is five times more prevalent in boys than in girls. Fisher writes:

> Women generalize; they synthesize; they take a more global perspective of anything they ponder. They think in webs of factors, not straight lines—web thinking. In contrast, men tend to focus on the goal; they discard what they regard as extraneous information and proceed toward their decision in a more linear, causal manner—what I call step thinking.[139]

Of course, there are exceptions that disprove all these generalizations. The evolutionary accounts for why these gender differences evolved may also be just-so stories. It is extremely difficult to disaggregate the biology of sex differences from the gendered roles inculcated through cultures. In his book *Women After All*, physician and anthropologist Melvin Konner explores the considerable research on innate sex and gender differences in men and women with this caveat:

> It's important to understand that similarities between men and women's brains are much greater than any differences; the differences that exist are unrelated to general intelligence, but they are tied to specific dispositions . . . men greatly exceed women in violence and driven sexuality.[140]

In all of this, remember that our differences—sex, gender, and otherwise—exist along bell curve distributions with long tails. There is an enormous plasticity in human biology, brains, and behavior. Cultural selection can shift the distributions of traits and behaviors to the right or the left on the distribution curves, for better or for worse, depending

---

[139] Ibid., Kindle 3371.
[140] Melvin Konner, *Women after All: Sex, Evolution, and the End of Male Supremacy* (New York: W,W, Norton, 2016), 229.

on the context for survival and reproduction. Identity politics only make sense if we remember that we are all of one species, more alike than different. Mother nature made us sexist and xenophobic, but that doesn't mean we must act that way. Mother nature gave our species many other endowments, including the possibility of transforming nature and our natures.

It is not clear how far we have wandered from our hunter-gatherer genes and behavior in the 10,000-year process of human self-domestication. Humans survive in complicated circumstances today that bear little resemblance to the lives of hunter-gatherers. While our hunter-gatherer genes, cognition, emotions, and behavior persist today, it is not always clear what constitutes our "innate" behaviors and dispositions. Getting to know your hunter-gatherer brain requires a lot of science, to be sure, but also nuance in interpreting the science. We can and should make tentative generalizations based on both nature and nurture, both biology and culture.

Evolution, for instance, has invested heavily in the fairer sex of our species. Higher pain tolerance, delayed gratification, ability to multitask, and better social skills—stereotypically female traits, whether manifested by women or men—are assets in today's business environment. The liberation of women from unwanted pregnancies may be one of the most significant sociological changes in the past century. Moreover, as fertility rates decrease around the world, all of this evolutionary energy invested in women is released to pursue education, careers, and service. Today, typically about 60 to 65 percent of university graduates around the world are female. A business team that does not include women as equals and leaders is at a significant disadvantage.

The predominance of testosterone in men also turns out to be a disadvantage for investors as it is linked to excessive risk taking. Many things influence the levels of testosterone in men (and women). It can vary depending on time of day, age, physical activity, sexual activity, and social status.[141] High-status men (and women) generate more testosterone (and can be more libidinous as a result). Winning also generates more testosterone. On the downside is cortisol, a stress

---

[141] Sylvia Ann Hewlett, "Too Much Testosterone on Wall Street?," Harvard Business Review, https://hbr.org/2009/01/too-much-testosterone-on-wall; Geoff Brumfield, "The Testosterone of Trading," Nature, http://www.nature.com/news/2008/080414/full/news.2008.753.html; Joao Medeiros, "The Truth Behind Testosterone: Why Men Risk It All," WIRED, http://www.wired.co.uk/article/why-men-risk-it-all.

hormone released when losing in social status, competition, or money. When the body generates the cortisol stress hormone, it makes us more risk averse. In the long run, too much cortisol also makes us sick. It seems hormones, especially testosterone and cortisol, make traders irrationally exuberant and overly pessimistic. The biochemistry turns out to be much the same in other mammalian species. It can be informative to study the trading floor in the same way ethologists study a baboon troop or neurogeneticists study mice brains.

The Cognitive Revolution

Somewhere along the way, our hominid ancestors developed impressive linguistic abilities. We don't know when or how our species' use of symbolic language evolved, because the soft tissues of our brains and vocal apparatus do not fossilize. And until written language evolved, spoken words also did not fossilize. We can, however, compare contemporary human anatomy with that of other primates today and make additional extrapolations from fossilized skulls of our hominid ancestors.

The larynx in humans is low in the throat, creating a more complex resonance chamber. Humans also have exquisite fine motor control of the tongue, lips, and breath. Enlarged brains were necessary for utilizing our enhanced vocal and auditory apparatus. In the course of 6 million years, the brains of our ancestors tripled in size, growing from 450 cm^3 to 1,300 cm^3. We do not know which came first, sophisticated vocalization or larger brains. No doubt, these coevolved, though not necessarily in a uniform and gradual process.

The growth of hominid brains also drove other physiological and cultural changes. Childbirth became more difficult, as big-headed babies have trouble passing through the mother's birth canal. Hominids adapted by giving birth to less developed infants with brains that grew after birth over a prolonged period of childhood dependency.

Human language, as distinguished from other kinds of animal communication, is especially subtle. Through a system of sounds and signs we are able to produce distinct sentences and meanings, share and store information about the surrounding world, and negotiate the social environment. Speech has many adaptive advantages.

A limited number of sounds can produce an infinite number of meanings. Language can be both precise and versatile. It allowed early hominids to coordinate action and share information about the world around them—which plants could be eaten, where animals could be hunted, how to make a particular tool. Moreover, it enabled knowledge and know-how to be passed on and accumulated across generations. "Biologically we are just another ape," writes anthropologist Terrance Deacon, "mentally we are a whole new phylum of organism."[142]

Big Historian David Christian marks symbolic language as the origin of collective learning, a major threshold in the story of our species and the planet.

> Humans as individuals are not that much cleverer than chimps or Neanderthals; but as a species we are vastly more creative because our knowledge is shared within and between generations. All in all, collective learning is so powerful an adaptive mechanism that one might argue it plays a role in human history analogous to that of natural selection in the histories of other organisms.[143]

Communication, however, was not just about practical matters of the hunter-gatherer life. It was also about the social life of the tribal group. Humans are uniquely social creatures, but cooperation is hard work. Anthropologist Robin Dunbar proposed a cognitive limit to the number of individuals with whom one can maintain social relations based on the relative size of the neocortex in primate species. Smaller brains mean smaller social groups. The "Dunbar Number" for humans is 150 individuals. Beyond 150 it is increasingly difficult to remember who is who and how they fit into the group. Beyond 150 individuals, cooperating groups require social hierarchies and enforced rules. Today, the Dunbar Number informs not just paleoanthropology, but also business management, military units, and social networks.

In his book *Grooming, Gossip, and the Evolution of Language*, Dunbar further proposes that language was a "cheap" replacement for social grooming. Nonhuman primates spend a lot of time grooming each other in order to chill out and promote group cohesion. Mutual back scratching is replaced in humans by "vocal grooming." Language allows humans to maintain social cohesion while freeing up hands to do other kinds of work. According to this theory, gossiping about others replaced grooming among humans as a form of social bonding. Indeed,

---

[142] Terrence W. Deacon, *The Symbolic Species: The Co-Evolution of Language and the Brain* (New York: Norton, 1997).
[143] Christian, *Maps of Time: An Introduction to Big History*, Kindle 3531-33.

gossip was also a powerful means for enforcing group norms and morals.[144]

Evolutionary theorists debate whether the coevolution of language, brains, vocal chords, and physiology was gradual or abrupt. We may never know. Cave art, ritualistic burials, and prehistoric sculptures suggest that by 40,000 years ago, humans already had other forms of complex symbolic thoughts. So it is likely that by this stage human symbolic language was already advanced. The rise of human languages set loose a positive feedback loop and an evolutionary arms race. Those individuals and groups that communicated better were more likely to survive and reproduce.

For Yuval Harari, however, the most important function of language in human evolution was the ability to create social fictions. It is precisely our ability to create social fictions and imaginary worlds that allowed us to scale cooperation from tens to thousands, to millions, and to now billions of people in our global civilization:

> Any large-scale human cooperation—whether a modern state, a medieval church, an ancient city or an archaic tribe—is rooted in common myths that exist only in people's collective imagination. . . . [N]one of these things exists outside the stories that people invent and tell one another. There are no gods in the universe, no nations, no money, no human rights, no laws, and no justice outside the common imagination of human beings.[145]

Harari calls these "networks of artificial instincts."[146] Outside of bacteria, we are the only species that can "flexibly cooperate" in large numbers because we can create imagined realities and shared, taken-for-granted rules. Religion, human rights, ethnicities, nations, and even languages are all fictions. Money is perhaps the most universal and important fiction of all. In the twenty-first century, human fictional realities now change the objective realities of the planet and our future evolution of the planet and ourselves.

---

[144] Dunbar, *Grooming, Gossip and the Evolution of Language.*
[145] Harari, *Sapiens: A Brief History of Humankind*, Kindle 464-71.
[146] Ibid., Kindle 2515.

Stone-Age Brains

If you look inside the human brain, you do not actually see cognition or emotions. There is nothing in the brain that you could recognize as anything like your experiences of talking, listening, reading, writing, understanding, and making complex decisions.

In dissecting a human brain, we first see large-scale structures. On the outside is the neocortex with areas labeled the frontal lobe, the parietal lobe, the occipital lobe, and the temporal lobe; and these are divided into two hemispheres, right and left, with a broad band of nerve fibers known as the corpus callosum connecting the two halves. If we peel away the neocortex, we discover the mesocortex and subcortical structures in the limbic system, including the thalamus, the amygdala, the hippocampus, and the cerebellum, all connected to the brain stem and the spinal cord. This much you probably already know. Images of the human brain and nervous system have become iconic in the modern world.

Because the brain has evolved over the deep time of evolution, we discover also layered evolutionary developments easily understood through the following cartoonish description. The subcortical structures are our "lizard legacy." The limbic system is our "furry little mammal" brain. The neocortex is our "monkey brain." And the frontal lobes represent "our higher-porpoise" brain.[147] While it is not necessary to remember all of the details of brain anatomy, it is helpful to remember this description of brain anatomy and evolution. Sensory data passes through our lizard, mammalian, and monkey brains before the thinking brain has a chance to cogitate.

Studying human brains in vivo presents all kinds of technical and ethical challenges. A lot of what we know about the specialized functions of different areas of the brain comes from observing survivors of traumatic brain injuries or stroke victims. In both cases, neuroscientists correlate the destruction of certain brain regions due to hemorrhaging or injury with the loss of particular mental functions, such as the loss of motor control, speech, or even particular parts of speech or sets of word concepts. The latter is known as aphasia.

---

[147] Michael Dowd, *Thank God for Evolution* (New York Plume, 2009).

Curiously, memory seems to be distributed throughout the brain and is not located in any particular region.

Because neurons function the same in mice and in men, because mammalian brains have similar structures, we have also learned a lot from animal studies. When we examine a brain under powerful microscopes, we see neurons and glial cells, which are also found throughout our central nervous system in the rest of the body. There are different types of neuronal cells, but they all share a basic structure. The cell body contains the nucleus and organelle. Neurons, unlike glial cells, have lots of dendrite "trees" and axon "arms." These connect to other neurons. This maze of connections ends in synapses, linking each neuron with hundreds or thousands of others. The neurons fire electrical charges in the form of chemical ions, which are mediated by a variety of neurochemicals produced endogenously by the brain. The chemicals produced in different areas of the brain are very important to how the brain functions.

Recent estimates suggest that here are 86 billion neurons in a mature human brain. Each neuron has on average about 1,000 synaptic connections.[148] A three-year-old child has about 10^{16} (10 quadrillion) synapses, but this happily decreases through "pruning" with age to a more manageable number, between 1 to 5 quadrillion synapses.[149]

The 1.5 kilograms of your brain, give or take, represents only 2 percent of your body weight and yet it consumes 15 percent of your cardiac output, 20 percent of your body oxygen, and about 25 percent of your body's glucose consumption. Even when you're just sitting around, the brain needs about 0.1 calories per minute; with intellectual activity, this can increase to as high as 1.5 calories per minute. From an evolutionary point of view, the human brain is an expensive item. In birth, the head's size makes it difficult for it to pass through the female pelvis, often resulting in the death of the infant or the mother. In life, the brain-mind requires a lot of extra food and care.

The advantage of big brains from an evolutionary perspective is the increased ability to integrate information from the body and environment in order to respond quickly to threats and opportunities.

[148] Christof Koch, *Consciousness: Confessions of a Romantic Reductionist* (Cambridge: MIT Press, 2012).

[149] Carvalho LR Azevedo FA, Grinberg LT, Farfel JM, Ferretti RE, Leite RE, Jacob Filho W, Lent R, Herculano-Houzel S, "Equal Numbers of Neuronal and Nonneuronal Cells Make the Human Brain an Isometrically Scaled-up Primate Brain," *Journal of Comparative Neurology* 513, no. 5 (2009); R.W. Williams, Herrup, K, "The Control of Neuron Number," *Annual Review of Neuroscience* 11 (1988).

Like lab rats, our brains are hard-wired so that food, sex, and other pleasures give us little doses of dopamine. Indeed, from the perspective of neuroscience, neurotransmitters are the very definition of "pleasure" and "pain." Evolution has programmed us to enjoy and seek out activities that promote survival and reproduction and to fear and avoid activities that threaten survival and reproduction. Most of this happens automatically and unconsciously.

The brain-mind is best understood as a kind of Rube Goldberg machine. Goldberg was an American cartoonist who was famous for depicting complex devices that performed simple tasks in convoluted ways. One such cartoon depicts a man eating his soup. The spoon is attached to a string that flips a cracker to a parrot that then activates water pouring into a bucket that activates a lighter that launches a rocket attached to a knife that turns on a clock with a pendulum that swings back and forth moving a napkin that now wipes clean the soup-eating man's mustache. The entire contraption is worn on the head of the mustached man as a kind of hat. Our brains are like this complex machine, except that it is worn inside our heads instead of outside. Neuroscientists today are developing algorithmic flow charts that map out neural processes. Something simple like engaging in meditation sets off an impossibly complex series of actions, reactions, and feedback loops.[150] We can be thankful that we do not need to be the least bit aware of any of these processes. Philosopher Daniel Dennett calls this "competence without comprehension." You have a wonderfully functional and competent brain that allows you to mindlessly perform lots of simple and complex mental activities every day. Most of what we comprehend about the brain's many competences, we have learned in recent decades. It is worth stopping a moment, however, to grok that the most complicated object in the known universe is sitting right between your ears.

Divided Self

We are not of one mind, but many. The sages of the past have long recognized a gap between desire and reason, between emotion and willpower. Plato, for instance, described the self with the metaphor of a charioteer controlling horses in which the horses represent unruly

---

[150] Andrew Newberg, "Religious and Spiritual Practices: A Neurochemical Perspective," in *Where God and Science Meet*, ed. Patrick McNamara (Westport, CT: Praeger, 2006).

desires and the charioteer the controlling rationality. Plato went on to develop the myth of the tripartite polis in *The Republic,* which many interpret as a metaphor for the individual soul. The majority of self is governed by desires and passions (the Workers). A smaller part is groupish and governed by collective virtues (the Guardians). And the smallest part of the self is governed by reason and rationality (the Philosopher-King).[151] Freud also understood the self to be divided into three parts. The Id is our instinctive desire for pleasure. The Ego is our conscious, rational self. The Superego is expectations and rules programmed by our families and societies in opposition to our Id. Each of us is a volatile mix of emotions and desires, reasons and restraints, often working at cross-purposes.[152]

Neuroscientist Antonio Damasio and others have shown that human rationality is driven by our emotions. Independent reason is a myth.[153] Social psychologist Jonathan Haidt describes the divided self with the Buddhist metaphor of the elephant and the rider. Our emotions lumber along like an elephant, while the rider tries to control and steer the huge beast. Haidt writes:

> Reason and emotion must both work together to create intelligent behavior, but emotion (a major part of the elephant) does most of the work. When the neocortex came along, it made the rider possible, but it made the elephant much smarter, too. [154]

Changing our mind-brain behavior turns out to be hard work. The elephant is big and clumsy, the rider small and weak. Moreover, the language of the elephant is "like/approach" or "dislike/withdraw." It makes these assessments automatically, mostly unconsciously, millions of times a day. Haidt describes our evolved animal nature as like having a "like-o-meter" running in our heads at all times that lights up with "flashes of pleasure and displeasure."[155]

---

[151] Plato, *The Republic*, trans. revised by C.D.C. Reeve G.M.A. Grube (Indianapolis, IN: Hackett Publishing Company, (ca. 380 b.c.e.) 1992).

[152] Sigmund Freud, *Civilization and Its Discontents* (New York: W.W. Norton, [1930] 1961).

[153] Antonio Demasio, *Descartes' Error: Emotion, Reason, and the Human Brain* (New York: Avon, 1995); *The Feeling of What Happens: Body, Emotion and the Making of Consciousness* (London: Vintage, 2000).

[154] Jonathan Haidt, *The Happiness Hypothesis: Finding Modern Truth in Ancient Wisdom* (New York: Basic Books, 2006).

[155] Ibid., Kindle 633.

These conclusions are not "just-so stories" of evolutionary adaptations in the past but are also supported by laboratory studies today. Recent empirical research into what is referred to as "affective priming" has given psychologists new insights into how the "like-o-meter" works. Since the 1980s, thousands of controlled studies have shown the power and limits of priming to unconsciously bias our thoughts and behaviors. The studies have been conducted with people of all ages, classes, ethnicities, and political affiliation.

A priming experiment involves exposing the subject to a priming effect before some test-taking exercise. The priming effect might be an image or a word flashed on a screen too quickly to be noticed or something seemingly unrelated in the background environment leading up to the task. The priming effect can be completely unconscious. The task then tests variable performance on psychological games and surveys in comparison with control groups. The experiments are a form of psychological theater and often involve confederates in the lab.

For instance, Kathleen Vohs at the University of Minnesota studies the unconscious, social, and psychological dimensions of money. One set of experiments involved playing Monopoly in unequal distributions of money. The actual test takes place after the game, when a confederate dropped pencils on cue to see who was more helpful in spontaneously picking them up: those primed with low money, those primed with high money, or a nonprimed cohort.[156] In another experiment, three-year-old children were give a crayon-sharing test, preceded by the priming, which involved sorting money or, in the case of the control, sorting something other than money. In summary, the studies show that unconscious money priming prompted self-reliance and hard work. Finger dexterity tasks improved after the money priming. Primed subjects were also less sensitive to physical pain. Money primes, however, also inhibit warm, interpersonal, and cooperative relations. Priming studies have proliferated in experimental psychology.

---

[156] Kathleen D Vohs, "The Meaning of Money," in *Paduano Seminar* (NYU Stern School2014); "The Poor's Poor Mental Power," *Science* 341, no. 969 (2013) (2013); Kathleen D Vohs, Nicole L. Mead, and Miranda R. Goode, "The Psychological Consequences of Money," ibid.314, no. 1154 (2006).

System 1 and System 2

In his book *Thinking, Fast and Slow*, behavioral economist Daniel Kahneman reviews the empirical research challenging the assumption, central to traditional economic theory, that humans are rational actors capable of maximizing self-interest. Instead, Kahneman shows that we have two general modes of thinking—fast and slow. These evolved for different reasons.

System 1 is fast, effortless, and unconscious. It looks for patterns and causations by association and creates stories to explain events. The advantage of system 1 is the speed of response in a crisis and its ability to routinize repetitive tasks. Associative thinking can also lead to creative and expansive ideas. The disadvantage of system 1 is that it makes errors; jumps to conclusions; and blindly follows emotions, wrong assumptions, and false causal links. System 1 thinking calls on a number of heuristics and biases, which while often right, can also lead to tragic failures in decision making.

System 2 is slow and effortful. It requires logic, deliberation, and abstract thinking. The advantage of system 2 is that it allows reflection on pros and cons, options and consequences. It can handle math, statistics, and reductive thinking. The disadvantage of system 2 is that it is slow and requires effort. Indeed, deploying system 2 can lead to decision fatigue.

Kahneman infers an evolutionary logic in trade-offs between system 1 and system 2 thinking:

> Jumping to conclusions is efficient if the conclusions are likely to be correct and the costs of an occasional mistake acceptable, and if the jump saves much time and effort. Jumping to conclusions is risky when the situation is unfamiliar, the stakes are high, and there is no time to collect more information.[157]

People have confidence in their decisions and assessments "by the coherence of the story they manage to construct from available information," Kahneman tells us. "Indeed," he continues, "you will often find that knowing little makes it easier to fit everything you know into a coherent pattern."[158] Kahneman notes that:

---

[157] Kahneman, *Thinking, Fast and Slow*, Kindle 1345.
[158] Ibid., Kindle 1494.

System 1 is indeed the origin of much that we do wrong, but it is also the origin of most of what we do right—which is most of what we do. Our thoughts and actions are routinely guided by System 1 and generally are on the mark. One of the marvels is the rich and detailed model of our world that is maintained in associative memory: it distinguishes surprising from normal events in a fraction of a second, immediately generates an idea of what was expected instead of a surprise, and automatically searches for some causal interpretation of surprises and of events as they take place.[159]

The phenomenon of "negativity bias" has also been extensively studied with lab subjects. Negativity bias is why the media sensationalizes conflicts and crises. If the news reported only on the positive things people did around the world, nobody would care to watch it. We are super-sensitive to threat and danger, which is not to say that we don't enjoy and seek our pleasures too. Evolution puts a premium on overreacting to perceived dangers, threats, and unknowns. The pain of losing invariably exceeds the pleasure of an equal gain.

Negativity bias is built into the structure of our brains. The neural impulses from our eyes and ears go first to the thalamus—our lizard legacy—before any higher cortical cognition gets to take a go at them. If danger is associated with the external stimulus, the amygdala—also our lizard legacy—is activated nearby with its direct connection to the brainstem and can initiate a fight-or-flight response, before the frontal neocortex is even aware of anything going on. The amygdala also changes how the frontal cortex thinks about any given pleasure or threat. The basic brain structure that we share with reptiles is thus calling the shots before any of our higher cortical regions and cognitive capacities even "know" or can "think" about what just happened microseconds before.[160]

Negativity bias is only one of our many cognitive biases in System 1. The Cognitive Biases Codex, an infographic created by John Manoogian III and Buster Benson, categorizes a few hundred named cognitive biases. Some sense of the meanings can be discerned from

---

[159] Ibid., Kindle 7057.
[160] Paul Rozin and E.B. Royzman, "Negativity Bias, Negativity Dominance, and Contagion," *Personality and Social Psychology Review* 5 (2001); Haidt, *The Happiness Hypothesis: Finding Modern Truth in Ancient Wisdom*; Kahneman, *Thinking, Fast and Slow*.

their names: confirmation bias, priming effects, framing heuristics, risk-aversion, inequity aversion, associative coherence, affect heuristics, availability effects, agency detection, and more. The authors classify cognitive biases into four fundamental dilemmas: humans encounter 1) too much information, 2) not enough meaning, 3) needs to act fast, and 4) needs to filter what we should remember. These decision-making heuristics make sense in terms of survival in the past but can be dangerously dysfunctional in the context of the modern world, particularly so for investors.

Buster Benson of Better Humans took 177 examples of cognitive bias from Wikipedia and regrouped them thematically by what problems the biases tried to solve. Benson writes:

> Every cognitive bias is there for a reason—primarily to save our brains time or energy. If you look at them by the problem they're trying to solve, it becomes a lot easier to understand why they exist, how they're useful, and the trade-offs (and resulting mental errors) that they introduce.[161]

Without going into detail, it is valuable to present this overview of Benson's functional analysis of our many varied cognitive biases:

Too much information
- We notice things already primed in memory or repeated often.
- Bizarre, funny, visually-striking, or anthropomorphic things stick out more than non-bizarre/unfunny things.
- We notice when something has changed.
- We are drawn to details that confirm our own existing beliefs.
- We notice flaws in others more easily than we notice flaws in ourselves.

---

[161] Buster Benson, "Cognitive Bias Cheat Sheet," BetterHumans.Coach.Me, https://betterhumans.coach.me/cognitive-bias-cheat-sheet-55a472476b18; John Manoogian III and Buster Benson, "Cognitive Biases Codex," DesignHacks.co, http://www.visualcapitalist.com/wp-content/uploads/2017/09/cognitive-bias-infographic.html.

Not enough meaning

- We project our current mind-set and assumptions onto the past and the future.
- We think we know what other people are thinking.
- We simplify probabilities and numbers to make them easier to think about.
- We imagine things and people we're familiar with or fond of as better.
- We fill in characteristics from stereotypes, generalities, and prior histories.
- We tend to find stories and patterns even when looking at sparse data.

We need to act fast

- To act, we must be confident we can make an impact and feel what we do is important.
- To stay focused, we favor the immediate, relatable thing in front of us.
- To get things done, we tend to complete things we've invested time and energy in.
- To avoid mistakes, we aim to preserve autonomy and group status, and avoid irreversible decisions.
- We favor simple-looking options and complete information over complex, ambiguous options.

What we should remember

- We edit and reinforce some memories after the fact.
- We discard specifics to form generalities.
- We reduce events and lists to their key elements.
- We store memories differently based on how they were experienced.[162]

---

[162] Benson, "Cognitive Bias Cheat Sheet".

Avoiding error and making better decisions and predictions in a complex world requires an unusual mind or, better yet, group of minds. Individuals can train themselves to be critical thinkers and to regularly exercise their system 2 brains (and a career in economics and finance requires a lot of training); but this may only scale up the magnitude of mistakes made.

In finance, mistakes are expensive, but only recognized after the fact. Individuals compensate for their finitude by cooperating with others through networks—cultural, economic, social. We outsource many of our mental functions, beliefs, assumptions, and behavior to others. It should be no surprise that when you look around your office at your colleagues, you will see that the collective is smarter and capable of accomplishing much more than any individual.

There is wisdom in the crowd, but that only applies when the crowd consists of a diversity of opinions, expertise, and perspectives.[163] Kahneman details how adversarial collaboration and algorithmic criteria lead to better decision-making, but notes that this is not the normal practice in most business settings.[164] In his TED talk, Ray Dailo argues for transparency and data-driven, group decision-making.[165] In their book *Superforecasting: The Art and Science of Prediction*, Philip Tetlock and Dan Gardner show how to structure groups and experts in order to maximize successful predictions in economics and politics.[166]

Luck of the Genes

Human personalities, characteristics, and abilities exist along bell curve distributions. That very diversity is adaptive in evolution and population genetics. The variations entail greater plasticity for our species as a whole in changing selective environments. The distributions apply also to the Big Five personality dispositions—

---

[163] James Surowiecki, *The Wisdom of Crowds* (New York: Anchor, 2005); Philip E. Tetlock and Dan Gardner, *Superforecasting: The Art and Science of Prediction* (New York: Crown Publishers, 2015).

[164] Kahneman, *Thinking, Fast and Slow.*

[165] Ray Dalio, "How to Build a Company Where the Best Ideas Win," TED, https://www.ted.com/talks/ray_dalio_how_to_build_a_company_where_the_best_ideas_win. See also *Principles: Life and Work* (New York: Simon & Schuster, 2017).

[166] Philip E. Tetlock and Dan Gardner, *Superforecasting: The Art and Science of Prediction* (New York: Crown Publishers, 2015).

extraversion, openness, conscientiousness, agreeableness, and neuroticism.[167]

Behavioral genetics has expanded our understanding of the biological basis of these personality traits. Several decades of studies on human twins—identical and fraternal, raised separately or together—confirm that at least 50 percent of your personality traits are in the luck of your genes.[168] Indeed, identical twins raised separately from birth and then reunited decades later have similar aesthetic, spiritual, physical, emotional, and political behaviors.[169] It ain't fair, but as Kahneman observes:

> If you are genetically endowed with an optimistic bias, you hardly need to be told that you are a lucky person—you already feel fortunate. An optimistic attitude is largely inherited, and it is part of a general disposition for wellbeing, which may also include a preference for seeing the bright side of everything. . . . Optimists are normally cheerful and happy, and therefore popular; they are resilient in adapting to failures and hardships, their chances of clinical depression are reduced, their immune system is stronger, they take better care of their health, they feel healthier than others and are, in fact likely to live longer.[170]

Your genetically determined personality traits are your "set points." You can't change your set points, but you can change the activities that you undertake and the conditions of your life. Research indicates that increasing an individual's sense of control over life also increases their life satisfaction and engagement.[171]

All of us experience a range of emotions—up and down, positive and negative—based on lived circumstances. It is just that we tend to return to our "set point." Research tracking lottery winners and recent paraplegics bear this out. Within a year of their good or bad luck, the

---

[167] P.T.J. Costa and R.R. McCrae, "Personality Continuity and the Changes of Adult Life," in *The Adult Years: Continuity and Change*, ed. M Storandt and G. R. VandenBos (Washington, D.C.: American Psychological Association, 1989).

[168] D.T. Lykken, *Happiness: What Studies on Twins Show Us About Nature, Nurture, and the Happiness Set-Point* (New York: Golden Books 1999).

[169] Haidt, *The Happiness Hypothesis: Finding Modern Truth in Ancient Wisdom*; S. Srivastava et al., "Development of Personality in Early and Middle Addulthood: Set Like Plaster or Persistent Change?," *Journal of Personality and Social Psychology* 84 (2003); Dean H. Hamer, *The God Gene: How Faith Is Hardwired into Our Genes* (New York: Anchor, 2005).

[170] Kahneman, *Thinking, Fast and Slow*, Kindle 4276.

[171] Haidt, *The Happiness Hypothesis: Finding Modern Truth in Ancient Wisdom*, Kindle 1819.

individuals generally return to their baseline prior to the life-changing event. We quickly grow accustomed to new circumstances and move back to our set point.[172] It seems that the anticipation of some pleasure or pain has more power than actually achieving some goal or experiencing some loss. The process of becoming rich is more pleasurable than actually being rich. The biochemistry of investing is much like gambling, including the possibility of addiction.[173]

Our Inner Demons

In his book *The Better Angels of Our Nature*, psychologist Steven Pinker exhaustively documents a remarkable decline in interpersonal violence in recent history and theorizes how this occurred. He lists and explores five "inner demons" that make violence such a prominent feature of human history. They are:

1. Predatory or instrumental violence
2. Dominance hierarchies
3. Revenge passions
4. Sadism
5. Ideology

When revenge passions and dominance hierarchies are also activated, otherwise normal people can be turned into sadists. Ideologies are especially dangerous, fanning the flames of intercommunal violence throughout human history. Ideological conflicts, which are often also religious conflicts, are like a perfect storm, harnessing all of our inner demons. Pinker writes:

> Means-ends reasoning becomes dangerous when the means to a glorious end include harming human beings. The design of the mind can encourage the train of theorization to go in that direction because of our drives for dominance and revenge, our habit of essentializing other groups, particularly as demons or vermin, our elastic circle of sympathy, and the self-serving biases that

---

[172] Lykken, *Happiness: What Studies on Twins Show Us About Nature, Nurture, and the Happiness Set-Point*; Haidt, *The Happiness Hypothesis: Finding Modern Truth in Ancient Wisdom*, Kindle 1670.

[173] Luke Clark et al., "Pathological Choice: The Neuroscience of Gambling and Gambling Addiction," *The Journal of Neuroscience* 33, no. 45 (2013).

exaggerate our wisdom and virtue. An ideology can provide a satisfying narrative that explains chaotic events and collective misfortunes in a way that flatters the virtue and competence of believers, while being vague or conspiratorial enough to withstand skeptical scrutiny. Let these ingredients brew in the mind of a narcissist with a lack of empathy, a need for admiration, and fantasies of unlimited success, power, brilliance, and goodness, and the result can be a drive to implement a belief system that results in the deaths of millions.[174]

Add some epidemiology and social contagion theory[175] and these mental processes can unleash a firestorm of destructive passions. Thus, humans become mindless zombies fighting over empty fantasies. Religions frequently fall and fail in just this way, in spite of noble teachings to the contrary. To prevent such eventualities, it helps to understand the currencies of hope and fear, rationalities and irrationalities, in the marketplaces of ideologies. Charlie Munger counsels us to seek to understand different political and philosophical points of view without necessarily ascribing. Avoid extreme ideologies and religions, however, because they "cabbages up one's mind."[176]

Our Better Angels

Our evolved human natures are part of the problem but also part of the solution. Pinker lists four "better angels" that work to mitigate and transcend our destructive passions:

1. Empathy
2. Self-Control
3. Moral Sense
4. Reason

Our inner demons and better angels have been battling it out for millennia. The mystery is why, in recent history, we have seen such a dramatic reduction in violence, a fact that Pinker documents in hundreds of pages of cited empirical studies. He argues that five

---

[174] Pinker, *The Better Angels of Our Nature: Why Violence Has Declined*, Kindle 556.
[175] Nicolas A. Christakis and James H. Fowler, *Connected: The Surprising Power of Our Social Networks and How They Shape Our Lives* (New York: Little, Brown and Company, 2009).
[176] Munger, "Usc Law School Commencement Address, May 1, 2007".

historical forces in the modern period have led not to a change in human nature but to a change in how that nature is expressed. The five forces are:

1. Leviathan—Government and the rule of law
2. Commerce—The win-win of economic trade
3. Feminization—The empowerment of women in society
4. Cosmopolitanism—Migration, travel, media, and globalization
5. Escalator of reason—Rational thinking is self-reinforcing

Contrary to our natural negativity bias and the daily onslaught of violence in the news media, Pinker presents convincing evidence that we live in one of the most peaceful periods in human existence. We are less likely to die due to violence than at any other time in human history at least since the beginning of agriculture and maybe before.[177]

Given the destructiveness of contemporary weapons, perhaps we shouldn't be too sanguine. The demons can be easily roused. The five historical forces can hardly be taken for granted in the future. People feel threatened in a fast-changing world. Our inner elephant is scared of mice and suffers from cable news–induced dementia.

Unfortunately, when threatened or injured, we tend to overreact. There is an evolutionary logic in tit-for-tat. The passions of revenge run deep. Politicians and pundits know how to push the buttons in our Stone Age brains to rally the people around the defense of flag and country, faith and tribe.

Primatologists see potential precursors in the behavior of chimpanzees. Male chimpanzees fight with each other and especially with neighboring troops. Like humans, chimpanzees are one of the few mammalian species that kill their own kind. Males sometimes "rape" females.[178]

Bonobos, on the other hand, live in troops dominated by two or three females. Bonobos use genital rubbing—nonreproductive sex— many times a day to decrease aggression and create social bonds within the group. Female-male, female-female, male-male, old-young, the bonobo troops "make love, not war." Bonobos also live in a more

---

[177] Pinker, *The Better Angels of Our Nature: Why Violence Has Declined.*
[178] Richard Wranghan and Dale Peterson, *Demonic Males: Apes and the Origins of Violence* (New York: Mariner Books, 1997).

resource-rich environment, so they need not compete as much for food.[179]

Much of the academic debate over violence and human nature can be summarized in the question of whether humans are (or should be) more like chimpanzees or bonobos—our two closest living relatives.

Natural Values, Natural Morality

Valuation is at the core of economics and finance. How does one ascribe value to some product or service, some asset or security? The fiction of money allows humans to ascribe numbers to their various "utility functions," as if they were interchangeable. Markets flatten the diversity and complexity of values, which are also moral and aesthetic judgments, making everything reducible to the mighty dollar, somehow equivalent based on price and preferences. It is a very useful fiction, but Big History reminds us that there are hierarchies of needs and preferences based on natural values of being a biological and social organism. Natural values start with food, shelter, community, and evolve into cultural values (i.e., "artificial instincts").

The idea of natural morality is not new. Medieval European scholars posited natural law ethics, separate from revealed ethics. Rational humans of any faith or culture could reach the same conclusions and codes of conduct. Revelation supported these natural moral precepts. The concept is still in vogue among many, mostly conservative religious jurists and politicians.

Today, however, we can re-envision natural morality based on scientific evidence. We can talk about an inborn "natural morality" that precedes religion and culture. Natural morality is based on instincts, emotions, and behavior associated with kinship, reciprocity, and dominance hierarchies. Primatologist Frans de Waal makes such an observation among chimpanzees and bonobos.[180] Paul Bloom and his colleagues at Yale University have undertaken studies to show that even preverbal babies show morally contextualized antisocial aversion and prosocial preference by the age of six months.[181] These infant studies also suggest that we are all intuitively dualist and inclined

---

[179] Frans de Waal, *The Bonobo and the Atheist: In Search of Humanism among the Primates* (New York: W.W. Norton, 2014).

[180] *Good Natured: The Origins of Right and Wrong in Humans and Other Animals* (Cambridge, MA: Harvard University Press, 1996).

[181] Paul Bloom, *Just Babies: The Origins of Good and Evil* (New York: Crown, 2013).

130

toward supernatural and teleological beliefs. "People everywhere," writes Bloom, "naturally have some tacit supernatural beliefs; these arise in children regardless of the culture."[182]

Cultural morality evolves on top of our natural morality. Religions, for instance, can be understood historically as one of the engines of prosocial evolution. Like morality, religion comes naturally to humans. A religious predisposition is embedded in our System 1 thinking. Science, like successful investing, by contrast, is hard, must be learned, and the content is often counterintuitive.[183] Science is embedded in System 2 thinking.

It is helpful to take an inventory of our "natural morality" in order to better define and operationalize the "new" human natures. In his book *The Righteous Mind*, Haidt develops a theory of innate-intuitive ethics, what he calls "moral taste buds."

- Harm/Care

- Fairness/Reciprocity

- In-group/Loyalty

- Authority/Respect

- Purity/Sanctity

Haidt builds his theory from the bottom up, showing the adaptive function of each moral-mental disposition in natural selection— individual and group—in our evolutionary past. Haidt's realism about our human nature, informed by so much contemporary science, can seem shocking to those who haven't considered the evidence before. Indeed, all of us walk around the days of our lives with elephant emotions running in the background.

---

[182] *Descartes' Baby: How the Science of Child Development Explains What Makes Us Human* (New York: Basic Books, 2009).
[183] Robert McCauley, *Why Religion Is Natural and Science Is Not* (2011); Pascal Boyer, *The Naturalness of Religious Ideas: A Cognitive Theory of Religion* (Berkeley: University of California Press, 1994).

Fig. 6.1 A Map of Moral Taste Buds

	Harm/Care	Fairness/ Reciprocity	Ingroup/ Loyalty	Authority/ Respect	Purity/ Sanctity
Adaptive challenges	Protect and care for young, vulnerable, or injured kin	Reap benefits of dyadic cooperation with non-kin	Reap benefits of group cooperation	Negotiate hierarchy, defer selectively	Avoid microbes and parasites
Proper domain (adaptive trigger)	Suffering, distress, or threat to one's kind	Cheating, cooperation, deception	Threat or challenge to group	Signs of dominance and submission	Waste products, diseased people
Actual domain (the set of all triggers)	Baby seals, Cartoon characters	Marital fidelity, broken vending machines	Sports teams one roots for	Bosses, respected professionals	Taboo ideas (communism, racism)
Characteristic emotions	Compassion	Anger, gratitude, guilt	Group pride, belonging, rage at traitors	Respect, fear	Disgust
Relevant virtues [and vices]	Caring, kindness, [cruelty]	Fairness, justice, honesty, trust-worthiness, [dishonesty]	Loyalty, patriotism, self-sacrifice [treason, cowardice]	Obedience, deference [disobedience, uppitiness]	Temperance, chastity, piety, cleanliness [lust, intemperance]

The five foundations of intuitive ethics (Haidt and Joseph, 2007, 392).[184]

Our "higher cognition" operates in social relations to rationalize and justify ourselves and our group identities. We all carry within us an inner defense lawyer, press secretary, and con artist. "Morality binds and blind us," according to Haidt. He summarizes our innate intuitive ethics thus:

> We lie, cheat, and cut ethical corners quite often when we think we can get away with it, and then we use our moral thinking to manage our reputations and justify ourselves to others. We believe our own post hoc reasoning so thoroughly that we end up self-righteously convinced of our own virtue. I do believe that you can understand most of moral psychology by viewing it as a form of enlightened self-interest, and if it's self-interest, then it's easily explained by Darwinian natural selection working at the level of

---

[184] Jonathan Haidt and C Joseph, "The Moral Mind: How 5 Sets of Innate Moral Intutitions Guide the Development of Many Culture-Specific Virtues, and Perhaps Even Modules," in *The Innate Mind*, ed. P. Carruthers, S. Laurence, and S. Stich (New York: Oxford University Press, 2007); Haidt, *The Righteous Mind: Why Good People Are Divided by Politics and Religion*, Kindle 2187.

the individual. Genes are selfish, selfish genes create people with various mental modules, and some of these mental modules make us strategically altruistic, not reliably or universally altruistic. Our righteous minds were shaped by kin selection plus reciprocal altruism augmented by gossip and reputation management.[185]

Haidt's scholarship helps us to better understand culture wars and clashing civilizations within and between nations. Taken together with Stephen Pinker's insights, our better angels may yet prevail in our uncertain futures. The cosmopolitanism of business and finance today is part of the social glue that keeps our global civilization from falling prey to our inner demons.

Caveats and Cautions

Each of us is a combination of nature and nurture. The more you understand the biology, the less you can separate nature and nurture. We should proceed, however, with some caution. It is dangerous to draw normative implications from evolution for our lives today, even though this is what we ultimately do.

Human evolution is complicated. Each of us is a complex dynamic system, embedded in emergent layers above and below in the Great Matrix. Physics and chemistry deal with incredibly simple systems compared to the complexity of our body-brain-minds or, for that matter, the superorganism of our global civilization. There are more disagreements and thus less understanding in the human sciences than in physics or chemistry. This is to be expected. The social implications of those debates are also potentially more significant. "The image of man affects the nature of man," wrote Rabbi Abraham J. Herschel. "We become what we think of ourselves."[186]

Confusing the "is" of nature with the "ought" of human values is referred to as the Naturalistic Fallacy.[187] In fact, there is no way *not* to relate the "is" and the "ought."[188] The only question is how. Let's be sure we use science to the best of our ability to get an accurate and

---

[185] Haidt, *The Righteous Mind: Why Good People Are Divided by Politics and Religion*, Kindle 3154.

[186] Abraham Heschel, *Who Is Man?* (Stanford, CA: Stanford University Press, 1965), 8.

[187] G.E. Moore, *Principia Ethica* (Cambridge, UK: Cambridge University Press, [1903] 1989); David Hume, *A Treatise on Human Nature* (Online, [1738]).

[188] Roy A. Clouser, *The Myth of Religious Neutrality: An Essay on the Hidden Role of Religious Belief in Theories* (Notre Dame, IN: University of Notre Dame Press, 2005).

properly nuanced account of the "is" of nature. Our understanding of human nature tends to morph into political economy, social policies, behavioral norms, and child-rearing practices.

In their book *Ecological Developmental Biology*, biologists Scott Gilbert and David Epel note that "if we think of ourselves as killer apes, certain behavioral phenotypes are acceptable that would not be socially allowed if we view humans as the current apex of an evolutionary trend towards cooperation."[189]

Coming out of epigenetics, developmental biology, and ecology, Gilbert and Epel take a more holistic view of the organism and its environment as mutually constitutive. Popular accounts of genetic determinism are too simplistic and misleading. The authors write:

> . . . the environment is not merely a filter that selects existing variations. Rather, it is a *source of variation*. The environment contains signals that can enable a developing organism to produce a phenotype that will increase its fitness in that particular environment. This isn't the view of life usually presented in today's textbooks or popular presentations of biology.[190]

This dovetails with our understanding of complexity economics. The economic environment is a source of variation for individual businesses, not simply an agent of economic selection.

Darwin's elegant algorithm can become a catechism. Random drift, universal struggle, survival, reproduction, and differential selection may be necessary but insufficient to explain the diversity and abundance of life.[191] Evolution includes symbiosis, multilevel selection, contextuality, recurrent mathematical patterns, chaos and complexity theory.[192] Along the way, we can banish the geneticist dogma of

---

[189] Gilbert and Epel, *Ecological Developmental Biology: Integrating Epigenetics, Medicine, and Evolution*, 415.

[190] Ibid., 8.

[191] Robert Wesson, *Beyond Natural Selection* (Cambridge, MA: MIT Press, 1991); David Depew and Bruce Weber, *Darwinism Evolving: Systems Dynamics and the Genealogy of Natural Selection* (Cambridge, MA: MIT Press, 1996); Simon Conway Morris, *Life's Solution: Inevitable Humans in a Lonely Universe* (New York: Cambridge University Press, 2003); Ian Stewart, *Life's Other Secret: The New Mathematics of the Living World* (Wiley & Sons, 1998); Susan Oyama, *The Ontogeny of Information* (New York: Cambridge University Press, 1985); *Evolution's Eye: A Systems View of the Biology-Culture Divide* (Durham, NC: Duke University Press, 2000).

[192] The French biologist Jean Baptiste Lamarck (1744-1829) proposed a theory of evolution prior to Darwin's theory of natural selection in the first decade of the 19th century. He proposed that acquired characteristics could be passed on to the next generations. We now know that this can happen indirectly. Lamarckianism has been a term of derision in Anglo-American biology.

"selfish genes," because genes do absolutely nothing by themselves. Indeed, the metaphor of "sharing genes' is equally valid.[193] Perhaps we should begin to see humanity as the current apex of cooperation, because it is both true and salubrious.

From the perspective of biology today, we need to reconceptualize the individual. The organism is not contained within the borders of epidermis, membranes, and genomes. The individual is always internally and externally composite and interactive. The individual is always an interdependent variable. The organism is always a "social construction."

Gilbert and Epel read biology as a dialectic between emergence and reduction, individuals and groups, cooperation and competition, species and environment, nature and nurture, self and no-self. It is process and relations all the way down. If that seems like a muddle, it is because that is what life turns out to be.

Mathematician and philosopher Alfred Whitehead warned:

> The aim of science is to seek the simplest explanations of complex facts. We are apt to fall into the error of thinking that the facts are simple because simplicity is the goal of our quest. The guiding motto in the life of every natural philosopher should be, Seek simplicity and distrust it.[194]

Our thoughts about nature become a kind of magic mirror to our present and future prospects. They can become self-fulfilling prophecies. We will continue to evolve and transform our human natures, including our genetic natures. Socially constructed human environments, both cultural and economic, also select for human characteristics and traits. We need to think of ourselves as a self-domesticated species still in process. What remains of our hunter-gatherer brains has been filtered through "artificial instincts" inculcated by cultures over millennia.

Our thinking and doing today are also literally transforming our planet, as humans engage in large-scale environmental engineering and prepare to embark upon large-scale genetic engineering of other species and ourselves. Gilbert and Epel call for an "ethics of flourishing and

---

[193] This deconstruction of the "selfish gene" into the "sharing gene" follows Rolston, *Genes, Genesis, and God: Values and Their Origins in Natural and Human History*.

[194] Alfred North Whitehead, *The Concept of Nature* (Cambridge: Cambridge University Press, [1920] 2010), 163.

well-becoming" adequate for the Anthropocene, "an ethic that can integrate both selfishness and otherness, as one might expect of a discipline where self and other mutually construct each other."[195]

Not just investors and fund managers, but really everyone should be aware of how they are predictably irrational and inclined to make misjudgments. Everyone should understand how situation and context can affect the variable flows of powerful endogenous chemicals in our brains and bodies—testosterone, endorphins, oxytocin, adrenalin, cortisol, and more—and how these hormones affect our judgment and behavior. Science is giving us a user-manual for our brains and bodies, as well as, our education and careers.

Our rationality is largely a slave to our emotions.[196] Our magnificent analytic minds are largely in the service of our cultural, political, and professional prejudices.[197] Understanding, and partially rising above our hunter-gatherer brains and behavior, provides a competitive advantage. We have inherited Stone Age cognition, psychology, and behavior, though we live now in a twenty-first-century global civilization. Investors need to pay close attention to these new insights as they impact their own judgments and behaviors, as well as those of others. Understanding the new human nature can be as important to investors as tracking balance sheets and market trends.

---

[195] Gilbert and Epel, *Ecological Developmental Biology: Integrating Epigenetics, Medicine, and Evolution*, 417.

[196] Demasio, *Descartes' Error: Emotion, Reason, and the Human Brain*; *The Feeling of What Happens: Body, Emotion and the Making of Consciousness*.

[197] Haidt, *The Happiness Hypothesis: Finding Modern Truth in Ancient Wisdom*; *The Righteous Mind: Why Good People Are Divided by Politics and Religion*.

Chapter 7:
The Big Lollapalooza

"Lollapalooza" is a fanciful word of unknown origins dating back to the 1890s. The term refers to "something or someone extraordinary, an outstanding example." Charles Munger uses the term "lollapalooza effect" to refer to occasions when multiple biases align in the same direction at the same time for good or for bad. Munger understands the success of Berkshire Hathaway to be a "confluence of factors in the same direction."[198] In the context of Big History, the last hundred years have been a really big lollapalooza with positive and negative consequences.

Our task is to grok the transformations of the last century, to gain a much- needed sense of perspective and proportion in assessing a current context and future possibilities. We have been through an extraordinary period of rapid growth in human populations and consumption patterns. The new developments have been big, multiple, and remarkable—fossil fuels, electricity, transportation, communications, construction, agriculture, public health, technology, education, finance, management, travel, recreation, entertainment, arts, and culture. Our lives are vastly different than a hundred years ago, let alone a thousand or ten thousand years ago.

Normal evolution would not have allowed this exponential growth to go on for long. Malthus and Darwin forbade it, but the laws of physics allowed it. Between the limits of natural selection and the possibilities of physics was human ingenuity applied with a whole heap of energy and matter. Humans have cheated the logic of evolution, at least for the time being. How did we accomplish this feat and how might we continue to do so?

Welcome to the Anthropocene

"Anthropocene" is the term used to label the most recent geological epoch, an era in which human activities begin to

---

[198] As quoted in Tren Griffin, *Charlie Munger: The Complete Investor* (New York: Columbia University Press, 2015).

dramatically impact Earth systems.[199] There is some debate about when this era began. Some say it began recently, with the creation of transuranic elements and plastics, both of which will leave traces over geological time scales. Others say it began with industrialization and the widespread use of fossil fuels, which will also leave geological traces in the deep time of our planet. Still others say that the Anthropocene began with the advent of agriculture or even with the controlled use of fire, both of which had a dramatic impact on regional ecosystems.

The exact dating of the Anthropocene is not really the point. The challenge lies in recognizing the dramatic quantitative and qualitative changes throughout human history that have transformed this planet. The human impact becomes particularly steep in the decades after World War Two, a period that is aptly referred to as "the Great Acceleration."[200] Human population growth is one dramatic indicator of this surge. By 1950, the population of the world was approximately 2.5 billion people. Today, the population is 7.3 billion. In not quite seven decades, a single lifetime, the population has increased almost threefold.

This increase in numbers included enormous improvements in longevity and quality of life. This was mostly accomplished through clean water, better sanitation, vaccinations, antibiotics, and refrigeration. We also learned how to produce and distribute more food for this rapidly expanding population. The possibilities today for travel, education, healthcare, recreation, entertainment, comfort, food, and culture far exceed any luxuries that rulers and royalty of the past might have enjoyed.

Let's look at some of statistics on the Great Acceleration compiled in 2014 by the International Geosphere-Biosphere Programme:

- Real Global GDP, measured in constant 2005 dollars, increased from US$4.4 trillion dollars in 1945 to US$50.1 trillion in 2010. This is an elevenfold increase.

---

[199] J. Zalasiewicz and et.al., "Are We Now Living in the Anthropocene?," *GSA Today* 18, no. 2 (2008).

[200] International Geosphere-Biosphere Programme, "Global Change," Royal Swedish Academy of Sciences, http://www.igbp.net/globalchange/greatacceleration.4.1b8ae20512db692f2a680001630.html.

- World Primary Energy Consumption increased from 90.8 exajoules in 1945 to 533.4 exajoules in 2008. This is 5.8-fold increase.

- Fertilizer consumption increased from 7.2 million tons in 1945 to 171.5 million tons in 2010. This is a 23.8-fold increase.

- Water consumption (irrigation, livestock, domestic, manufacturing, and electricity water withdrawals) increased from 1.14 thousand km^3 in 1945 to 3.87 thousand km^3. This is a 3.4-fold increase.

- Global Paper Production increased from 74.15 million tons in 1960 to 398.77 million tons in 2010. This is a 5.3-fold increase.

- Motor Vehicles increased from 177 million vehicles in 1966 to 1,281 million vehicles in 2009. This is a 7.2-fold increase.

- The number of Large Dams increased from 5,106 large dams in 1945 to 31,635 large dams in 2010. This is a 6.2-fold increase.

- Global tourism increased from 25.3 million arrivals in 1950 to 939.9 million arrivals in 2010. This is a 37-fold increase.

- Telephones increased from 713,000 landlines in 1950 to 6.48 billion mobile and landlines in 2010. This is an increase of 9,056-fold.
  -

Let's add to these statistics with some data from the UN Food and Agricultural Organization:

- Marine Fish Catch increased from 14 million tons in 1950 to 64 million tons in 2010. This is a 4.5-fold increase.

- Cattle stocks grew from 942 million head in 1961 to 1,453 million head in 2010. This is a modest 50 percent increase.[201]

- Pig stocks grew from 406 million in 1961 to 974 million in 2010. This is a 2.3-fold increase.

- Chicken stocks grew from 3.9 billion birds in 1961 to 20.1 billion in 2010. This is a 5.1-fold increase. [202]

All of this activity—human production and consumption—meant increased human-generated entropy. The energy consumed and dissipated also drives a manifold increase in pollution and the degradation of local bioregions.

Soil erosion, for instance, carries away 75 billion tons of topsoil and degrades 10 million hectares every year.[203] Erosion is caused by wind, rain, and gravity. Plowed farmland and overgrazed pastures are especially vulnerable. Erosion results in clogged and polluted waterways, increased flooding, and ultimately the destruction of previously arable land.

Erosion is only one aspect of the larger problem of soil degradation, which occurs also through the depletion of organic material and essential minerals, the buildup of salt from prolonged irrigation, and compaction of soil from heavy farm machinery. Soil erosion and degradation significantly reduce crop yields and, along with other human pollution, are dramatically increasing nitrogen-fed eutrophication of rivers, lakes, estuaries, and costal zones around the world.[204][205]

Soil is not dirt. It is a living organism, a thin blanket of life on the surface of land that sustains other plant and animal life. A handful of soil contains billions of microorganisms feeding off plant and animal decay, even as they provide nutrients for continued plant growth.

---

[201] FAOstats, "Live Animals Data Set," Food and Agricultural Organization of the United Nations, http://www.fao.org/faostat/en/#data/QA.

[202] Wendy Broadgate et al., "The Great Acceleration Data," http://www.igbp.net/globalchange/greatacceleration.4.1b8ae20512db692f2a680001630.html.

[203] David Pimentel and Michael Burgess, "Soil Erosion Threatens Food Production," *Agriculture* 3, no. 3 (2013).

[204] FAO, "Soils Are Endangered, but the Degradation Can Be Rolled Back," Food and Agricultural Organization of the United Nations, http://www.fao.org/news/story/en/item/357059/icode/.

[205] H Eswaran, R. Lal, and P.F. Reich, "Land Degradation: An Overview," USDA Natural Resources Conservation Service, https://www.nrcs.usda.gov/wps/portal/nrcs/detail/soils/use/?cid=nrcs142p2_054028.

140

Everywhere we look on earth, we encounter microbiomes that are the foundational scaffolding for all plant and animal life.

You will recall that it is possible to use DNA to encode binary information and that a kilogram of DNA could store all of the digital information in the world.[206] Think of a kilogram of living topsoil as something approaching that same complexity. Soil contains staggering quantities of living, organized information.

It takes a long-time to build up topsoil. The last ice age stripped the topsoil down to the bedrock for much of the Northern Hemisphere, so most of the topsoil in these previously glaciated regions has accumulated over the last 20,000 years. Throughout the history of agriculture, soil erosion and degradation far exceeded the rate of replenishment. Humanity may soon find itself bereft of suitable agricultural land, even as we struggle to grow enough to feed the expanding population.

The Big Lollapalooza, the Anthropocene, the Great Acceleration—however we demarcate this period in recent history—is noteworthy also as a period of remarkable economic growth. Between 1950 and today, it would have been hard not to make money on long-term investments during a period in which economies around the world rapidly expanded. Investors, of course, want to know if they can expect continued economic growth and in what sectors, entities, and regions.

In order to anticipate future scenarios, we need to better understand how we got to this moment in the cultural evolution of our species and the natural history of our planet. How can we explain our species' rapid rise? How did we cheat the logic of Malthus and Darwin by growing exponentially in numbers and consumption?

The Secret of Our Success

In the last chapter we already explored some of the factors in human evolution that propelled us to the heights of complexity through the mastery of dense and intense flows of energy, matter, and ingenuity. Big Historians would agree that the foundation of our success story is our unique capacity to create and use symbolic language. Language enabled the possibility of speaking about and coordinating actions around the objective world—plants, animals, skills, relationships, threats, and opportunities—and describing

---

historical and future outcomes. This was an evolutionary advantage. That being said, language also gave rise to complex social relations. Humans are great cooperators, even as we compete with each other. A deeper look at several different, though complementary, interpretations of the secret to our recent success helps to better understand how we came to our current circumstances. This brief overview tracks and combines the analyses of several different Big Historians under the following headings:

- Collective Learning
- Network Effects
- Imaginary Worlds and Artificial Instincts
- Energy-Matter Capture
- Information-Ingenuity Capture
- Gene-Culture Coevolution of Collective Brains

Collective Learning

No other species excels in the use of symbolic languages, through which we are able to communicate and accumulate knowledge and skills from one generation to the next. We are the beneficiaries of long lineages of discoveries, inventions, and skills acquired and passed down by our ancestors over tens of thousands of years. We build upon the achievements of our contemporaries and previous generations.

The real story of evolution is as much about cooperation as it is about competition.[207] Humans are the most amazing cooperators, and collective learning is the prime example thereof. Because of collective learning, cultural evolution is a win-win over the long arc of human history, even though economic markets, ethnic conflicts, class struggle, and political disputes frequently involve win-lose tradeoffs.[208] Learning is how we survive, thrive, and, ultimately, reproduce our genes and our cultures.

---

[207] Lynn Margulis, "Symbiogenesis and Symbioticism," in *Symbiosis as a Source of Evolutionary Innovation*, ed. Lynn Margulis and R. Fester (Cambridge, MA: MIT Press, 1994); *Symbiotic Planet: A New Look at Evolution* (New York: Basic, 1998); Scott F. Gilbert and David Epel, *Ecological Developmental Biology: Integrating Epigenetics, Medicine, and Evolution* (Sunderland, MA: Sinauer Associates, 2009).
[208] Robert Wright, *Nonzero: The Logic of Human Destiny* (New York: Vintage, 2001).

Collective learning is why "all hell breaks loose" during the Great Acceleration of the past century.[209] Collective learning is one of the main engines of economic growth.[210] You and I didn't invent agriculture, metallurgy, or arithmetic. We didn't invent the wheel or the automobile, the light bulb or the phonograph, the smartphone or the GPS satellites. The list goes on and on. But here it all is, our amazing portfolio of knowledge and know-how that grows with compounded interest. Every culture, every domesticated plant and animal, every work of literature and art, every technology, every artifact, every language, including these words, is the common inheritance of humanity. In economic terms, collective learning is a positive externality—the more people who use the resource, the more value it generates.

In his book *Maps of Time*, David Christian points to collective learning as the key to the rapid rise of our species. Collective learning begins with language and accelerates with the rise of agriculture and ever-larger permanent settlements. Christian shows how collective learning became a positive feedback loop in human cultural evolution. He writes:

> First, with the appearance of cities and states, human societies became more diverse than ever before. And diversity itself was a powerful motor of collective learning, for it increased the ecological, technological, and organizational possibilities available to different communities, as well as the potential synergies of combining these technologies in new ways. But states also increased the *scale* of human interactions. Because they were so much larger than all earlier human communities, their powerful gravitational fields sucked in resources, people, and ideas from great distances. By doing so, agrarian civilizations created vast new networks of exchange. These count as the era's second main structural feature. Networks of exchange that were more extensive, more varied, and more dynamic than those of any earlier era increased both the scale and variety and the potential synergies of collective learning.[211]

---

[209] Eric D. Beinhocker, *The Origin of Wealth: Evolution, Complexity, and the Radical Remaking of Economics* (Cambridge Harvard Business Press, 2006).

[210] David Warsh, *Knowledge and the Wealth of Nations: A Story of Economic Discovery* (New York: Norton, 2006).

[211] Christian, *Maps of Time: An Introduction to Big History*, 284.

The vast majority of the knowledge and know-how that runs our twenty-first-century global economy has been passed on by previous generations, added to, accumulated, and distributed laterally across geographies.[212] And as the transfer of information got cheaper, first with the printing press and later with the internet, collective learning became practically free for the taking. The problem is that there is so damn much of it. Technical proficiencies often require decades of specialized training to master.

Network Effects

In their book *The Human Web*, historian William McNeill and his son J. R. McNeill, also a historian, take a systems approach to explaining the rapid rise of our species. Webs are sets of connections linking people together. These connections take many forms: kinship, friendship, cooperation, rivalry, enmity, and chance encounters. They involve common worship, economic exchange, ecological exchange, political cooperation, and military competition. These networks always involve the communication and use of information, and with it the transfer of useful technologies, crops, goods, ideas, and diseases. The authors' systems approach to world history allows them to make a number of important observations about large patterns in cultural evolution:

(1) All webs involve cooperation and competition, both of which are sustained by communication. This can be seen already in hunter-gatherer societies, where small bands of humans transmitted local knowledge about edible plants and ecologies, organized cooperative hunting of large game, and developed exogamous marriages with neighboring tribes, as well as cooperative aggression and defense against competing groups of humans.

(2) Those groups that achieve more efficient communication and cooperation improve their competitive advantages and survival prospects. Cooperating groups tend to grow and in so doing also begin to lose internal cohesion, often leading to collapse and succession. For

---

[212] Science is a quintessential example of collective learning, because it is so obviously cumulative and international. As the Pakistani Nobel Physics Laureate Abdus Salam said, "Scientific thought and its creation is the common and shared heritage of mankind."

instance, larger and larger metropolitan webs grew over the past 6,000 years because urban cultures had (a) economic advantages via specialization of labor and exchange, (b) military advantages via larger, well-equipped warriors with better technology, and (c) epidemiological advantages via frequent exposure to a wider array of diseases that built up their immunities over many generations.

(3) Metropolitan webs tended to expand and grow in scale because of improved communication and transportation technologies. This can be seen today in the development of modern communication, air travel, and global capitalism. The worldwide cosmopolitan web has left no part of the world untouched.

(4) Human communication, cooperation, and competition also shape the Earth's history, not just human history, beginning with the deliberate use of fire, coordinated hunting of large animals, and the domestication of plants and animals. This process of changing the ecologies of the world has accelerated dramatically in the past centuries through the harnessing of more and more of the earth's energy and material flows for our human purposes, leading to a vast expansion of the human population and a great remaking of the geology and the biosphere.

The McNeills conclude by calling for another widening of the human web, uniting humans more intimately and less destructively with nature and other cultures.[213]

Imaginary Worlds and Artificial Instincts

Yuval Harari, like others, sees language as the key to our becoming world-dominating super-cooperators. The miracle of human language, however, is not just about accumulating knowledge and know-how. Language also enabled the possibility of speaking about fictional worlds. Ancient cave paintings and petroglyphs from around the world suggest that by 40,000 years ago, we were not only budding artists, but also storytellers. Storytelling is how we scaled up our

---

[213] J. Robert McNeill and William H. McNeill, *The Human Web: A Bird's-Eye View of World History* (New York: W.W. Norton, 2003).

cooperative behavior. The key to our success is as much collective fiction making as it is collective learning.

Small groups of intimate humans can cooperate without hierarchies, but beyond this low threshold, cooperation requires a group fiction to maintain social order and cohesion. Here, language makes possible the rapid rise of our species. For Harari, it is precisely our ability to create social fictions and imaginary worlds that allowed us to scale cooperation from tens to thousands, to millions, and to now billions of people in our global civilization:

> Any large-scale human cooperation—whether a modern state, a medieval church, an ancient city or an archaic tribe—is rooted in common myths that exist only in people's collective imagination. . . . [N]one of these things exists outside the stories that people invent and tell one another. There are no gods in the universe, no nations, no money, no human rights, no laws, and no justice outside the common imagination of human beings. [214]

Harari calls these "networks of artificial instincts."[215] Outside of bacteria, we are the only species that can "flexibly cooperate" in large numbers because we can create imagined realities and shared taken-for-granted rules. Religion, human rights, ethnicities, nations, and even languages are all fictional. Money is perhaps the most universal and important fiction of all. In the twenty-first-century, in the wake of the scientific revolution and the Great Acceleration of the past century, human fictional realities are now changing the objective realities of entire ecosystems and our own future evolution.

"[T]he way people cooperate [and compete] can be altered by changing the myths," writes Harari. "Under the right circumstances myths can change rapidly."[216] How might the new narrative of Big History alter our many competing myths in order to promote a healthier, safer, and more compassionate world? What are the right circumstances for rapid change? How might these be strategically advanced? These are some of the big questions that led me to the philosophical and social scientific study of religion. We still have a long way to go in our exploration of the new narrative of Big History before we can productively begin to answer those questions.

---

[214] Harari, *Sapiens: A Brief History of Humankind*, 464-71.
[215] Ibid., Kindle 2515.
[216] Ibid., Kindle 551.

Energy Capture

In his book *Big History and the Future of Humanity*, anthropologist Fred Spier frames the rapid rise of our species as a case of energy capture. The rise of agriculture, for instance, is "concentrating useful bio-solar collectors (plants) and bio-energy converters (animals) within certain areas to improve the conversion of solar energy into forms of bio-energy that were helpful for maintaining or improving human complexity."[217]

As we have already discussed, the flow of energy is essential for maintaining and growing pockets of complexity that run uphill in a universe that is otherwise always running downhill (entropy). Life probably began, and certainly took hold, at alkaline thermal vents in the primordial oceans by harnessing chemical and heat energy from the Earth's core.[218] Life grew exponentially, but was initially limited by this energy source. By figuring out how to tickle a photon from the sun and turn it into food energy, life could continue to grow and become more complex. Without photosynthesis, life would have stalled, plateaued, and possibly died out long ago. Photosynthesis is the most important innovation in the history of the planet. Everything that follows is parasitic on the energy economy of photosynthesis, including our brains and collective learning. All our dreams and desires, our thinking and doing, are directly or indirectly powered by plants.

Photosynthesis converts carbon dioxide and water into carbohydrates (food energy) and oxygen. Thus, photosynthesis progressively removed methane and carbon dioxide from the primordial planet and increased concentrations of oxygen in the atmosphere and oceans. Initially, this had cataclysmic results—it led to the greatest pollution and extinction crisis in natural history. First, with the decline in greenhouse gases, the earth cooled and the oceans froze into a "snowball Earth." Second, because oxygen is chemically reactive, it oxidized the membranes of the anaerobic bacteria that populated the early Earth.

Life eventually adapted to these new conditions by creating membranes that could resist oxygen and, later, harness the chemical power of oxygen through respiration, thus greatly increasing the efficiency of the biochemical-energy cycle inside the cell.

---

[217] Spier, *Big History and the Future of Humanity*.
[218] Lane, *The Vital Question: Energy, Evolution, and the Origins of Complex Life*.

In his book *Energy: The Engine of Evolution*, Frank Niele analyzes the thermodynamics of life from early prokaryotes to our global civilization. Life depends on three "energy regimes," which appear sequentially—the Thermal Regime, the Phototropic Regime, and the Aerobic Regime.[219] These all appeared first at the scale of single-celled organisms, prior to the evolution of complex multicellular organisms. The energy economies of evolution were all directly or indirectly dependent on these processes, until humans came along.

It began with the controlled use of fire. Fire mastery improved human diets, as cooking expanded the number of foods that could be hunted, gathered, eaten, and digested. Fire also protected our ancestors from predators and expanded the range of ecosystems in which humans could flourish. Finally, fire mastery let loose a series of coevolutionary developments, as the hearth provided a new context for social bonding, tool making, planning, symbolic language, and other cognitive enhancements. No other species has learned to control fire. Niele calls this the Pyrocultural Regime.

The domestication of plants and animals, beginning only 10,000 years ago, was another leap in the capture of energy-matter. The evolution of agriculture led to larger, sedentary communities with surpluses that could support specialized classes of laborers, including ruling elites, standing armies, and priestly castes, which extracted the surplus production through conquest and tribute-taking. Specialization, competition, cooperation, and trade led to numerous technological developments, including the harnessing of the kinetic energy of wind and water that also contributed to our increased energy consumption. This is the Agrocultural Regime.

About 200 years ago, the burning of fossil fuels during industrialization marked the next energy revolution. Note that coal, oil, and gas are products of photosynthesis that have been accumulated, concentrated, and transformed over geological time scales. It is fair to say that pretty much everything we touch, eat, wear, use, and do in the modern world is directly or indirectly touched by fossil fuels. Niele calls this the Carbocultural Regime. He goes on to explore the necessity and possibilities of an evolving Heliocultural Regime.

The logic of harvesting more solar energy to grow human complexity is compelling from the perspective of Big History—but, of course, that transition will require huge investments and further

---

[219] Niele, *Energy: Engine of Evolution.*

innovations in the decades to come. Over 7 billion humans now consume in aggregate 18 trillion watts of energy in a variety of forms—fossil fuels (coal, oil, gas); hydropower; nuclear power; renewables (solar, wind, biomass, biofuels, and geothermal); and, of course, the food we eat. Without this energy constantly running through our global civilization's arteries, the world would collapse. Our cities, industries, transportation, agriculture—indeed, every aspect of our contemporary lives—depend on this tremendous flow of energy.

Those reading this book are likely energy rich, relative to others throughout human history and in our contemporary world. You have effortless access to electricity and the internet. You have potable water pumped into your home and your waste safely disposed. You have an enormous quantity and variety of food at your disposal, cultivated, processed, and shipped from distant places to your local grocery store. You likely have access to travel great distances by bike, car, bus, train, ship, and airplane. Remove one of these from your life and you would starkly come to understand true "luxury" by its absence.

Information-Ingenuity Capture

As discussed, the quantity of information-ingenuity on our planet has been growing by leaps and bounds. This is true of life's rising complexity and the recent rising complexity of human culture. Moreover, the Earth-bound growth of information-ingenuity manifests aspects of exponentiality, as we saw in the chapter on the Great Matrix.

Like other big historians, Cesar Hidalgo understands the rise of symbolic language and collective learning among humans as the threshold resulting in an accelerating adventure of discovery and invention. "Humans," writes Cesar Hidalgo, "are special animals when it comes to information, because unlike other species, we have developed an enormous ability to encode large volumes of information outside our bodies."[220] Human artifacts, not just the written word, can be thought of as a form of embodied information—manufactured physical orders serving some human function. The story of human artifacts begins with wood-stone tools and cave paintings and now extends to global positioning satellites and megacities. Look around. Most of the objects in your immediate environment, including these

---

[220] Hidalgo, *Why Information Grows: The Evolution of Order, from Atoms to Economies*, Kindle 285.

words, are what Hidalgo calls "crystalized imagination." Earlier we explored the exponential nature of energy density flow in evolution and culture. We examined the Great Acceleration of the last century and the manifold growth in human population and consumption patterns leading to the Anthropocene. Now we need to grok similar jumps in order of magnitude of information-ingenuity through the course of human history. "People," writes Hidalgo, "are the ultimate incarnation of the computational capacities of matter."[221]

Cultural evolution has limitations and constraints that make the growth of knowledge and know-how uneven in human history and the contemporary world. Learning occurs in social and cultural networks. Learning occurs over a prolonged period of childhood dependency. Much of it happens by absorption. Children naturally learn their mother tongue and acquire cultural norms. We evolved to learn best from people who are similar to us. Learning requires trust. Individuals with social prestige within the group are seen to be trustworthy sources of relevant knowledge. Trust is a big issue in social psychology and the scaling of human cooperation.

Today, learning often includes decades of formal training in order to gain technical mastery of a specific domain. Hidalgo introduces the term "personbyte" to indicate the theoretical maximum amount of knowledge that any single person can acquire. An individual can only acquire so much in a lifetime. It is in the nature of collective learning that knowledge and know-how are trapped in social networks. And social networks are difficult to copy.

Hidalgo runs the Observatory of Economic Complexity at MIT. Among their many projects are the graphic visualization of imports and exports between countries—for instance, Chile and South Korea, or Brazil and China. Hidalgo introduces the notion of a net balance of embodied imagination (manufactured products) in international trade. Some countries are net importers of "crystallized imagination." Other countries are net exporters. "The more prosperous countries," write Hidalgo, "are those that are better at making information grow."[222]

More precisely, it is the growth of ingenuity, not merely the growth of information as code, that matters in evolution and economics. In computer programming, for instance, ingenuity can be maximized through clever algorithms, and perhaps also less code, less

---

[221] Ibid., Kindle 2488.
[222] Ibid., Kindle 1864.

memory, and less processing. Evolutionary, technological, and economic elegance is captured in my aphorism "minimize entropy, maximize creativity."

Hidalgo also introduces the term "firmbyte" as a theoretical limit on how much knowledge and know-how any single company can command. This limit is why networks of firms are needed to manufacture complex goods and to provide complex services. The firmbyte limit scales more than the personbyte limit, because firms vary dramatically in size and complexity. As networks grow within and between companies, so do the transaction costs. The scaling adds friction and inefficiencies to production and exchange, but also the possibilities of creating more complex products and services with more "crystallized imagination."

Cheaper links favor larger networks and the concentration of knowledge and know-how. Larger networks of people and companies are able to embody more knowledge and know-how, but transaction costs may also scale, putting a drag on productivity. "Certain societies can save substantially on transaction costs," writes Francis Fukuyama, "because economic agents trust one another in their interactions and therefore can be more efficient than low trust societies, which require detailed contracts and enforcement mechanisms."[223] Trust is an essential ingredient in lubricating and scaling complex economic manufacturing.

Recall Eric Beinhocker's understanding of the importance of both physical and social technologies in economic growth. Hidalgo reminds us that physical technologies are themselves products of social learning and that it is the accumulation of knowledge and know-how that drives evolution and economics. He writes:

> So it is the accumulation of information and of our ability to process information that defines the arrow of growth encompassing the physical, the biological, the social, and the economic, and which extends from the origin of the universe to our modern economy. It is the growth of information that unifies the emergence of life with the growth of economies, and the emergence of complexity with the origins of wealth.[224]

---

[223] Francis Fukuyama, *Trust: Human Nature and the Creation of Prosperity* (Boston: Free Press, 2008), 352.

[224] Hidalgo, *Why Information Grows: The Evolution of Order, from Atoms to Economies*, Kindle 222.

Gene-Culture Coevolution of Collective Brains

In his book *The Secret of Our Success*, anthropologist Joseph Henrich reminds us that genes and culture coevolve. We are a self-domesticated species. Like our domesticated animals, humans today are different from our wild forebears long ago. Human cultures are a form of decentralized eugenics—controlled breeding—and have for millennia been selecting for prosocial attributes. Henrich writes:

> Recognizing that we are a cultural species means that, even in the short run (when genes don't have enough time to change), institutions, technologies, and languages are coevolving with psychological biases, cognitive abilities, emotional responses, and preferences. In the longer run, genes are evolving to adapt to these culturally constructed worlds, and this has been, and is now, the primary driver of human genetic evolution.[225]

Somewhere along the way, Henrich argues, early humans crossed the Rubicon into "superorganism" status, whereby survival and reproduction became entirely dependent on the cultural transmission of knowledge. From there, a positive feedback loop took hold, as group competition selected for societies with better cooperators. The coevolution of genes and culture resulted in something unique in evolution. Humans are the first species to develop "collective brains."

> All human societies, whether they live as hunter-gatherers or not, are entirely dependent on culture . . . humans are at the beginning of a major biological transition, the formation of a new kind of animal. In our species, the extent and sophistication of our technical repertoire—and of our ecological dominance—depends on the size and interconnectedness of our collective brains. In turn, our collective brains depend heavily on the packages of social norms and institutions that weave together our communities, create interdependence, foster solidarity, and subdivide our cultural information and labor. These social norms, which were gradually selected by intergroup competition over eons, have domesticated us to be better rule followers, as well as

---

[225] Joseph Henrich, *The Secret of Our Success: How Culture Is Driving Human Evolution, Domesticating Our Species, and Making Us Smarter* (Princeton: Princeton University Press, 2015), 314-15.

more attentive parents, loyal mates, good friends (reciprocators), and upstanding community members. Like the cells in our bodies, all human societies possess a division of labor and information, with different subgroups specializing in different tasks and cultural knowledge.[226]

The secret of our species' dramatic rise is all of these factors—symbolic language, collective learning, network effects, social fictions, energy- and ingenuity-capture, gene-culture coevolution, collective brains, and more. There is little disagreement on the basics among Big Historians, but the different emphases mentioned above help us to better understand how our species cheated the evolutionary logic of Malthus and Darwin by growing exponentially in the last century. Past performance, however, is no guarantee of future success.

---

[226] Ibid., 318.

Chapter 8:
Existential Challenges

In spite of the stellar rise of our species, many existential challenges face us in the future. We have a lot of potential catastrophes to consider—both anthropogenic and nonanthropogenic challenges to our future prospects.

Anthropogenic Existential Challenges:

- weapons of mass destruction
- rising greenhouse gases
- runaway artificial technology
- biotech run amok
- self-replicating nanotechnology
- cyber insecurity
- pandemics
- social anarchy
- overpopulation
- mineral depletion
- collapse of global economic markets.

Natural Existential Challenges:

- sun flares
- impact events
- supervolcanos
- mega-earthquakes
- massive tsunamis
- evolved pathogens
- Earth wobbles
- changing climates.

Like the White Queen in Lewis Carroll's *Through the Looking Glass*, I find it useful to imagine these "impossibilities" a little bit each day. "When I was younger I always did it for a half an hour a day," the Queen tells Alice. "Why sometimes I believed as many as six impossible things before breakfast."[227] It is not bad to think of impossibly dark possibilities. Contemplating one's own death, or the death of billions, feels impossible, even though it is a certainty from the day of our birth. Reflecting on death is an important spiritual practice in many different traditions—one that investors should also remember. A little bit each day is a way to focus life on really important matters. Taking the White Queen's lead, I try to do my imaginings before breakfast, so I can spend the rest of my day focusing on the positive things in the world. So many disasters to contemplate! In the next two sections I offer contrarian considerations of the prospects of climate change and human population growth.

Peak Humanity

I was born in 1957. Eisenhower was president. The Soviet Union launched Sputnik. The Cold War was heating up, even as McCarthyism literally died out. Science and technology were all the rage. Leonard Bernstein's *West Side Story* debuted on Broadway. *Leave It to Beaver,* with its vision of the ideal American family, premiered on television.

There were 2.8 billion people alive in 1957 and 172 million of them were Americans. In 2011 demographers figure that the world's population reached 7 billion. There are two and a half times more people alive on the planet now than in 1957. Here in the United States, the population is now at 326 million.

At the beginning of the Common Era (C.E.), the number of humans living on this planet was about 130 million, distributed across the globe. Rome and Xi'an would have been the largest cities in the world, each with an estimated population of 400,000.

It would not be until 1800 that the world population reached 1 billion. In 1930 we reached 2 billion. Today we are at 7.3 billion. The largest city today is Tokyo, with 32 million inhabitants. Seoul, Mexico City, and New York vie for the next largest with around 20 million each. These numbers, and the sciences and societies behind them, are profoundly important to understanding the trajectory of humanity on its recent unprecedented growth spurt. It is important to know in some detail how we got here and what scenarios might lie in store for the planet and its people over the next hundred years.

---

[227] Lewis Carroll, *Through the Looking Glass* (Project Gutenberg, 1871).

Population growth is a factor of three trends: birth rates, life expectancy, and the mortality or death rate. Global fertility rates have dropped from 5 or more children per woman post–World War II to 2.5 children per woman today. At the same time, life expectancy at birth has gone up and mortality rates have gone down. This is great news. Fewer children are born, they are less likely to die in childhood, and we tend to live longer lives.

The surge in human population in the last century is primarily the result of three factors:

1. Sanitation and civil engineering, the unsung heroes of public health, from which we derive clean drinking water and safe sewage disposal;

2. Modern medicine, particularly vaccinations, through which we have dramatically reduced occurrences of communicable diseases;

3. Increased agricultural production through the use of hybrid crops, petrochemicals, irrigation, and industrialization at economies of scale in a now global food market.

Since the 1950s, life expectancy at birth around the world increased from about 47 years to 68 years. In North America, life expectancy is now about 78 years. Mortality rates are closely related to life expectancy, but significantly different in how they impact age distributions and growth within a population. How long you linger on this planet, when and how you die—for instance, before or after reproduction—all end up impacting population growth. Infant mortality is more significant in demography than old-age mortality.

Longer-living humans and declining fertility rates are creating challenging demographic and economic issues, such as increased pension payouts, skyrocketing health care costs, and a smaller labor force to support the elderly. Of course, at some point, mortality rates are 100 percent.

Demographers develop prediction models based on these factors, noting also the distribution of age groups within a population. Most models predict that the world population will peak at around 9 to 10 billion by 2050. From 7 billion to 9 billion people doesn't seem like a big deal, but what it means in the larger context of Big History is that humanity must grow as much food over the next 40 years to feed itself as it has grown over the last 10,000 years since the rise of agriculture. Presumably we will have to do so with less waste, less water, fewer petrochemicals, less nitrogen, and less soil erosion.

Population growth, however, is uneven. Seventy percent of the population growth in the next forty years is predicted to take place in extremely poor countries, while many of the rich countries are now stable or in demographic decline. In economics, a growing population also tends to grow the economy, as it requires more economic activity. And more people are also seen as a resource to spur growth. More humans provide more labor, more productivity, more consumption, and more creativity. Human population growth is thus an engine of economic growth, not simply an economic burden.

Decreasing birth rates have huge implications for economic growth and environmental well-being. Education, health care, family planning, urbanization, and, especially, increased opportunities for adolescent girls and women are all highly correlated with lower fertility. Families are desiring and deciding to have fewer children, and they now have the means and know-how to make those decisions. If fertility rates drop from 2.5 today down to 1.6 in the near future, then peak humanity will occur around 8 billion by 2025 and will actually decrease to 5 billion by 2100. Exponential patterns work going up and could also work coming down.[228]

Environmentalists might applaud such a scenario—a planet with 2 billion fewer people than today at the turn of the next century —as it seems like fewer people would relieve some of the pressure on the planet's ecosystems. Indeed, one of the ways to increase energy density flow is to decrease the mass of the system, i.e., the mass of humans on the planet.

The economic consequences of such a population decline, however, could be catastrophic in the short term. It is not clear that we can have economic growth with a declining population. If economies don't grow, then paying off debt becomes an exponential burden, unleashing a downward economic spiral. Peak humanity may involve a difficult economic and demographic deleveraging that will span an entire generation.

---

[228] United Nations, "World Population Prospects: The 2012 Revisions," (New York: UN Department of Economic and Social Affairs, 2012); Leslie Roberts, "9 Billion?," *Science* 333, no. 6042 (2011).

The collapse of our global economy is, counterintuitively, also likely to be devastating for our global environment, as desperate people aren't likely to care much about protecting the planet. And economic factors also help drive the decisions of families to have fewer children. It seems that we are in a triple-bind between containing population growth, protecting the environment, and growing economies.

The prospect of declining fertility also raises evolutionary concerns about the future of humanity on a soon-to-be child-scarce planet. Children are literally the future of our species. Children humanize us. They inspire adults to be nurturing and future oriented. We need a planet with fewer children in a world that invests more in those few children, even though they may be someone else's children. Fostering that kind of altruism and long-term commitment unfortunately runs contrary to our tribal instincts and hunter-gatherer mentality.

At some point, human population on Earth will peak, for as Darwin observed, any exponential growth curve within a finite space cannot continue forever, for "the world cannot hold them all." It may happen sooner than we anticipate, perhaps later. It may plateau for a while or it may start to decline and rise again. The future history will involve rates of births, deaths, and lives lived at rates, ranges, and intensities that we cannot know in advance. Flat and declining populations, however, are already having an economic impact on a number of countries.

Climates Change

Climate changing is hardly front-page news for geologists. It is the whole story from beginning to end. Geologists read this story from the text of rock, mud, water, ice, and air, in the half-lives of radioactive isotopes, in the orientation of magnetic sediments, in geological deposits, and in the traces of ancient glaciers, mountain ranges, canyons, craters, fossils, bygone oceans, and tectonic plates. The 4.5-billion-year-old-Earth story is one of continuous and dramatic metamorphoses on a time scale difficult to imagine, unless, of course, you happen be a geologist. We are the first generation to know this about our past and future planet.

These dynamics and others have been at work on the earth since its beginning. The Earth wobbles on its axis. The planet is ever so slightly out of kilter. The wobbles have a periodicity, known as the

Milankovitch Cycle. This is why ice ages come and go with irregular regularity. As ice ages advance, enormous glaciers extend down from the poles and suck up the oceans of our planet, turning them into mile-deep rivers of moving ice that sculpt the contours of continents. As the ice ages recede, the land rises and melting water refills our planetary bathtubs. Since the last glacial maximum some 20,000 years ago, ocean levels have risen some 160 meters to today's levels. A grassroots movement to "stop Earth wobbles" is not likely to succeed, no matter how sincerely felt.

Under the weight of the ice sheets and oceans, the Earth's crust bends and buckles, rises and falls. Variations in the volume of liquid water on the Earth are *eustatic* changes, i.e., depending on the distribution of glaciated ice, atmospheric water, ocean water, and geologically bounded water captured in aquifers, lakes, soil, and rock. The shape of the ocean floor and land mass, however, can also dramatically affect sea levels. These *isostatic* changes (i.e., changes in shape of the Earth's crust) in sea levels are caused by changes in the contours of Earth's ocean basin and continents, which can increase or decrease the volume of the global bathtub and the height of the land mass. When the ocean basin is smaller, global sea levels rise everywhere. The ocean cup runneth over onto all of the continents. Or, as the case may be in the reverse, sea levels can also drop dramatically depending on the shape of the ocean floor, as the Earth's crust warps, cracks, and bends.

Our sun, too, is dynamic, sometimes overly exuberant in bathing the Earth with excess solar energy, and sometimes providing too little. Solar flares present a special challenge to our technologically advanced civilization, as the electromagnetic pulse from a major solar flare hitting Earth has the capacity to destroy much of the electronic infrastructure upon which our civilization now depends.

A single supervolcano can ruin your whole day, dumping volcanic ash meters deep over entire continents, causing widespread earthquakes and tsunamis and mucking up the upper atmosphere so as to create a "nuclear winter," and possibly a runaway feedback loop giving rise to an instant ice age. Our common ancestors survived just such a catastrophe 74,000 years ago, when Mount Toba, a supervolcano in Sumatra, exploded. By this time in our wanderings out-of-Africa, our ancestors had followed the coastlines along the Middle East and South Asia, settling as far as Southeast Asia and Australia. The supervolcano changed everything overnight for our ancestors. It dumped six meters of volcanic ash over much of South Asia. The massive eruption also brought on an instant ice age. Humanity was reduced to a mere 10,000 individuals, a story written in our mitochondrial DNA. And yet, we, and the other flora and fauna, survived. And as the sky cleared and ice slowly retreated over millennia, we resumed our migrations and expansions.[229]

The Earth has experienced large impact events throughout its history. Large asteroids and comets occasionally smash into the Earth. A major impact event can set lose earthquakes, volcanic eruptions, tsunamis, and the onset of an instant ice age. We may soon have the technological means to detect and deflect large impact events, but we are not going to stop platetectonics, supervolcanos, solar flares, and Earth-wobbles. The Holocene—the 10,000 years since the last ice age—will not last forever. Indeed, it may already be over.

On the one hand, significant climate change will be a disaster of unimaginable magnitude for most humans. On the other hand, of all the large mammals, humans are most likely to survive future climatic disasters. Much of the flora and fauna may require our help to survive and thrive on the other side of catastrophe. What should concern us most about future evolutionary bottlenecks is the information-ingenuity that may be lost—what we have accomplished in 10,000 years of human civilization—and how it will be passed on through the eye of an evolutionary needle. Humans need a lot more than just our genes to survive and thrive on the other side of future catastrophes. I maintain that constructing a resilient global civilization that can bounce back from geological disasters will also significantly reduce fossil fuel consumption. The larger perspective offered here supports efforts to reduce the impact of anthropogenic climate change without framing the political conflict as an eco-apocalyptic battle between forces of light and darkness.

All rock is ultimately metamorphic rock. This includes the concrete, steel, and glass monuments of human engineering and architecture built in cities around the world. I often imagine my beloved New York City, and every other city at some point in the future, crushed under mile-thick glacier ice, someday under the ocean again, or perhaps absorbed back into the molten core of the Earth through normal plate tectonics. A geologist knows that it is only a

---

[229] Stanley H. Ambrose, "Volcanic Winter, and Differentiation of Modern Humans. Bradshaw Foundation. ," Bradshaw Foundation, http://www.bradshawfoundation.com/stanley_ambrose.php.

matter of time—hot or cold, fast or slow, sea levels up or down, round and round the Sun we go—before there are dramatic changes on our restless and exuberant planet. Maybe this will happen soon, maybe suddenly, and maybe not for a long, long time, at least relative to the scale of human life, but it will happen, if the past is any guide.

Life, as we learned, also changes climates, most dramatically in the Great Oxidation Event. The rise of photosynthesizing microbes 2 billion years ago resulted in an increase in atmospheric oxygen, causing a "snowball" Earth. Life also gave rise to the formation of large hydrocarbon deposits hundreds of millions of years ago, which we have been digging up and burning over the last two centuries to fuel humanity's exponential growth spurt. The result is increased levels of carbon dioxide, methane, and nitrous oxide in the atmosphere, which have increased the heat-retention properties of the Earth system and caused an international political uproar over the dangers of human-caused climate change.

Again, we are the first generation to know this about our past and future planet. Most of the details were discovered only over the last fifty years by scientists working in diverse disciplines. Perhaps our panic about anthropogenic climate change can be understood as a way of denying and channeling this larger and more unsettling truth. We delude ourselves into thinking that by merely reducing the emission of greenhouse gases, we can control our restless planet. The new geology is simply too frightening to face head on. Climates do change. We don't know when it will happen, only that it will. Sooner or later, fast or slow, hot or cold, wet or dry, this card will eventually be dealt, again and again throughout our big future.

Useless Arithmetic

The sciences of modeling and predicting climate change provide an important case study in the challenges of making economic models and predictions. It turns out that we are not very good at predicting or managing environmental changes. The problems are endemic to all modeling of complex natural and human systems, including economic markets. Predictions from *any* computer simulations of *any* complex reiterative dynamic processes are constrained by unknown parameters and the chaotic properties of the evolving systems.

In their book *Useless Arithmetic: Why Environmental Scientists Can't Predict the Future,* Orrin H. Pilkey and Linda Pilkey Jarvis discuss the limits of climate change models. There are about fifteen major climate change models used by scientists around the world today. Favored are *bottom-up models*, involving a long chain of events and very complicated computer simulations with enormous data inputs run on supercomputers. This approach uses a great aggregation of models, and models of models, all the way up. In other words, it is also models all the way down. The assumption here is that the more variables included in the meta-model, the better the meta-model. Another approach, the minority view, favors *top-down models,* which focus only on larger systems and simplify, average, estimate, and test, but do not presume to include every potentially relevant variable at greater resolution with ever more detail. Economists, investors, and other living things, take note—our global economy also defies accurate and quantitative prediction because of its complexity.

In the case of climate change, a short list of variables and feedback loops might include the following:

- the absorption of CO_2 by the ocean (resulting in ocean acidification)
- the heat exchange between the oceans and the atmosphere
- the effect of cloud cover
- other variations in the Earth's albedo
- ocean current circulation
- local climate perturbations
- arctic ice melt
- release of methane from melting arctic tundra
- health of phyloplankton
- variations in amounts and types of precipitation
- variable rates of carbon absorption by plants
- long-term climate cycles.

Any of these variables could accentuate or ameliorate climate change and could do so with runaway dynamics. Personally, I lean agnostic to pessimistic on the prospects for near-term climate change resulting from anthropogenic causes. It may not be all that bad. It may even be worse than we imagine. It may already be too late. We have no way of knowing, in spite of the many billions of dollars invested in the climate change prediction industry. Whether sea levels go up or down, the Pilkeys warn:

What a daunting task faces those who choose to predict the futures of the sea-level rise! We have seen that the factors affecting the rate are numerous and not well understood. Even if our understanding improves, the global system simply defies accurate and quantitative prediction because of its complexity . . .

Assumption upon assumption, uncertainty upon uncertainty, and simplification upon simplification are combined to give an ultimate and inevitably shaky answer, which is then scaled up beyond the persistence time to make long-term predictions of the future of sea-level rise. Aside from the frailty of the assumptions, there remains ordering complexity: the lack of understanding of the timing and intensity of each variable.[230]

The American Petroleum Institute, however, should take no pleasure over these limitations to the global climate-change prediction industry and the impassioned advocates for reducing fossil fuel consumption. Anthropogenic climate change is a real concern. And, furthermore, the same types of modeling errors and known unknowns presumably also call into question industry models of global petroleum reserves and the future value of those reserves.

No matter how much data is collected or how sophisticated the computer program, science cannot deterministically model and predict complex dynamic systems. Long-term predictions about the Earth's climate are about as useful as long-term predictions of economic markets. There are too many variables, too many feedback loops between variables, and the system is dynamic in ways that we do not understand and cannot fully represent through mathematics. Investors should already understand this merely by reading the history of economics and finance.

The Pilkeys advocate a qualitative methodology that merely seeks to predict tendencies, directions, and magnitudes of possible changes. A supercomputer simulation is not required to document actual glacial declines around the world over the last few decades. Before-and-after photographs of Muir Lake, Alaska, from the 1940s and today provide compelling evidence for major changes. Several decades of space telemetry and ground observations in the Antarctic reveal disturbing

---

[230] Orrin H. Pilkey and Linda Plkey-Jarvis, *Useless Arithmetic: Why Environmental Scientists Can't Predict the Future* (New York: Columbia University Press, 2007), 82.

short-term trends. Over a three-year period, the West Antarctic Ice Sheet lost 36 cubic miles of ice per year. The complete melting of the West Antarctic Ice Sheet alone would produce a 13-foot global eustatic rise in sea level, perhaps accompanied by isostatic changes in the contours of the ocean basins that could accentuate or mitigate the impact.[231]

Of course, many things can be predicted with a great deal of accuracy. On March 20, 2019, the sun will rise in New York City at 7:00 a.m. and set at 7:08 p.m. And on that day, the sun will reach an altitude of 49.2 degrees above the horizon. The sun will be at a distance of 92,570,000 miles from Earth. Also on March 20, 2019, we can accurately predict a full moon rising at 7:04 p.m., setting at 6:49 a.m., at a distance of 223,395 miles from Earth.

It is comforting that many things can be known with certainty. Regularity and reproducibility have traditionally been seen as hallmarks of science. I count on it every time I log into this computer, get on an airplane, or take an elevator to the eighth floor. Predictive success is thought to be the sine qua non in most science, technology, and engineering fields. In some domains, however, science is going to need to let go of prediction and certainty.

Two things have changed in the recent past that now affect how we approach prediction and certainty:

1. the rise of complexity and
2. the rise of computation.

Environmental and human processes, including economic markets, have always been complex. This is not new. It is just that now we have a lot more insights and background information. We know a lot more of the details, so we are compelled by the known facts at every turn to ask more and more complex questions. This is true in many disciplines, including economics and finance.

The complexity challenge also arises because of the availability of the computer. Every scientific discipline has been dramatically changed over the last forty years by the growing power and availability of computers. Scientists, like investors, can now collect and query enormous data sets and run computer simulations. Without computers, there would be an epistemic bias toward asking simpler questions and

---

[231] Ibid., 78.

ignoring questions that were thought to be beyond the capabilities of science. Today, science is bumping up against horizons of complexity and chaos that may be, in principle, beyond reduction and prediction.

Whether we are forecasting economic markets or climate change, we need to be aware of how the models employed can distort our understanding of reality. There are two sources of this distortion— human frailty and finitude, on the one hand, and the nature of complex and chaotic systems, on the other hand.

The human factors include all of the cognitive biases of our hunter-gatherer brains—the System 1 heuristics—along with any number of technical mistakes, uncertain quality assurance, and debugging challenges that creep into the coding of complex algorithms. Moreover, algorithms have agendas— algorithmic biases based on important assumptions, pessimist and optimist biases, and political advocacy biases.

These human frailties are then compounded and confounded by the very nature of complex adaptive systems. We may understand how complexity and chaos function, but not in a way that allows for useful prediction. Complexity errors result from the nature of complexity itself, not frailty or lack of acuity on the part of the researchers. Our models necessarily make assumptions about partially known and unknown relationships, expressed in the ordering of variables with different valences, intensities, and vectors. Mitigating and reinforcing feedbacks are built into the models. No matter how large the data sets—the size of the data set is normally really important for reliable research—when it comes to simulating the climate or the economy, it ends up being models all the way down. What we simulate in the supercomputers is not nature, but the model itself, often mistaking the map for the terrain. This is what Alfred North Whitehead labeled "the fallacy of misplaced concreteness."[232]

Every model or simulation must solve two problems. First, what is the ordering of complexity in the system, the timing and intensity of different parameters? And second, how does one best represent this ordering of these parameters and complexities mathematically on a computer? Algorithms need to be imagined. Relationships defined. Data collected. Data analyzed. Values assumed. Code written. Models tested. Simulations run. And all of this—the algorithms, the lines of

---

[232] Alfred North Whitehead, *Science and the Modern World* (New York: Free Press, [1925] 1967), 52.

code, sets of data, computer storage and processing—have all been growing exponentially over the last four decades. In the end, though, the computer model is only simulating and testing itself. What is represented on the computer is not the actual complex natural phenomenon.

The Pilkeys advocate *qualitative modeling*, which at best can be used only to predict general directions of change and possible magnitudes. Qualitative modeling will not presume to offer a numerical answer with a range of error. The approach asks *why*, *how*, and *what if.* Qualitative modeling can also use large data sets, computer simulations, and lots of useful arithmetic, but they are used to explore different *scenarios*, *contingencies*, and *normative* relationships. At the end, there is more humility and uncertainty, multiple scenarios, and no hard-and-fast predictions. The authors offer the following chart as a typology of qualitative versus mathematical modeling. Value investors and other living beings might well apply these insights to every aspect of their work.

Scenario Planning	Strategic Planning or Mathematical Modeling
Qualitative input	Quantitative input
Exploits uncertainties	Minimizes uncertainty
Long-range planning	Short-term planning
Multiple answers	Single answer
Planning for the future	Predicting the future
Hypothetical events	Predetermined goals

233

The bad news about complex predictions is that we don't know anything with certainty and may never know anything concrete at all— neither about future climate change, nor about storing radioactive waste over eons, managing declining fisheries, invasive weed species, or untangling complex genetic bureaucracies. Science is butting its head against horizons of complexity that we may not be able to hack. Few are willing to accept such epistemic limitations. It runs counter to the very ethos of science. And yet complexity and chaos theories suggest that certain kinds of problems cannot be solved with bigger data sets,

---

[233] Pilkey and Plkey-Jarvis, *Useless Arithmetic: Why Environmental Scientists Can't Predict the Future*, 200.

better code, more powerful supercomputers, fewer flawed humans, and less politicized science.

Complexity is not just more; it is something new. The really creative processes in the world tend to be complex distributed systems, not amenable to deterministic modeling This is the greatest challenge for science today. It is also a challenge to applied ethics, because the consequences of actions cannot always be known in advance. The precautionary principle—"do no harm"—must reckon with unknown and unintended consequences along with the unknown opportunity costs of doing nothing.

Science produces lots of useful and reliable predictions. Mathematical modeling works well with simpler systems, like plotting the motion of the stars and planets in the evening sky or stress-engineering concrete and steel bridges under variable loads and conditions. Multiply the variables, however, add a lot of feedback loops, and grow the complexity of a system and the questions posed, and suddenly predictive modeling becomes an exercise in futility. Predictive modeling cannot yield valid predictions for any complex natural and human-related processes. The story is about approaching limits to science in the domain of the complex.

A conclusion to be drawn is that humanity is now thrust willy-nilly into the role of managing the Earth, even though we don't really know what we are doing. Humans will never have the complete *know-how*, even though we certainly have increased our *can-do*. Humans have themselves become an important variable in the planetary evolution of the planet. In his environmental history of the twentieth century, J. R. McNeill reflects on our dilemma.

> The human race, without intending anything of the sort, has undertaken a gigantic uncontrolled experiment on the earth. In time, I think, this will appear as the most important aspect of twentieth-century history, more so than World War II, the communist enterprise, the rise of mass literacy, the spread of democracy, or the growing emancipation of women.[234]

This uncertainty does not relieve us of the responsibilities and risks of taking action. We must and will make choices. We have to

---

[234] J.Robert McNeill, *Something New under the Sun: An Environmental History of the Twentieth-Century World* (New York: W.W. Norton & Company, 2000).

imagine and seek desirable outcomes. Let us try to model, design, and build for sustainable and resilient futures. We have the possibility of anticipatory adaptation, if we begin to think in terms of Big History and the big challenges that we face.

How should governments, business, and citizens respond to the real and perceived threat of global climate change? Perhaps the question is as perplexing as asking how one would plan for and respond to a dramatic nonanthropogenic climate change.

For my part, we need to deemphasize anthropogenic climate change and look at other variables. There are many compelling arguments for radically increasing efficiencies and reducing fossil fuel consumptions. These reasons do not depend on prognostications of climate models. Reducing fossil fuel consumption improves local environmental air and water quality. It increases health, safety, and quality of life. It slows resource depletion. Reducing fossil fuel consumption improves the bottom line for individuals, corporations, and entire economies. There are also important national security interests in reducing fossil fuel imports. We don't need a global climate change scare in order to justify, rationalize, or motivate what should already be obvious and sound public and private policy. It is in the best interest of the United States and the world to dramatically reduce fossil fuel consumption, especially through increased efficiency, while also developing alternative energy sources. As discussed, the prime directive of evolution is to minimize entropy while maximizing creativity.

Remember that humans are being asked to make major political and economic decisions in response to the perceived and presumably real threat of anthropogenic climate change. And that is just the tip of the iceberg, so to speak, of the many and varied complex ways that humans and nature interact. We need to accept that things will not stay the same, that the world will change in dramatic and unpredictable ways. These transformations, for good and for bad, may make sense in hindsight, but could not have otherwise been predicted. This is true of evolution, climate change, the movements of economic markets, and the odyssey of an individual life lived.

The Next Leap in Energy-Matter-Ingenuity

Based on the observed pattern in biological evolution and in cultural evolution, we can hypothesize a new energetic leap in human-generated energy density flows. This will be accomplished in part by a reduction in human population, by new efficiencies in generating and using energy, and by new technologies that will allow humans to more directly harvest solar energy. We can extrapolate that this will be accompanied by a commensurate jump in information-ingenuity density flows. We already have intimations of the next big lollapalooza, though not enough to pick winners and losers in the transformations ahead.

In the end, humans must do what all life does so exquisitely. We must innovate to capture energy-matter flows for the construction of greater complexity. The critical inputs to economic growth are energy, matter, and ingenuity. The task of investors and other living things is to capture a tiny slice of that flow and, in so doing, to act as membrane-like allocators of resources among organelles in a vast global exchange system.

Humans now consume at a rate of 18 trillion watts of energy in a variety of forms—fossil fuels (coal, oil, gas), hydropower, nuclear power, renewables (solar, wind, biomass, biofuels, and geothermal), and, of course, the food that the 7.3 billion of us eat. Without energy constantly running through the arteries of our global civilization, the world would collapse. Our cities, industries, transportation, agriculture—indeed, every aspect of our contemporary lives—depend on this tremendous flow of energy.

In order to meet the demands of a still-growing population and the desperate needs of the energy poor, the world will need to increase its energy production by about 50 percent in the next two decades. Note that this is most easily and economically accomplished through increased efficiency and not through increased production.[235] Emerging markets—China, India, Brazil, and others—also aspire to achieve much higher standards of living, comparable to those in the United States and Europe. All of this increased demand occurs alongside of concerns about anthropogenic climate change caused primarily by the burning of fossil fuels.

It may be that greater energy efficiency has survival value at different stages of our cosmic story and that we should start measuring

---

[235] Eric D. Beinhocker and Jeremy Oppenheim, "Economic Opportunities in a Low-Carbon World," McKinsey & Company, http://www.mckinsey.com/client_service/sustainability/latest_thinking/economic_opportunities_in_a_low_carbon_world; IEA, "Energy Efficiency Market Report 2014," (Paris, France: International Energy Agency, 2014)..

those efficiencies in terms of energy density flows. Few of us think about energy flows in our daily lives. We drive to the supermarket to buy our groceries that we store in a refrigerator and cook on the stove. Calculating the flow of energy in our morning breakfast, including multiple conversions of energy from one form to another along the entire journey from field to supermarket to body, requires a new kind of scientific literacy and accounting principles.[236]

Elegance in evolution is achieved when we do more for less with the emphasis being on more, smaller, and faster. Productivity growth in economics is also a more-for-less proposition. Evolution and ecology have a lot to teach us about how to achieve sustainable economic growth and a resilient planetary civilization.

Big History offers an interesting vantage point for thinking about energy policies and solutions for the twenty-first century that can lead to a healthier, cleaner, smarter, wealthier, and a more creative global civilization. "Minimize entropy, maximize creativity" is the new ethical, aesthetic, and pragmatic first principle, evolution's prime directive.

---

[236] Smil, *Energy in Nature and Society*.

Chapter 9:
The Bottom Line

We live in a layered world of selectively permeable membranes, barriers, and borders through which energy, matter, and ingenuity are channeled and directed by living cells, organisms, ecologies, corporations, and cultures. In commerce, economics, and finance, we have become very sophisticated in representing these flows as money, but never forget that behind it all is a flux of real energy, matter, and ingenuity that we have only recently come to understand and enumerate. This fundamental insight about evolution and economics, however, gives us little contextual insight into the diverse pathways actualized in any particular evolutionary or economic niche. The question remains: how does applied Big History provide an edge for investors and entrepreneurs? What is the bottom line?

And it is at this point that I feel less like an informed outsider and more like an imposter. During my career, I have built a large and diversified intellectual and experiential portfolio— hence the ambition of this book—but my own investment portfolio is modest and mostly managed by TIAA-CREF. There are many technicalities and details about which I lack understanding. In this last chapter, this Big Historian is going to take what he has learned to develop some normative insights about investing and business in a complex world. I do so for lay investors as well as for those with vast formal training and experience working in business, finance, and economics. I find this daunting on both accounts.

Perhaps I should include some boilerplate legal disclaimer at this point as one might find in other financial publications and presentations. Nothing contained in this book constitutes investment advice or offers any opinion with respect to the suitability of any security or asset class. The views expressed in this book should not be taken as advice to buy, sell, or hold any security or asset class. Any strategy described herein is for illustrative purposes. No representation or warranty, express or implied, is made or given to the information cited in this book as to the accuracy, completeness or fairness of such information, and no responsibility or liability is accepted for any such information. And most important, past performance of an investment, strategy, fund, economy, species, and planet is not a guarantee of future results.

Creating and Capturing Value

From the macro perspective, there is no lack of energy, matter, and potentially also ingenuity to drive future evolutionary complexification and economic growth on our restless planet. From a practical perspective, however, an increase in consumption is generally at the expense of other entities in the eat-and-be-eaten food chains and economic markets.

There are two sides to the dramas of evolution and economics. On the one hand, other living beings must die so that we may eat and live. Other economic entities must also lose so that we may profit. There is zero-sum competition in life and in markets between winners and losers. A buyer must exist for every seller and often this means a profit gained through someone else's loss. Economic markets could not otherwise exist. Natural selection and economic selection require as much. There is a tragic dimension to evolution, economics, and life. Economic markets, like nature, can indeed be "red in tooth and claw." It is the great Eucharistic law—eat and be eaten. Economics remains a dismal science.

From a different vantage point, however, the dramas of evolution and economics are actually epic stories of progress measured in exponential leaps in cooperation, creativity, and complexity. In a world of increasing prosperity, the cooperative side to economics (and evolution) poses a fundamentally different moral, aesthetic, and value proposition for entrepreneurs, investors, and other living things. This sets off a non-zero-sum dynamic of win-win in which exchange creates benefits for many parties, floating all boats and increasing productivity, incomes, and wealth. This is the larger story of evolution and our species' rapid rise.

Competition and cooperation are two aspects of the real world. We should avoid fuzzy thinking about either side of this dialectic, remembering always that in the end we all die. From the beginning of the universe, the certainty of death and taxes was mandated by the laws of thermodynamics. In the dialectic between competition and cooperation, however, the win-win of cooperation is the more creative and dynamic force behind evolution in general and our species' remarkable success in particular.

Parasites or Symbionts

People who work and win in finance are often perceived by the larger society as parasites sucking the blood out of the rest of the otherwise productive economy.[237] The reality is much more complicated. Indeed, from the perspective of Big History, all living beings are in the business of extracting and consuming matter, energy, and ingenuity from their environment. We're all parasites sucking our existence and complexity out of the great thermodynamic flux.

If we include pension and sovereign funds, then the people who directly or indirectly buy, own, and sell securities constitute a significant, albeit privileged, portion of humanity today. If we include the insurance industry in this equation, then the portion of humanity directly and indirectly invested in the financial instruments is larger still. We might expand this circle further by including government spending and debt as a critical component of finance that extends the circle to include all citizens. Indeed, anyone with a bank account, a credit card, a mortgage, a student loan, or a wallet full of cash is already a cog in this enormous, complex, distributed system.

Together, financial services and insurance constitute about 7 percent of the US GDP,[238] but they play a significant role in enabling all other sectors of the economy to function. Finance may not be the engine of capitalism, but it is a vital lubricant without which the engine would freeze up. Furthermore, most of the money in circulation, as already discussed, is created by private lenders, not governments. Institutional and individual investors—buyers and sellers, winners and losers, debtors and creditors—provide three important functions in the economic superorganism of humanity.

First, the market acts like a membrane in a cell or an organism, transporting energy-matter-ingenuity to where it creates income-wealth-value. The financial service industry enables the distribution of real goods and services around the world in real time. The world would not function without this complex allocation system, any more than a cell could survive without its selectively permeable membranes. Seven percent of GDP is a relatively small transaction cost for the function of this amazingly productive economic superorganism.

---

[237] Matt Taibbi, "The Great American Bubble Machine," *Rolling Stone*, 4/5/2010 2010.
[238] Analysis, "U.S. Gdp by Year."

The second function of the market of buyers and sellers, lenders and borrowers, is to select winners and losers. Here the market functions much like the forces of natural selection in evolution to "blindly" promote the most adaptive and eliminate the least adaptive enterprises. No wonder that people resent bankers, hedge fund managers, and investors. They play the part of the grim reaper in economic selection—often benefiting from the failure of others.

The third function of the global finance industry is to consume, create, and spread information-ingenuity around the world. Markets promote innovation. They are not particularly efficient, except in this sense of dispersing knowledge and know-how around the world. Indeed, markets are not particularly fair, as they tend to concentrate wealth in the hands of the few.[239] Capitalism provides neither according to needs nor according to merit.[240] What global capitalism does well is promote innovation-adoption-adaptation. Financial services thus selectively speed up the global distribution of information and ingenuity.

This macro perspective on finance says nothing about what the appropriate compensation should be for CEOs, hedge fund managers, bankers, and investors of all sorts. Of course, there are huge differences in scale between a teacher hoping to retire on a modest pension and a top hedge fund manager taking home over a billion dollars in any given year. This macro perspective does not inform us about how the rewards and losses should be shared within a firm among employees or how the earnings should be taxed by the larger society, nor does it tell us what regulations are appropriate for protecting us from the vices and follies of others. I only want to emphasize that the 7 percent "transaction fee" on the entire economy is not necessarily excessive. Indeed, it is a bargain. And while extreme wealth results for the few within this economic system, no one gets to take this wealth beyond the grave. And as long as there is social mobility, a shared tax burden, and philanthropic charity, the social contract that sustains free markets and free societies may yet endure.

---

[239] Thomas Piketty, *The Economics of Inequality* (Cambridge, MA: Belknap Press, 2015).

[240] Giacomo Corneo, *Is Capitalism Obsolete?: A Journey through Alternative Economic Systems* (Cambridge, MA: Harvard University Press, 2017).

Species of Specialization

The most important economic investment that individuals make is in their education and career choices. This is where you will spend most of your time and probably earn most of your money. Because of the exponential growth in collective learning, knowledge and know-how are abundant, expansive, and inexpensive. The problem is that there is so damn much information and ingenuity out there. Acquiring competency in any particular domain can take decades of social learning. Professions that require extensive training, certification, and licensing generally return higher compensation than other jobs. Specialized careers function much like a moat that ensures scarcity, leading to higher compensation. Presumably you have chosen a career that matches your talents and passions with your needs for income and security. Hopefully you have also garnered surplus income that you saved and invested.

If finance and economics are not your area of expertise, you may best be served by simply buying index funds with low management fees. Specialized mutual funds and exchange-traded funds allow one to further focus your investments in economic sectors and diverse geographies, but don't delude yourself that you're competent to actively manage your portfolio. It takes a lot of research and due diligence to beat the market averages. Little ole you will be competing with hedge funds, investment banks, and mutual funds that employ armies of researchers and analysts with many years of training and experience. Even professionals in finance generally prefer to hire others to manage their investments (and are sometimes also restricted from buying and selling individual stocks because of access to insider information). It is probably a good idea to have two or three separate investment managers as a hedge to incompetence and possible maleficence. Moreover, all that time and effort spent on studying the market is a huge opportunity cost in time and energy that could have been spent doing something more productive, less risky, and more enjoyable. It is one thing if you enjoy religiously reading financial news, but maybe you would rather be spending your free time playing with your children, working in the garden, getting some exercise, or binge watching the latest Netflix movie.

Little Bets, Big Wins

A little bet at the right time and place can lead to fabulous fortunes—Netflix being a recent example. Netflix (NFLX) went public in May 2002 at $15 per share. After two stock splits— 2004 (2:1) and 2015 (7:1)—an initial purchase of 100 shares would now be 1400 shares trading recently above $400 per share. In sixteen-years your initial investment of $1,500 would have returned $560,000 not including dividends, or a 35,000 percent return on investment over sixteen years.

The easiest way to get rich quick would be to have been smart or lucky enough to buy and hold several hundred shares of Netflix in 2002. The history of stock markets includes many more such examples.

Apple stock at the 1980 IPO price of $22 per share. There have been four stock splits, so your original 100 shares grew to 5,600 shares valued today at around $175 per share, or $980,000. This is a 30,000 percent increase in value over thirty-seven years on your original investment, and that is not including dividends paid out annually.[241]

Similarly, if you were smart or lucky enough to buy 100 shares of Amazon at $18 per share when it went public in 1997, you would also be very fortunate. After three stock splits, you would now own 1,200 shares of Amazon recently trading at around $1,500 per share, or $1,800,000. This is a 100,000 percent increase over twenty-one years of your original investment of $1,800. Similar stories could be told about Facebook, Google, and others. Unfortunately, those boats have already set sail.[242]

Smart people are out there now looking for the next big thing with the possibilities of scaling and exponential growth. These days, more and more of the shares of startups are locked up in advance by venture capital and private equity shops, so the exponential possibilities will be fewer for other investors if and when the shares go public. [243]

Anticipating the next big thing is not an easy or certain business. Many a startup has crashed and burned. In 1996, the more obvious Internet search engines to invest in were Yahoo!, Magellan, Lycos, Infoseek, AltaVista, Excite, and the once-ubiquitous AOL platform.

---

[241] "Macrotrends," http://www.macrotrends.net/stocks/research.
[242] Ibid.
[243] Vito Racanelli, "Big Ipo Gain? Don't Bet on It," *Barron's*, September 18, 2017 2017.

Google was launched in 1998, operating initially as just another search engine for the growing content on the Internet. Similarly, Facebook was a latecomer to social networking, replicating functions and services already provided by Friendster and MySpace. And when Amazon began in 1997, the idea of giving one's credit card information online seemed strange and dangerous to most consumers. Few could envision the larger disruption in retail shopping and exponential possibilities that inspired Jeff Bezos to start selling books online. Similar stories can be told about most technological innovations leading to new industries in the history of electricity, automobiles, and more. While the profits can be enormous, there end up being a lot of failed enterprises and investors along the way.

Exponentiality is more easily achieved over a longer time horizon. A modest 3 percent inflation-adjusted rate of return on investment will double in value after twenty-four years. Over fifty years, the value quadruples. Intergenerational wealth will accrue twentyfold over a hundred-year timeline. At this point, exponentiality begins to look absurd. Two hundred years in on our 3 percent annual return, your descendants would be looking at a 400-fold increase in the initial investment. You don't need to be a master of the universe or quant-rocket scientist to win at this long game. You need only disciplined saving, a diversified portfolio, competent managers, and a longer time horizon.

Albert Einstein is reputed to have called "compound interest the most powerful force in the universe."[244] From the perspective of Big History—the flows of energy, matter, and ingenuity in evolution and economics—compounding processes leading to exponential leaps are certainly part of our past history and future possibilities. Exponentiality is part of the possibility space of Earth and its creatures for as long as our Sun provides. In finance, exponential returns-on-investment is the holy grail.

Picking Winners

Thoughtful entrepreneurship and investing requires knowing something about the competitive and innovation space in different economic sectors—food, water, energy, transportation, technology,

---

[244] Einstein quotes about "compound interest" begin to appear after his death in writing and without citation. The quote is probably apocryphal.

construction, manufacturing, real estate, consumer goods, medicine, education, entertainment, and so forth. In this case, knowing "all the big ideas from all the big disciplines," as Charlie Munger advised, also means understanding in broad brushstrokes some details about all the major sectors of the global economy.

Vaclav Smil is one of my guides. In his many books, Smil provides an overview of the global flows of energy, matter, and ingenuity from the Industrial Revolution to today. His work makes investors familiar with how different sectors evolved and are evolving. It was not self-evident to me before reading Smil, for instance, that there is a global shortage of sand—a particular kind of river sand suited for use in concrete. And the world is consuming a lot of concrete.[245]

In his book *The Nature of Value*, Nick Gogerty introduced the concept of "ino" as a unit of innovation and the key to value creation in economic history (which we explored in chapter four). Gogerty cites Larry Keeley and his co-authors at the Doblin Group, who studied over 2,000 successful innovations in businesses and categorized them into ten types. Innovations in these ten areas can lead to unique business capabilities and competitive outcomes:

1. Profit Model
2. Network
3. Structure
4. Process
5. Product Performance
6. Product System
7. Service
8. Channel
9. Brand
10. Customer Engagement[246]

Try using this list to enhance your SWAT analysis (strengths, weaknesses, assets, threats) of a particular company in a particular economic cluster. Remember that we are trying to understand

---

[245] Smil, *Energy in Nature and Society*; *Making the Modern World: Materials & Dematerialization* (New York: Wiley, 2013).

[246] Gogerty, *The Nature of Value: How to Invest in the Adaptive Economy*, Kindle 1136; Larry Keeley et al., *Ten Types of Innovation: The Discipline of Building Breakthroughs* (New York: Wiley, 2013).

competitive advantages and disadvantages within a cluster. A cluster analysis gives a fuller understanding of the value proposition along with the probabilistic space of future scenarios for any particular enterprise in that competitive space. Unique capabilities in these ten domains provide the edge for a company in the face of competition. Remember that innovations in general float all our economic boats in the long run; but innovations in particular—innovations that are difficult to replicate, that have barriers to entry—lead to economic success in the short run for particular companies and their shareholders.

If an economic cluster is highly competitive and fully developed, Gogerty notes, the businesses therein have lower rates of return. Most of the value in such clusters will be realized by the consumer and not by the enterprises in that cluster. A crowded business environment may also involve a lot of turnover, as companies fail because of these narrow margins. This describes the restaurant industry in New York City and the steel industry on a global scale over the past fifty years. In some clusters, over time, there will be consolidation into a few super-organizations through mergers, acquisitions, network effects, and economies of scale.

Diversification

Building a diversified portfolio is one of the hallmarks of successful investing. The received wisdom advises maintaining a variable distribution among stocks, bonds, fixed income, and cash holdings depending on life circumstances, time horizons, and formulaic percentages. Stocks are further broken down into large, medium, and small capitalized firms. Additional diversification is achieved by distributing holdings across economic sectors—energy, food, manufacturing, transportation, health care, real estate, retail, tech, mining, and so on.

Publicly traded stocks are not the only game in town. The larger investment landscape includes trading in commodities, currencies, bonds (private and public, secured and unsecured debt), private equity, options, and derivatives. It is also possible to directly trade on macroeconomic trends such as the volatility index (VIX). Retail investors may not have access to many of these instruments, as they are only marketed to institutional and qualified investors. In all these exchanges, investors can also diversify internationally across geographies and nations. A competitive space exists within each of these economic clusters and international markets. However, one cannot and should not try to inhabit every economic niche. Each becomes its own area of expertise and specialization.

Even more important than having a diversified portfolio is having a diversified mind. To thrive in finance, one must cultivate diverse competencies. Mathematics and applied sciences are enormous cognitive assets that take effort to build and maintain. Individuals in finance typically work in teams, so they also need skills in cooperation and communication. And financial services are perhaps the most international and culturally diverse industry in the world today. Members of this group need to be proficient in all of the humanistic disciplines, including history, politics, religion, culture, sociology, psychology, and linguistics. The undergraduate curriculum for a career in finance today is a broad and rigorous liberal arts education.[247]

There is a pattern in ecology that might also be applied to managing portfolios and diversified minds. The r/K theory tracks the trade-offs between having many offspring with low parental investment or fewer offspring with higher parental investment. Mouse reproduction follows an r-selection strategy, with many offspring in a litter, a short gestation period, less parental care, and a short time until sexual maturity. Whales, elephants, and humans follow a K-selection strategy, with few offspring, a long gestation period, longer-duration parental care, and a long period until sexual maturity.

Humans are actually on a K-selection extreme—more so than ever in the contemporary world. In the past two generations, we've gone from fertility rates of 5-plus children per woman to 2.5 children per woman. There are many factors that account for this stunning drop in fertility rates, including an economic response to the increased costs of parenting caused by migrations from rural and agricultural societies to urban and capitalist societies. In many instances, childhood dependency in humans now requires parental investment all the way through graduate school. This may be a case of diminishing return on investment.

Portfolio diversification is a mix of r/K selection strategies. Place of employment is generally a K-selection situation for the individual. A person's job requires a great deal of time and energy and presumably provides significant returns. Saving and investing is a way of

---

[247] Robert Hagstrom, *Investing: The Last Liberal Art* (New York: Columbia Business School, 2013).

diversifying beyond your pay check (and beyond whatever stocks and options you may hold in your company). An r-selection investment strategy entails a scattered approach with minimal capital outlay to many different securities in the expectation that some fraction will survive and thrive. This is easily achieved by holding index funds. On the other hand, selecting individual companies to hold in your portfolio is a K-selection proposition. You are laying out a lot more effort in selecting and monitoring the company and the market. In a nutshell, r/K selection strategies in population biology are analogous to the Pareto Principle in finance (i.e., that 80 percent of return in a portfolio comes from 20 percent of the investments).

A diversified portfolio is a way of inhabiting multiple niches in the economic ecologies and hedging against losses. A diversified mind is a way of synergizing with others to innovate in the business of creating and capturing value.

The Alphas and the Rest of Us

The managers of successful hedge funds, mutual funds, and investment banks tend to be smart contrarians. Being contrarian is essential to beating the averages. By definition, you cannot outperform the market by following the crowd. Being smart is essential to not being beaten in the process. As the adage goes, luck favors the prepared mind. Being smart, in this context, includes some mastery of analytic and mathematical thinking, attention deficit hyperactivity disorder (ADHD) perhaps with a touch of creative dyslexia, voracious reading, an active memory, and a competitive streak.

The successful fund manager is also smart and contrarian when it comes to politics and religion. Charlie Munger counsels the avoidance of "extremely intense ideology" because it turns your mind into "cabbage." Don't get too worked up for or against any particular religious, political, or economic orthodoxy. Munger advocates inversion—turning a problem upside down or inside out—as a way of gaining clarity. He counsels us to articulate the other person's perspective better than they might do so themselves before forming our own opinion. This ability to consider many sides of a heated argument is similar to the skill involved in analyzing negative and positive scenarios for any given investment decision.[248]

---

[248] Munger, "Usc Law School Commencement Address, May 1, 2007".

The alpha fund managers often have big, competitive egos. At a certain point, it is not really about the money anymore, but about social status in relation to your peers who are playing the same game. The 0.1 percenters at the top are not comparing themselves to the 99.9 percent. The game is all about return-on-investments and growing portfolios.

Conspicuous consumption can be a manifestation of this competitiveness and our status-conscious hunter-gatherer brains. It is also a way to diversify assets. Real estate, jewelry, car collections, art, and so forth are some of the ways that the superrich and the rest of us turn dollars into tradable stuff, not to mention enjoyment.

The alphas, however, are fundamentally frugal creatures. They climbed to the top by shopping for bargains, preserving capital, and reinvesting. The ratio of securities-to-stuff is weighted heavily on the securities side. Late in life, status-and-charity fortuitously aligned in named endowments at universities, hospitals, museums, concert halls, public broadcasting, human services, and more.

And because our hunter-gatherer brains are finely attuned to social status and dominance hierarchies, to winning and losing, pleasure and pain, and approaching and fleeing, the successful investor needs also to cultivate a Daoist-like detachment from the results of his or her decisions.[249] Surely, one should learn from one's mistakes, but the anticipatory anxiety and post hoc anguish of losing diminish one's cognitive capacities. A big win also distorts our perceptions and decision-making. Both hope and fear turn out to be swindlers in the game of buying and selling securities.

Poker isn't the right analogy to successful fund management. Instead, think of what it takes to play and win bridge tournaments. In bridge competition, partners rotate through twenty-four boards each with a different deal of the cards. Everyone has an opportunity to play identical hands over twenty-four iterations, hence the term "duplicate bridge." Moving from table to table, partners are scored on their relative performance. The players' skills over the course of a tournament, rather than the luck of any particular deal of the cards, is decisive in determining the winners. There is no such thing as bluffing in bridge; instead, it is a game of skill against the backdrop of incomplete knowledge and probabilities. The bridge master beats the poker player in the long game of investing.

---

[249] The Daoist term in Chinese is wei wuwei, which means "engaged non-engagement" or "active non-action."

Michael Mauboussin, now Director of Research at Blue Mountain Capital, adjunct professor of finance at Columbia University Business School, and chairman of the Board of Trustees at the Santa Fe Institute has had a distinguished career. His many books and essays are always insightful. In a 2016 essay written while still head of Global Financial Strategies at Credit Suisse, Mauboussin looks back on his thirty-year career in finance and offers his "Reflections on the Ten Attributes of Great Investors." There is a lot to this essay, but in summary the ten attributes are:

1. Be numerate and understand accounting
2. Understand value (the present value of cash flow)
3. Properly assess strategy (or how a business makes money)
4. Compare effectively (expectations versus fundamentals)
5. Think probabilistically (there are few sure things)
6. Update your views effectively (beliefs are hypotheses to be tested, not treasures to be protected)
7. Beware of behavior biases (minimizing constraints to good thinking)
8. Know the difference between information and influence
9. Position sizing (maximizing the payoff from the edge)
10. Read (and keep an open mind)[250]

On the last point—read—this book is also an invitation to go my sources and dig deeper. Read Mauboussin and other authors discussed in this book. My cursory reviews do them insufficient justice.

While it may not be given to all of us, or desired, to be the next investment wizard and master of the universe, it is worth noting the personality, character traits, virtues, and skills of those who succeed in these careers. Many of these attributes are worth cultivating for their own sake, even if you don't work in finance.

Teams Work

If you do work in finance or manage a business, then you are a specialist involved in a team sport. Teams are how we overcome the personbyte limits to acquiring knowledge and know-how. And properly

---

[250] Michael J Mauboussin, "Thirty Years: Reflections on the Ten Attributes of Great Investors," (New York: Credit Suisse Global Financial Strategies, 2016).

structured, teams are also how we compensate for the weaknesses of our hunter-gatherer brains. Teams are how you create a diversified group mind. Generalists and diverse specialists need each other to create, innovate, and grow productivity and profits.

The investment team has been described as a "heterarchical collaboration."[251] This is reflected in the open architecture of the trading floor in which managing directors, junior analysts, and everyone in between operate in small groups without a visible hierarchy. Structuring an effective investment team requires that we *not* defer to authority or group think. Managers should cultivate and reward disagreements and debate within their teams. Building a diversity of perspectives within the team should also include gender diversity, because men and women really do think and behave differently. Ray Dalio, the founder of Bridgewater whom we encountered in chapter 4, advocates "radical transparency" in team decision-making.[252] Philip Tetlock also advocates a team approach consisting of differently minded specialists and generalists building a distributed intelligence through the exploration of multiple scenarios, possibilities, and probabilities.[253]

That means that you need a diverse team of experts who interact, share, and actively debate the decisions at hand—examining the challenges and opportunities from different perspectives; using multiple models at both micro- and macro scales; considering the effect of feedback loops and the possibility of unintended consequences; and combining analytic, associative, and inductive thought and decision-making processes. Economics and finance, like human evolution more broadly, are as much about how we cooperate within groups as they are about competition between groups. If the individuals in a group can become better cooperators, the investment team will be more competitive.

Inventing the Future

Innovation is the key to growing businesses and economies; but innovation is not necessarily easy to come by. In his book *Where Good*

[251] Daniel Beunza and David Stark, "How to Recognize Opportunities: Heterarchical Search in Trading Rooms," in *The Sociology of Financial Markets*, ed. Karin Knorr Cetina and Alex Preda (Oxford: Oxford University Press, 2004).
[252] Dalio, *Principles: Life and Work*; "How to Build a Company Where the Best Ideas Win".
[253] Tetlock and Gardner, *Superforecasting: The Art and Science of Prediction*.

Ideas Come From, Steven Johnson argues that innovation is the result of diversified minds ruminating over problems and possible solutions.

> The long-zoom approach lets us see that openness and connectivity may, in the end, be more valuable to innovation than purely competitive mechanisms. Those patterns of innovation deserve recognition—in part because it's intrinsically important to understand why good ideas emerge historically, and in part because by embracing these patterns we can build environments that do a better job of nurturing good ideas, whether those environments are schools, governments, software platforms, poetry seminars, or social movements. We can think more creatively if we open our minds to the many connected environments that make creativity possible.[254]

Here, too, something analogous to the r/K ratio in animal reproductive strategies might apply. The 80 percent of your learning across diverse disciplines help empower the 20 percent in which you have specialized. Johnson continues:

> If there is a single maxim that runs through this book's arguments, it is that we are often better served by connecting ideas than we are by protecting them . . . when one looks at innovation in nature and in culture, environments that build walls around good ideas tend to be less innovative in the long run than more open-ended environments. Good ideas may not want to be free, but they do want to connect, fuse, recombine. They want to reinvent themselves by crossing conceptual borders. They want to complete each other as much as they want to compete.[255]

In his book *Out of Control: The New Biology of Machines, Social Systems, and the Economic World*, Kevin Kelly offers a formula for complex creativity in nature and societies. He calls these "The Nine Laws of Gods." To be a creator, one needs to lose control of one's finest creations, hence the book's title "out of control." Kelly offers the following guidelines to would-be innovators and creators of elegant complexity:

---

[254] Steven Johnson, *Where Good Ideas Come From: The Natural History of Innovation* (New York: Riverhead Books, 2010), 21.
[255] Ibid., 22.

1. Distribute being;
2. Control from the bottom up;
3. Cultivate increasing return;
4. Grow by chunking;
5. Maximize the fringes;
6. Honor your errors;
7. Pursue no optima, have multiple goals;
8. Seek persistent disequilibrium; and
9. Change changes itself.[256]

These "Nine Laws of God" might well serve portfolio and business managers. As the title of Kelly's book implies, the first step in nine (or twelve) is to admit that you are out of control (i.e., powerless). The world is complex. Markets are fundamentally unpredictable. Life is fragile and finite. I imagine that these nine laws apply as much to the internal workings of investment teams and organizations as well as to the kind of investment portfolio one should build. Kelly's nine laws can also be understood as a formula for building diversified minds and perhaps also a robust ethical and moral framework.[257]

Distribute being, pursue no optima, grow by chunking, cultivate increasing returns, honor your errors—all of this translates into investments in complexity across all asset classes: small to large cap stocks, junk bonds to guaranteed securities, real estate and index funds, commodities and currencies. Thematically, it moves across diverse sectors and geographies, tracking macro and micro movements of the portfolio as an ecosystem of interrelated parts. Investing in complex situations and securities is now the best way to preserve and build capital in a complex world. Play both the creative and destructive sides in diverse economic ecologies and scales. This, at least, is how the big hedge funds achieve alpha and earn their fees.

As the baseball legend and pithy sage Yogi Berra once quipped, "It is tough to make predictions, especially about the future." And

---

[256] Kelly, *Out of Control: The New Biology of Machines, Social Systems, and the Economic World.*.
[257] William J. Grassie, "Wired for the Future: Kevin Kelly's Techno-Utopia," *Terra Nova: Nature and Culture* 2, no. 4 (1997).

yet predicting the future is the job of investors. Political scientist Phillip Tetlock created prediction tournaments (about the future, no less!) and found that expert forecasters were only slightly better than chance in getting predictions right. Indeed, his studies suggest that there is an inverse relationship between the media fame of the expert and the accuracy of their predictions.[258] Another reason not to watch television news.

In their book *Superforecasting: The Art and Science of Prediction*, Philip Tetlock and Dan Gardner went on to study the traits and behaviors that resulted in better predictions.[259] Tetlock uses the tale of foxes and hedgehogs to illustrate the traits of super forecasters. "A fox knows many things, but a hedgehog one big thing," wrote the Greek poet Archilochus over 2,500 years ago.[260] In his prediction tournaments, Tetlock found that

> . . . low scorers look like hedgehogs: thinkers who "know one big thing," aggressively extend the explanatory reach of that one big thing into new domains, display bristly impatience with those who "do not get it," and express considerable confidence that they are already pretty proficient forecasters, at least in the long term. High scorers look like foxes: thinkers who know many small things (tricks of their trade), are skeptical of grand schemes, see explanation and prediction not as deductive exercises but rather as exercises in flexible "ad hocery" that require stitching together diverse sources of information, and are rather diffident about their own forecasting prowess.[261]

It may be that economic forecasting follows more rigorous rules than predicting political outcomes and events. There is certainly more "data" to study and deploy in making economic predictions. The general rule, however, holds. Foxes make better forecasters. They "aggregate perspectives."[262] A diversified mind is a critical cognitive asset for investors and foxes. This book is an extended exercise in building a diverse toolkit, critical thinking,

---

[258] Philip E. Tetlock, *Expert Political Judgment: How Good Is It? How Can We Know?* (Princeton, NJ: Princeton University Press, 2005).

[259] Tetlock and Gardner, *Superforecasting: The Art and Science of Prediction.*

[260] Isaiah Berlin, *The Hegdehog and the Fox* (London: Weidenfeld & Nicolson, 1953).

[261] Tetlock, *Expert Political Judgment: How Good Is It? How Can We Know?*

[262] Tetlock and Gardner, *Superforecasting: The Art and Science of Prediction*, 77.

learning agility, and extending the possibilities of creative innovation.

Bad Things Happen to Good Investors

In contemplating investment decisions, investors should pay close attention to the dynamics of feedback, time delays, and tipping points. Economies, we have learned, are complex adaptive systems. Investors can anticipate, but not predict, oscillating patterns of overshoot, collapse, chaos, and the emergence of new equilibria. The frequency, amplitude, and duration of those patterns are impossible to forecast with any certainty, but significant enough to require preparation. By paying attention to these larger dynamics, we might better understand and prepare for these episodes, surviving Nassim Taleb's "Black Swans" and turning them into Didier Sornette's "Dragon King" opportunities.[263]

Debt obligations limit one's future possibilities. This is true of individuals, corporations, and governments. Whether it is buying on margins or carrying a mortgage, debt is generally incurred with the expectation that it will be easier to repay with continued growth. When growth rates stall or decline, however, as we have recently experienced, then this debt can quickly turn into an exponential burden, pulling individuals, corporations, and nations into a downward spiral. Excessive leverage in an economy is also dangerous, because the system is so interconnected on a global level that minor failures of corporations, banks, and nations will tend to reverberate and amplify around the world in a self-reinforcing, negative feedback loop. Debt is inherently destabilizing, even though debt is what keeps the monied economy running.

We need to build what Nassim Taleb calls "antifragility" into our economies, portfolios, and lives.[264] This means limiting leverage and keeping enough capital in reserve that investors can reenter the market after minor and major disruptions, when stocks and securities are likely to be significantly underpriced and a gradual economic rebound can be expected. Investors must have staying

---

[263] Nassim Nicholas Taleb, *The Black Swan: The Impact of the Highly Improbable*, 2nd ed. (New York: Random House, 2010); Didier Sornette, "Financial Crisis Observatory," ETH Zurich, http://www.er.ethz.ch/fco.

[264] Taleb, *The Black Swan: The Impact of the Highly Improbable*; Nassim Nicholas Taleb, *Antifragile: Things That Gain from Disorder*, Kindle ed. (New York: Random House, 2012).

power as well as earning power. In investing, as in economics and ecology, it would be better to change the rhetoric. Rather than talking about sustainable futures, let's talk about resilient futures—scenarios in which individuals, businesses, portfolios, and societies bounce back from disruption stronger, more adaptive, and more adept than they were before.

Disaster Preparedness

Because information spreads so rapidly today, because technological innovation is on a hyperbolic trajectory, because the flow of Big Money is growing ever more intense, investors can well expect more volatility than ever before in the coming decades. We just don't know what or when. There are so many radically different, but plausible, scenarios for the short- and long-term futures for each investment and the world as a whole.

Zooming in and out with the help of Big History is also a reminder that complex adaptive systems can be extremely fragile. Don't take human civilization for granted. The great deleveraging and natural disasters in our future will not be pretty, but it is a sure thing from the perspective of economic and ecological histories.

The rich buy super-yachts not just for recreation and status, but as a way to escape to distant lands in times of crisis. They keep money in offshore accounts and stashes of gold and silver bullion. Some have private jets ready to take them to well-stocked estates in New Zealand. Others keep a country home and their guns ready in expectation of the social chaos that will ensue, when the electricity fails, transportation halts, and food supply lines dry up. You don't need to be rich to hedge your bets. Disaster preparedness minimally means storing a month's worth of emergency water and other supplies. Depending on the nature of the disaster, one might flee the chaos or hunker down in place, each requiring different tactics suited to the location and circumstances.[265]

Don't panic in advance or otherwise become too obsessed with survival. Sometimes, one is in the wrong place at the wrong time. In the end, we all die anyway. Negativity bias, as we learned, is one of the major cognitive heuristics that gets investors and the rest of us

---

[265] "How to Prepare for Emergencies," American Red Cross, http://www.redcross.org/get-help/how-to-prepare-for-emergencies/make-a-plan.

into trouble. Maintaining intellectual and emotional equanimity does not come easily to humans. It is not in the nature of our evolved Paleolithic cognition and emotions. Getting to know your hunter-gatherer brain and partially overcoming your evolved biases may provide the most important edge of all for investors in particular and humanity in general at this moment in our cultural evolution.

Investing in Values

The term "value investing" is well worn in finance. It is an investment strategy first articulated by Benjamin Graham and David Dodd in their 1934 book *Security Analysis*.[266] The strategy involves buying securities at a discount of their "intrinsic" value by conducting careful analyses of a company's "fundamentals." Value investing is generally a long-term strategy of buy and hold.

For a philosopher, "investing in values" is more a complicated question than studying price-to-earning ratios. Human values are hotly debated within and between countries in cultural wars and clashing civilizations. What does "values investing" mean in this broader sense? What is the purpose of accumulating income and wealth? What are the human values we seek to maximize in our life through our careers and investments? Are there "universal" values to uphold?

It helps to do an inventory of many different kinds of values that humans share, before getting lost in the flat monetization of value by economic markets. Economic values are not all equal, even though the use of money would lead us to think of them as equivalent and interchangeable.

Take Maslow's hierarchy of needs as one kind of guide.[267] At the base of Maslow's pyramid are physiological needs for survival—the food and water needed to sustain life. Some businesses specialize in providing these needs, albeit today in a complex, global manufacturing and supply chain. Subsistence is essential, though today this involves hunting and gathering in the aisles of your local supermarket.

In Maslow's pyramid, the next level addresses the needs for safety and security—for instance, shelter, clothing, and protection from harm. Again, some businesses specialize in providing for these needs.

---

[266] Benjamin Graham and David Dodd, *Security Analysis* (New York: McGraw-Hill, 1934).
[267] Abraham H. Maslow, *Motivation and Personality* (New York: Harper & Brothers, 1954).

Humans have traded in caves and yurts for suburban houses and urban high-rise apartments, but the function provided is still essential for human well-being.

Next in Maslow's pyramid, we encounter social and psychological needs for love and belonging, which are required if individuals are to thrive. Once the purview of the hunter-gatherer tribal unit, social needs today are provided by complex networks of families, friends, schools, congregations, clubs, and all manner of affiliations, including, especially, one's place of work.

At the top of Maslow's pyramid are needs for esteem and self-actualization. In the context of economic plenty, the relative importance of each layer inverts the pyramid, if not the actual causal hierarchy. Fundamental biological needs can be taken for granted in wealthy societies, whereas the roles of esteem and self-actualization loom ever larger. Much of our economic activity today is focused not on the necessities of life, but on providing goods and services for esteem and self-actualization. Much of advertising is about connecting the top of Maslow's pyramid to products and services provided on the lower levels.

Fundamental Values

It is pretty much universally the case that people everywhere prefer health over sickness, freedom over slavery, prosperity over poverty, education over ignorance, empowerment over powerlessness, pleasure over pain, justice over injustice, easy over hard, and living over dying. Missing from the list are three other universal preferences: humans prefer belonging over isolation, meaning over meaninglessness, and certainty over uncertainty. We might well expand this list. We may disagree about the degree and interpretation of these terms, but not about the basic principles. How much is enough? When is enough too much? And, critically, how do we decide when these universal preferences conflict with one another in actual life as they necessarily do?

In economic terminology, we can refer to these values as "utility functions." The problem is that these various goods invariably conflict with each other. We cannot maximize all goods simultaneously. Trade-offs are necessary as we negotiate the satisfaction of our conflicting aspirations and desires.

One of the unfortunate side effects of money is the illusion that all values can be represented interchangeably and reduced to a mere number. This is certainly not the case. Sacred, moral, and aesthetic values transcend cost-benefit analyses. And while there is much disagreement about what counts for good, true, and beautiful values around the world, these are potent categories that profoundly shape human behavior beyond the ken of transactional economic analyses.

I am convinced that our material needs, as well as our spiritual aspirations, are best served by limited forms of government. Individuals should have the freedom to produce and consume, negotiate and exchange, and worship and express themselves according to their own preferences and abilities. The role of government is critical in protecting private-property rights and individual liberties in such a free society and free economy. Limited government can also regulate commerce, communication, and other services in an effort to increase efficiencies, including goods and services such as education, transportation, and environmental protection. Limited government can also promote forms of social insurance. In the latter categories are police and national defense, but also healthcare and services for the poor. Moreover, limited government can also create rules, regulations, and enforcement to protect us from our frailties, follies, and vices. Limited government adds value to the economy, for instance by funding and promoting scientific research and technological innovation. Taxes are the price of civilization. It is reasonable that those who benefit most from civilization pay a larger share of the costs.

These convictions place me ambiguously somewhere between libertarianism and democratic socialism. For me, the detailed policy implications are pragmatic considerations to be debated, not immutable ideological principles. I note that these classical liberal values are under threat around the world today. The financial services industry, one of the most cosmopolitan industries in the world today, has a big stake in protecting and improving free societies.

Impact Investing

The destructive side of evolution and economics is necessary and presumably also ultimately creative in the long run, but what is good for your portfolio may not be good for your soul or society. Shorting a particular company, for instance, is a different value proposition from going long. Investing in the hopes of an enterprise's failure is ethically distinct from investing in the hopes of an enterprise's success. In fact, investors piling-on can hasten the collapse of a company that might not otherwise fail.

There are lots of investment opportunities for providing social goods and creating new wealth. Given the choice, why wouldn't you prefer, on balance, to invest in companies that also provide for social goods while returning a sustainable profit to shareholders? Social impact investing adds good karma to your bottom line and helps make a better world.

We need to also consider "anti-social impact investing" that exploits human frailties. Profiting from addictions (tobacco, gambling) and violence (slavery, arms exports, gladiator sports) are morally compromised. Exploiting vulnerable populations (young, old, poor, uninformed) is also beyond my moral ken. Short of government regulations and restrictions, however, you will need to decide for yourself whether to invest and profit from such businesses.

In truth, however, the web of interconnections in evolution and economics means that there is no morally pure vantage point from which one can live, work, and invest. Don't let your sacred and moral values delude you into fuzzy thinking, as if these issues were all black and white.

Creating a Little Big History

High school students in the Bill Gates–funded Big History Project are asked at the end of the course to write a short essay on a "Little Big History" of their choice. The curriculum covers nine thresholds in emergent complexity from the Big Bang to the present. The student's essay might start with something contemporary and familiar—sneakers, coffee, horses, smartphones, pizza, etc.—but must then include at least three of the nine thresholds in explaining how the object or commodity functions and how it evolved.[268]

This, then, is your homework assignment—to create a Little Big History for the valuation of your business. This book is itself a long "Little Big History" for the financial services industry, but the challenge now is to do the same within each industry and company. In the corporate setting, the process might begin as a group brainstorm that leads to a sense of common purpose, as well as new ideas for

---

[268] Gates et al., "The Big History Project".

marketing and product development. It can be otherwise hard to see the significance of one's work—a small cog in a big organization and big economy—without these larger perspectives.

As New York University Business School professor Aswath Damodaran explores in his book *Numbers and Narratives*, the valuation of a business is always also a story told. Financial numbers and accounting formulas are presented as evidence for a particular and plausible future outcome. Good storytellers are more likely to raise capital and keep the company's valuation high. A case in point is Amazon, which until recently never made a profit and yet the company's stock valuation has soared into the stratosphere.[269] Your company's Little Big History is more fodder for effectively telling your story.

Our Big Future

Human civilization began fitfully some 10,000 years ago. The Great Acceleration started its steep climb a mere 100 years ago. Earth has another billion years, give or take, before our Sun turns into a Red Giant. At that time, Earth will become too hot and uninhabitable. Perhaps our descendants will have the technological means to build new homes in our solar system farther away from the Sun. If they succeed in such a migration, then our descendants may well have a 5-billion-year future time horizon before the Sun uses up all its fuel and goes completely cold. Whether 1 billion or 5 billion, these future time horizons are difficult to grok. Our descendants have the possibility of an incredibly big future.

[N.B., unless there are major new discoveries overturning fundamental physics as we now understand it, accompanied by commensurate technological innovations, interstellar travel will forever remain science fiction. Wishful thinking does not make for good investing or good science. As much as I enjoy watching Star Trek and imagining such futures, the Earth and this solar system will forever be our home.]

Imagining the next billion years of evolution, including human evolution, is an impossible task. I only note that the Sun has sufficient fuel to support Earth-based complexity for another billion years,

---

[269] Aswarth Damodaran, "Numbers and Narratives: Modeling, Storytelling, and Investing," in *CFA Institute*, ed. NYSSA (Boston2014).

perhaps much longer. The far future inevitable—death—is not as interesting or important as the far future possible—life more abundant. Our descendants have the possibility of an inconceivably big future on this blessed planet. We now know that our cities and civilization, like all complex adaptive systems, will come and go and need to be continually rebuilt. In the process, we must seek to minimize entropy and maximize creativity (e.g., ingenuity, work, value). As we rebuild, let us build in resilience—the ability to bounce back stronger and more adept than we were before. And ultimately, this may mean leaving Earth for more distant shores within our solar system.

We now know that climates do change and, like our ancestors, our descendants will also face evolutionary bottlenecks. Of all the large mammals, however, we are the most likely to survive and thrive again on the other side of those geological transitions—slow or fast, hot or cold, dry or wet, anthropogenic or natural. Indeed, the other flora and fauna may need our help reestablishing themselves on the other side of major planetary catastrophes.

Our greatest vulnerability as a species is also our greatest asset. Humans developed collective learning and thus knowledge and know-how that can grow exponentially with each passing generation. Every child, however, is also born without language and learning. Each generation must be taught anew, if our species is not to forget what we have been so fortunate to recently learn. Collective learning is thus our greatest strength, but always at risk of being forgotten or diminished in future bottlenecks.

Guaranteeing our big future, as best we can today, is the greatest return on investment that we can possibly imagine. The most valuable asset we can leave our descendants, to help them meet the challenges they will surely face, is this grand scientific story we have been so fortunate to recently learn—the greatest, truest, and most practical story ever told. Their gift back to us from that big future is more meaning, purpose, and value in our lives today.

The Bottom Line

The product of the evolutionary and economic processes, for you and other living things, should be life more abundant, more beautiful, more complex. In the end, it is not about me and mine, or even you and yours. Collectively, we carry in our genes and minds all future possibilities, even as our ancestors did for us. Life does not follow us to the grave. It continues without us. Our individual sojourns are brief, but spectacular—each individual a remarkable node of complexity and subjectivity. Each life is an incredible opportunity within the context of our long and fortuitous evolution histories.

In the end, economic and evolutionary processes are not merely a flux of energy, matter, and ingenuity, but also an immaterial flux of ever more truth, beauty, and goodness. And while we have partially enumerated truth through this exploration of Big History, beauty and goodness remain precious mysteries.

The bottom line turns out to be as much a spiritual practice as an investment or business strategy. Build diversified minds. Develop enhanced mathematical, statistical, and analytic skills. Think dynamically in terms of processes and relationships. Cultivate critical curiosity. Pay attention to your hunter-gatherer instincts. Compensate as necessary. Turn groupishness upside-down and inside-out to enhances deductive, inductive, and associative decision-making. Do not be seduced by hope or fear. Be a hopeful pessimist or better a considered optimist. Learn from your losses with grace. Take your gains with humility. Limit leverage. Seek exponentiality through multiple optima. Innovate. Prepare for disasters. Be resilient. Clarify your fundamental values, monetary and otherwise. Nurture the better angels of your nature. Practice gratitude. Grok Big History!

Acknowledgments

This book had a long gestation in which I have received much assistance and inspiration from others. Big History, by whatever name, has been a major academic interest of mine since my undergraduate studies at Middlebury College in the 1970s. And as already alluded to in the first chapter, I wrote a dissertation on the hermeneutics of Big History for my doctorate in religion at Temple University.[270] The teachers and intellectual heroes in my education are too many to mention and have been elsewhere acknowledged. [271] When it comes to my more recent explorations of Big History in the context of economics and finance, however, I need to credit a number of people.

Through my academic work on religion and science, I came to know John Mark Templeton (1912-2008), one of the original mutual fund managers and great value investors of the twentieth century.[272] Templeton was a classic long-term, value investor, noted also for his spiritually grounded optimism. He wrote folksy books and imagined what "progress in religion" and "humility in theology" would mean for humanity. John Templeton was my benefactor for many years. He funded what was essentially a twelve-year postdoctoral position running the Metanexus Institute and serving on the Advisory Board of his foundation. Through this work, supported by a staff of seventeen at one point and with over 400 projects based at universities in 45 countries, I was able to dramatically expand my understanding of the diverse disciplines and perspectives that constitute the story of our universe, the wonders of human evolution, and the contemporary world. Templeton's vision and generosity made this immense journey possible for me and many others. He provided both the ideas and the means to transform religions and the world in many positive ways.

My association with Mitch Julis is more recent, but also important, as he challenged me to embark upon this endeavor. Julis and his partners manage Canyon Partners, a successful Los Angeles-based hedge fund with $25 billion under management. A few years back I gave a talk on Big History at their annual research retreat, specifically

---

[270] Grassie, *Reinventing Nature: Science Narratives as Myths for an Endangered Planet*.

[271] See the acknowledgments in my book *The New Sciences of Religion: Exploring Spirituality from the Outside in and Bottom Up* (New York: Palgrave Macmillan, 2010).

[272]

on why it matters to investors. This was my first foray into applied Big History and finance. Mitch challenged me to go further with the topic, suggesting books and forwarding a steady stream of articles on value investing and complexity economics. His support and guidance allowed me to devote a year of research dedicated to this book. Consider this book then a modest and belated repayment on a debt owed.

There were others who gave me critical feedback along the way. I am especially grateful to David Christian, Robert Friedberg, Nick Gogerty, Ursula Goodenough, Chris Goulakos, Gerry Ohrstrom, Rosmarie Maran, Peter Salas, and Dexter Senft, for reading and commenting on earlier drafts and sections. This saved me from making mistakes and helped to expand my understanding of complexity in nature and economics. These generous readers significantly improved the end product, but of course, are not responsible for any mistakes, misunderstandings, and debatable views that may remain.

This is the second book that I have worked on with my copyeditor Meenakshi Venkat. As a somewhat dyslexic writer, I am especially grateful for her assistance in cleaning up the final manuscript and bringing it to press.

My wife, Rashmini Yogaratnam, has had a longstanding career in the financial services industry. I developed tremendous respect for the caliber and hard work of the people in finance through observing Rashmini and meeting her colleagues. Thanks to her, I also had a front row seat to the 2008 financial crisis. Rashmini has supported me throughout this long endeavor. More than anyone, I owe this book to her for both inspiration and support.

I end by acknowledging "all my relations" in the manner of the native peoples of North America. It is a spiritual practice of giving thanks by carefully naming and appreciating each relation—animal, vegetable, and mineral. Praise is offered to the elemental properties and natural kinds—the four directions, the rivers and the oceans, the forests and the meadows, the sun and the stars, the moon and the seasons, the birds of the air, the fish of the sea, the four-footed creatures—each by name.

In an age of science, the lists of "all our relations" have grown dramatically in scales and complexity from the microcosmic to the macrocosmic. Together through collective learning, we are the first generation to piece together the real world and its epic evolutionary past. Each exists within a vast matrix of causal relations at different scales— biophysical, familial, psychological, cultural, socioeconomic, educational, professional, and technological—that create and sustain our lives and the world around us. Each also has the possibilities of self-creative, albeit constrained choice, within these determinative matrices. And our choices and behavior aggregate into large wholes—ecologies and economies. Markets are not just economic, but also aesthetic, political, moral, ecological, and personal. To grok "all our relations" has been a source of great wonder and pleasure in my life, as I hope reading this book is for you.

William Grassie
New York, NY
September 21, 2018

About the Author

William Grassie was born in 1957 in Wilmington, Delaware, where he attended public schools. Billy was the fifth of six children born to Canadian immigrants. His father and step-father, and many of his neighbors, worked in Wilmington's booming chemical industries. During his school years, he hitchhiked some 30,000 kilometers throughout North America and Europe. He has worked as a newspaper boy, farm hand, house painter, dish washer, janitor, night watchman, golf caddy, caretaker of multiply handicapped children, apprentice in a ceramic studio, camp counselor, beekeeper, computer consultant, real estate manager, and general contractor, among other jobs. Along the way, he developed passions for hiking, skiing, sailing, scuba, dance, yoga, languages, and international travel.

Grassie received his bachelor's in political science from Middlebury College in 1979, after spending his junior year abroad at the Hebrew University in Jerusalem. He then worked for ten years on nuclear disarmament, citizen diplomacy, community organizing, and sustainability issues primarily based in Philadelphia, Pennsylvania. In 1983 he worked with *Aktion Sühnezeichen Friedensdienste* in West Berlin and traveled extensively in East Germany and Poland.

Grassie received his doctorate in religion from Temple University, where he wrote a dissertation entitled *Reinventing Nature: Science Narratives as Myths for an Endangered Planet* (1994). Grassie taught undergraduate religion courses at Temple throughout his five-years as a doctoral student. He continued teaching at Temple University for another five-years as an assistant professor in the Intellectual Heritage Program—a two-semester, writing-intensive introduction to the humanities required of all undergraduates. Grassie also taught as a visiting professor at Swarthmore College, Pendle Hill, and the University of Pennsylvania. A recipient of academic awards and grants from the American Friends Service Committee, the Roothbert Fellowship, and the John Templeton Foundation, Grassie served also as a Senior Fulbright Fellow in the Department of Buddhist Studies at the University of Peradeniya in Kandy, Sri Lanka, in 2007–2008.

Grassie was the founding director of the Metanexus Institute, which promotes scientifically rigorous and philosophically open-ended exploration of foundational questions. Metanexus has worked with partners at some 400 universities in 45 countries and published an online journal available at www.metanexus.net.

William Grassie has authored numerous essays and books, including *The New Sciences of Religion: Exploring Spirituality from the Outside In and Bottom Up* (2010); *Politics by Other Means: Science and Religion in the 21st Century* (2010); *H+/-: Transhumanism and Its Critics* (co-editor) (2010); and, most recently, *Applied Big History: A Guide for Entrepreneurs, Investors, and Other Living Things* (2018).

More information available at www.grassie.net.

Bibliography

Bibliography

"Adenosine Triphosphate." *Wikipedia* (2018). https://en.wikipedia.org/wiki/Adenosine_triphosphate.

Ambrose, Stanley H. "Volcanic Winter, and Differentiation of Modern Humans. Bradshaw Foundation. ." Bradshaw Foundation, http://www.bradshawfoundation.com/stanley_ambrose.php.

Analysis, Bureau of Economic. "U.S. Gdp by Year." Washington, D.C.: U.S. Department of Commerce, 2017.

Ariely, Dan. *Predictably Irrational: The Hidden Forces That Shape Our Decisions.* New York: HarperCollins, 2009.

Azevedo FA, Carvalho LR, Grinberg LT, Farfel JM, Ferretti RE, Leite RE, Jacob Filho W, Lent R, Herculano-Houzel S. "Equal Numbers of Neuronal and Nonneuronal Cells Make the Human Brain an Isometrically Scaled-up Primate Brain." *Journal of Comparative Neurology* 513, no. 5 (4/10/2009 2009): 532-41.

Barbour, Ian. *Religion in an Age of Science: The Gifford Lectures 1989-1991.* Vol. Volume One, San Francisco: Harper, 1990.

Baumeister, Roy. *Evil: Inside Human Creulty and Aggression.* New York: Macmillan, 1996.

Beinhocker, Eric D. *The Origin of Wealth: Evolution, Complexity, and the Radical Remaking of Economics.* Cambridge Harvard Business Press, 2006.

Beinhocker, Eric D., and Jeremy Oppenheim. "Economic Opportunities in a Low-Carbon World." McKinsey & Company, http://www.mckinsey.com/client_service/sustainability/latest_thinking/economic_opportunities_in_a_low_carbon_world.

Benson, Buster. "Cognitive Bias Cheat Sheet." BetterHumans.Coach.Me, https://betterhumans.coach.me/cognitive-bias-cheat-sheet-55a472476b18.

Berlin, Isaiah. *The Hegdehog and the Fox.* London: Weidenfeld & Nicolson, 1953.

Berry, Thomas, and Brian Swimme. *Universe Story, The: From the Primordial Flaring Forth to the Ecozoic Era.* San Francisco, CA: Harper, 1992.

Beunza, Daniel, and David Stark. "How to Recognize Opportunities: Heterarchical Search in Trading Rooms." In *The Sociology of Financial Markets*, edited by Karin Knorr Cetina and Alex Preda. Oxford: Oxford University Press, 2004.

Bianconi, Eva, Allison Piovesan, and et al. "An Estimation of the Number of Cells in the Human Body." *Annals of Human Biology* 40, no. 6 (2013): 463-71.

Bloom, Paul. *Descartes' Baby: How the Science of Child Development Explains What Makes Us Human.* New York: Basic Books, 2009.

———. *Just Babies: The Origins of Good and Evil.* New York: Crown, 2013.

Bohan, Elise, Robert Dinwiddie, Jack Challoner, Colin Stuart, Derek Harvey, Rebecca Wragg-Sykes, Peter Chrisp, *et al. Big History.* New York: DK, 2016.

Boyer, Pascal. *The Naturalness of Religious Ideas: A Cognitive Theory of Religion.* Berkeley: University of California Press, 1994.

Broadgate, Wendy, Owen Gaffney, Lisa Deutsch, Cornelia Ludwig, and Will Steffen. "The Great Acceleration Data." http://www.igbp.net/globalchange/greatacceleration.4.1b8ae20512db692f2a680001630.html.

Brumfield, Geoff. "The Testosterone of Trading." Nature, http://www.nature.com/news/2008/080414/full/news.2008.753.html.

Buchanan, Mark. *Forecasts: What Physics, Meteorology, and the Natural Sciences Can Teach Us About Economics.* Kindle ed. New York: Bloomsbury USA, 2014.

Buffett, Warren. "Berkshire Hathaway Annual Report." Omaha: Berkshire Hathaway, 2002.

Carroll, Lewis. *Through the Looking Glass.* Project Gutenberg, 1871.

Carroll, Sean. *The Big Picture.* New York: Dutton, 2017.

Cartwright, John. *Evolution and Human Behavior: Darwinian Perspectives on Human Nature.* New York: Palgrave, 2000.

Chaisson, Eric. *Cosmic Evolution: The Rise of Complexity in Nature.* Cambridge, MA: Harvard University Press, 2001.

———. "Energy Rate Density as a Complexity Metric and Evolutionary Driver." *Complexity* 16, no. 3 (2011): 27-40.

———. "Energy Rate Density. Ii. Probing Further a New Complexity Metric." *Complexity* 17, no. 1 (2011): 44-63.

————. *Epic of Evolution: Seven Ages of the Cosmos.* New York: Columbia University Press, 2006.

————. "Using Complexity Science to Search for Unity in the Natural Sciences." In *The Self-Organizing Universe: Cosmology, Biology, and the Rise of Complexity*, edited by Lineweaver, Davies and Michael Ruse. New York: Cambridge University Press, 2012.

Christakis, Nicolas A., and James H. Fowler. *Connected: The Surprising Power of Our Social Networks and How They Shape Our Lives.* New York: Little, Brown and Company, 2009.

Christian, David. *Maps of Time: An Introduction to Big History.* Berkeley, CA: University of California Press, 2004, 2011.

Clark, Luke, Bruno Averbeck, Doris Payer, Guillaume Sescousse, Catherine A. Winstanley, and Gui Xue. "Pathological Choice: The Neuroscience of Gambling and Gambling Addiction." *The Journal of Neuroscience* 33, no. 45 (2013): 17617-23.

Clouser, Roy A. *The Myth of Religious Neutrality: An Essay on the Hidden Role of Religious Belief in Theories.* Notre Dame, IN: University of Notre Dame Press, 2005.

Cobb Jr., John B., and Herman Daly. *For the Common Good: Redirecting the Economy toward Community, the Environment, and a Sustainable Future.* Boston: Beacon Press, 1989.

Corneo, Giacomo. *Is Capitalism Obsolete?: A Journey through Alternative Economic Systems.* Cambridge, MA: Harvard University Press, 2017.

Costa, P.T.J., and R.R. McCrae. "Personality Continuity and the Changes of Adult Life." In *The Adult Years: Continuity and Change*, edited by M Storandt and G. R. VandenBos, 45-77. Washington, D.C.: American Psychological Association, 1989.

Cowen, Tyler. *Average Is Over: Powering America Beyond the Age of the Great Stagnation.* Dutton Adult, 2013.

————. *The Great Stagnation: How America Ate All the Low-Hanging Fruit of Modern History, Got Sick, and Will (Eventually) Feel Better.* New York: Penguin eSpecial from Dutton, 2011.

Dalio, Ray. *How the Economic Machine Works.* Westport, CT: Bridgewater Associates, 2013.

————. "How to Build a Company Where the Best Ideas Win." TED, https://www.ted.com/talks/ray_dalio_how_to_build_a_com pany_where_the_best_ideas_win.

———. *Principles: Life and Work.* New York: Simon & Schuster, 2017.

Daly, Herman E., and Joshua Farley. *Ecological Economics: Principles and Applications.* Second ed. Washington: Island Press, 2011.

Damodaran, Aswarth. "Numbers and Narratives: Modeling, Storytelling, and Investing." In *CFA Institute*, edited by NYSSA. Boston, 2014.

Darwin, Charles. *The Origin of Species.* Online, 1859.

Dawkins, Richard. *The Blind Watchmaker: Why the Evidence of Evolution Reveals a Universe without Design.* New York: Norton, 1986.

———. *The God Delusion.* New York: Houghton Mifflin, 2006.

De Long, Edward. "Deciphering the Ocean's Microbiome." Simons Foundation, 2017.

de Waal, Frans. *The Bonobo and the Atheist: In Search of Humanism among the Primates.* New York: W.W. Norton, 2014.

———. *Good Natured: The Origins of Right and Wrong in Humans and Other Animals.* Cambridge, MA: Harvard University Press, 1996.

Deacon, Terrence W. *The Symbolic Species: The Co-Evolution of Language and the Brain.* New York: Norton, 1997.

Demasio, Antonio. *Descartes' Error: Emotion, Reason, and the Human Brain.* New York: Avon, 1995.

———. *The Feeling of What Happens: Body, Emotion and the Making of Consciousness.* London: Vintage, 2000.

Dennett, Daniel C. *Breaking the Spell: Religion as a Natural Phenomenon.* New York: Viking, 2006.

———. *Darwin's Dangerous Idea: Evolution and the Meaning of Life.* New York: Simon & Schuster, 1995.

———. *From Bacteria to Bach and Back.* New York: W.W. Norton, 2017.

Depew, David, and Bruce Weber. *Darwinism Evolving: Systems Dynamics and the Genealogy of Natural Selection.* Cambridge, MA: MIT Press, 1996.

Diamond, Jared. "The Worst Mistake in the History of the Human Race." *Discover Magazine*, 1999.

Dowd, Michael. *Thank God for Evolution.* New York Plume, 2009.

Dunbar, Robin. *Grooming, Gossip and the Evolution of Language.* Cambridge: Harvard University Press, 1996.

Dyer, Gwynne. *War: The Lethal Custom.* New York: Carroll & Graf, 1985, 2004.

Ellis, George F.R. *How Can Physics Underlie the Mind? Top-Down Causation in the Human Context.* New York: Springer, 2016.

Eswaran, H, R. Lal, and P.F. Reich. "Land Degradation: An Overview." USDA Natural Resources Conservation Service, https://www.nrcs.usda.gov/wps/portal/nrcs/detail/soils/use/?cid=nrcs142p2_054028.

EurekaAlert. "Pinpointing Where Seizures Are Coming from, by Looking between the Seizures." news release, 2017, https://www.eurekalert.org/pub_releases/2017-05/bch-pws050117.php.

Extance, Andy. "How DNA Could Store All the World's Data." Nature, http://www.nature.com/news/how-dna-could-store-all-the-world-s-data-1.20496.

FAO. "Soils Are Endangered, but the Degradation Can Be Rolled Back." Food and Agricultural Organization of the United Nations, http://www.fao.org/news/story/en/item/357059/icode/.

FAOstats. "Live Animals Data Set." Food and Agricultural Organization of the United Nations, http://www.fao.org/faostat/en/#data/QA.

Ferguson, Niall. *The Ascent of Money: A Financial History of the World.* Kindle ed. New York: Penguin Press, 2008.

Fisher, Helen E. *Anatomy of Love: A Natural History of Mating, Marriage, and Why We Stray.* New York: W.W. Norton, 2016.

Freud, Sigmund. *Civilization and Its Discontents.* New York: W.W. Norton, [1930] 1961.

Fukuyama, Francis. *Trust: Human Nature and the Creation of Prosperity.* Boston: Free Press, 2008.

Galbraith, John Kenneth. *Money: Whence It Came, Where It Went.* New York: Houghton Mifflin, 1975, 1995.

Gates, Bill, David Christian, Andrew Cook, and et al. "The Big History Project." http://www.bighistoryproject.com.

Georgescu-Roegen, Nicholas. *The Entropy Law and the Economic Process.* Cambridge, MA: Harvard University Press, 1971.

Gershenson, Carlos. "Complexity Digest." Complex Systems Society, https://comdig.unam.mx/.

Gilbert, Scott F., and David Epel. *Ecological Developmental Biology: Integrating Epigenetics, Medicine, and Evolution.* Sunderland, MA: Sinauer Associates, 2009.

Gleick, James. *Chaos: Making a New Science.* New York: Penguin, 1987.

Gogerty, Nick. *The Nature of Value: How to Invest in the Adaptive Economy.* New York: Columbia Business School, 2014.

Gorntz, Vivien. "Sea Level Rise, after the Ice Melted and Today."
Goddard Institute for Space Studies (2007).
http://www.giss.nasa.gov/research/briefs/gornitz_09/.

Graham, Benjamin. *The Intelligent Investor.* New York: Harper,
1949.

Graham, Benjamin, and David Dodd. *Security Analysis.* New York:
McGraw-Hill, 1934.

Grassie, William J. *The New Sciences of Religion: Exploring
Spirituality from the Outside in and Bottom Up.* New York:
Palgrave Macmillan, 2010.

———. *Reinventing Nature: Science Narratives as Myths for an
Endangered Planet.* Philadelphia: doctoral dissertation,
Temple University Department of Religion, 1994.

———. "Wired for the Future: Kevin Kelly's Techno-Utopia." *Terra
Nova: Nature and Culture* 2, no. 4 (1997): 91-101.

Gregorian, Vartan. "Colleges Must Reconstruct the Unity of
Knowledge." *Chronicle of Higher Education* 50, no. 39
(6/4/2004 2004): B12.

Griffin, Tren. *Charlie Munger: The Complete Investor.* New York:
Columbia University Press, 2015.

Hagstrom, Robert. *Investing: The Last Liberal Art.* New York:
Columbia Business School, 2013.

Haidt, Jonathan. *The Happiness Hypothesis: Finding Modern Truth in
Ancient Wisdom.* New York: Basic Books, 2006.

———. *The Righteous Mind: Why Good People Are Divided by
Politics and Religion.* New York: Random House, 2012.

Haidt, Jonathan, and C Joseph. "The Moral Mind: How 5 Sets of
Innate Moral Intutitions Guide the Development of Many
Culture-Specific Virtues, and Perhaps Even Modules." In
The Innate Mind, edited by P. Carruthers, S. Laurence and S.
Stich. New York: Oxford University Press, 2007.

Hamer, Dean H. *The God Gene: How Faith Is Hardwired into Our
Genes.* New York: Anchor, 2005.

Harari, Yuval Noah. *Sapiens: A Brief History of Humankind.* Kindle
ed. New York: HarperCollins, 2015.

Haught, John. *God after Darwin: A Theology of Evolution.* Boulder,
CO: Westview, 2000.

Henrich, Joseph. *The Secret of Our Success: How Culture Is Driving
Human Evolution, Domesticating Our Species, and Making Us
Smarter.* Princeton: Princeton University Press, 2015.

Heschel, Abraham. *Who Is Man?* Stanford, CA: Stanford University
Press, 1965.

Hewlett, Sylvia Ann. "Too Much Testosterone on Wall Street?" Harvard Business Review, https://hbr.org/2009/01/too-much-testosterone-on-wall.

Hidalgo, Cesar. *Why Information Grows: The Evolution of Order, from Atoms to Economies.* New York: Basic Books, 2015.

"How to Prepare for Emergencies." American Red Cross, http://www.redcross.org/get-help/how-to-prepare-for-emergencies/make-a-plan.

Hume, David. *A Treatise on Human Nature.* Online, [1738].

IEA. "Energy Efficiency Market Report 2014." Paris, France: International Energy Agency, 2014.

"Institute for New Economic Thinking." https://www.ineteconomics.org/.

Johnson, Steven. *Where Good Ideas Come From: The Natural History of Innovation.* New York: Riverhead Books, 2010.

Judson, Olivia. "The Energy Expansion of Evolution." *Natue Ecology & Evolution* 1 (2017).

Kahneman, Daniel. *Thinking, Fast and Slow.* New York: Farrar, Straus and Giroux, 2011.

Keeley, Larry, Ryan Pikkel, Brian Quinn, and Hele Walters. *Ten Types of Innovation: The Discipline of Building Breakthroughs.* New York: Wiley, 2013.

Kelly, Kevin. *Out of Control: The New Biology of Machines, Social Systems, and the Economic World.* New York: Addison-Wesley, 1994.

Koch, Christof. *Consciousness: Confessions of a Romantic Reductionist.* Cambridge: MIT Press, 2012.

Konner, Melvin. *Women after All: Sex, Evolution, and the End of Male Supremacy.* New York: W,W, Norton, 2016.

Kurzweil, Ray. *The Singularity Is Near: When Humans Transcend Biology.* New York: Penguin Books, 2005.

Lane, Nick. *The Vital Question: Energy, Evolution, and the Origins of Complex Life.* New York: W.W. Norton & Company, 2015.

Lefranc, Marie-Paule, and et.al. "Amino Acids." *International Immunogenetics Information System* (2015). http://www.imgt.org/IMGTeducation/Aide-memoire/ UK/aminoacids/abbreviation.html.

Lykken, D.T. *Happiness: What Studies on Twins Show Us About Nature, Nurture, and the Happiness Set-Point.* New York: Golden Books 1999.

"Macrotrends." http://www.macrotrends.net/stocks/research.

Malthus, Thomas Robert (1766-1834). *An Essay on the Principle of Population.* 1798, 18032 1826, 1830 ed. London: J. Johnson, 1798.

Manoogian III, John, and Buster Benson. "Cognitive Biases Codex." DesignHacks.co, http://www.visualcapitalist.com/wp-content/uploads/2017/09/cognitive-bias-infographic.html.

Maslow, Abraham H. *Motivation and Personality.* New York: Harper & Brothers, 1954.

Mauboussin, Michael J. "Thirty Years: Reflections on the Ten Attributes of Great Investors." New York: Credit Suisse Global Financial Strategies, 2016.

McCauley, Robert. *Why Religion Is Natural and Science Is Not.* 2011.

McNeill, J. Robert, and William H. McNeill. *The Human Web: A Bird's-Eye View of World History.* New York: W.W. Norton, 2003.

McNeill, J.Robert. *Something New under the Sun: An Environmental History of the Twentieth-Century World.* New York: W.W. Norton & Company, 2000.

Medeiros, Joao. "The Truth Behind Testosterone: Why Men Risk It All." WIRED, http://www.wired.co.uk/article/why-men-risk-it-all.

Milo, Ron, and Rob Phillips. "Cell Biology by the Numbers." Garland Science, 2015.

"The Money Project." Visual Capitalist, http://money.visualcapitalist.com/worlds-money-markets-one-visualization-2017/.

Moore, G.E. *Principia Ethica.* Cambridge, UK: Cambridge University Press, [1903] 1989.

Morris, Simon Conway. *Life's Solution: Inevitable Humans in a Lonely Universe.* New York: Cambridge University Press, 2003.

Munger, Charles. "Usc Law School Commencement Address, May 1, 2007." Genius.com, http://genius.com/Charlie-munger-usc-law-commencement-speech-annotated.

Nations, United. "World Population Prospects: The 2012 Revisions." New York: UN Department of Economic and Social Affairs, 2012.

Newberg, Andrew. "Religious and Spiritual Practices: A Neurochemical Perspective." In *Where God and Science Meet*, edited by Patrick McNamara, 15-32. Westport, CT: Praeger, 2006.

Niele, Frank. *Energy: Engine of Evolution.* New York: Elsevier, 2005.

"The Observatory of Economic Complexity." MIT, https://atlas.media.mit.edu/en/.

"Otc Derivatives Statistics at End of 2014." (2014). http://www.bis.org/publ/otchy1405.pdf.

Oyama, Susan. *Evolution's Eye: A Systems View of the Biology-Culture Divide.* Durham, NC: Duke University Press, 2000.

———. *The Ontogeny of Information.* New York: Cambridge University Press, 1985.

Piketty, Thomas. *The Economics of Inequality.* Cambridge, MA: Belknap Press, 2015.

Pilkey, Orrin H., and Linda Plkey-Jarvis. *Useless Arithmetic: Why Environmental Scientists Can't Predict the Future.* New York: Columbia University Press, 2007.

Pimentel, David, and Michael Burgess. "Soil Erosion Threatens Food Production." *Agriculture* 3, no. 3 (2013): 443-63.

Pinker, Steven. *The Better Angels of Our Nature: Why Violence Has Declined.* New York: Viking, 2011.

Plato. *The Republic.* Translated by revised by C.D.C. Reeve G.M.A. Grube. Indianapolis, IN: Hackett Publishing Company, (ca. 380 b.c.e.) 1992. (427?-347? B.C.E.).

Potts, Malcom, and Thomas Hayden. *Sex and War: How Biology Explains Warfare and Terrorism and Offers a Path to a Safer World.* Kindle ed. Dallas, TX: BenBella Books 2008.

Prigogine, I., and Isabelle Stengers. *Order out of Chaos : Man's New Dialogue with Nature.* New York, N.Y.: Bantam Books, 1984.

Prigogine, Ilya, and Gregoire Nicolas, eds. *Self-Organization in Nonequilibrium Systems: From Dissipative Structures to Order through Fluctuations.* New York: Wiley, 1977.

Primack, Joel R., and Nancy Ellen Abrams. *The View from the Center of the Universe: Discovering Our Extraordinary Place in the Cosmos.* New York: Riverhead, 2006.

Programme, International Geosphere-Biosphere. "Global Change." Royal Swedish Academy of Sciences, http://www.igbp.net/globalchange/greatacceleration.4.1b8ae20512db692f2a680001630.html.

"Proteins." *Wikipedia* (2017). https://en.wikipedia.org/wiki/Protein.

Racanelli, Vito. "Big Ipo Gain? Don't Bet on It." *Barron's*, September 18, 2017 2017.

Ridley, Matt. *The Evolution of Everything: How New Ideas Emerge.* New York: HarperCollins, 2015.

Roberts, Leslie. "9 Billion?". *Science* 333, no. 6042 (29 July 2011 2011): 540-43.

Rolston, Holmes. *Genes, Genesis, and God: Values and Their Origins in Natural and Human History.* New York: Cambridge University Press, 1998.

Roser, Max. "Ethnographic and Archaeological Evidence on Violent Deaths." OurWorldinData.org, https://ourworldindata.org/ethnographic-and-archaeological-evidence-on-violent-deaths/.

―――. "Gdp Growth over the Last Centuries." University of Oxford, https://ourworldindata.org/gdp-growth-over-the-last-centuries/.

Rozin, Paul, and E.B. Royzman. "Negativity Bias, Negativity Dominance, and Contagion." *Personality and Social Psychology Review* 5 (2001): 296-320.

Russell, Bertrand. *An Outline of Philosophy.* New York: Routledge, 1993.

Ryan, Christopher, and Cacilda Jetha. *Sex at Dawn: How We Mate, Why We Stray, and What It Means for Modern Relationships.* New York: Harper Collins, 2012.

"Santa Fe Institute." https://www.santafe.edu/.

Sapolsky, Robert M. *Behave: The Biology of Humans at Our Best and Worst.* New York: Penguin, 2017.

Schrödinger, Erwin, and Roger Penrose. *What Is Life? With "Mind and Matter".* New York: Cambridge University Press, 2003.

Sender, Ron, Shai Fuchs, and Ron Milo. "Revised Estimates of the Number of Human and Bacteria Cells in the Body." *PLOS Biology* (2016).

Shobhit, Seth. "The World of High Frequency Algorithmic Trading." Investopedia, https://www.investopedia.com/articles/investing/091615/world-high-frequency-algorithmic-trading.asp.

Smil, Vaclav. *Energy in Nature and Society.* Cambridge, MA: MIT Press, 2007.

―――. *Making the Modern World: Materials & Dematerialization.* New York: Wiley, 2013.

Smith, Adam (1723-1790). *An Inquiry into the Nature and Causes of the Wealth of Nations.* London: Methuen and Co., 1776.

"Society for Worldwide Interbank Financial Telecommunication (Swift)." Wikipedia, http://en.wikipedia.org/wiki/Society_for_Worldwide_Interbank_Financial_Telecommunication.

Sornette, Didier. "Financial Crisis Observatory." ETH Zurich, http://www.er.ethz.ch/fco.

Soros, George. *The Alchemy of Finance.* New York: Wiley, 2003.

Spier, Fred. *Big History and the Future of Humanity.* New York: Wiley-Blackwell, 2011.

Srivastava, S., Oliver P. John, S.D. Gosling, and J. Potter. "Development of Personality in Early and Middle Addulthood: Set Like Plaster or Persistent Change?". *Journal of Personality and Social Psychology* 84 (2003): 1041-53.

Statistics, Bureau of Economic. "Quarterly Gross Domestic Producti by State, 2005-2013." U.S. Department of Commerce, http://blog.bea.gov/category/gdp-by-state/.

Stewart, Ian. *Life's Other Secret: The New Mathematics of the Living World.* Wiley & Sons, 1998.

Taibbi, Matt. "The Great American Bubble Machine." *Rolling Stone,* 4/5/2010 2010.

Taleb, Nassim Nicholas. *Antifragile: Things That Gain from Disorder.* Kindle ed. New York: Random House, 2012.

Taleb, Nassim Nicholas *The Black Swan: The Impact of the Highly Improbable.* 2nd ed. New York: Random House, 2010.

Tattersall, Ian. *Becoming Human: Evolution and Human Uniqueness.* New York: Harcourt Brace, 1998.

Templeton, Lauren, and Scott Philllips. *Investing the Templeton Way: The Market-Beating Strategies of Value Investing's Legendary Bargain Hunter.* New York: McGraw-Hill Education, 2008.

Tetlock, Philip E. *Expert Political Judgment: How Good Is It? How Can We Know?* Princeton, NJ: Princeton University Press, 2005.

Tetlock, Philip E., and Dan Gardner. *Superforecasting: The Art and Science of Prediction.* New York: Crown Publishers, 2015.

Thaler, Richard. *Misbehaving: The Making of Behavioral Economics.* New York: W.W. Norton, 2015.

"The Trouble with Gdp." *The Economist,* 2016.

Vohs, Kathleen D. "The Meaning of Money." In *Paduano Seminar.* NYU Stern School, 2014.

———. "The Poor's Poor Mental Power." *Science* 341, no. 969 (2013) (2013).

Vohs, Kathleen D, Nicole L. Mead, and Miranda R. Goode. "The Psychological Consequences of Money." *Science* 314, no. 1154 (2006).

Warsh, David. *Knowledge and the Wealth of Nations: A Story of Economic Discovery.* New York: Norton, 2006.

Weatherford, Jack. *The History of Money: From Sandstone to Cyberspace.* Kindle ed. New York: Crown Publishing Group, 2009.

Wesson, Robert. *Beyond Natural Selection.* Cambridge, MA: MIT Press, 1991.

West, Geoffrey. *Scale: The Universal Laws of Life, Growth, and Death in Organisms, Cities, and Companies.* New York: Penguin Books, 2017.

"Wfe Annual Statistics." World Federation of Exchanges, https://www.world-exchanges.org/home/index.php/statistics/annual-statistics.

Whitehead, Alfred North. *The Concept of Nature.* Cambridge: Cambridge University Press, [1920] 2010.

———. *Process and Reality.* New York: Free Press, [1929]1978.

———. *Science and the Modern World.* New York: Free Press, [1925] 1967.

Wigner, Eugene. "The Unreasonable Effectiveness of Mathematics in the Natural Sciences." *Communications in Pure and Applied Mathematics* 13, no. 1 (1960).

"Wikipedia." Wikipedia Foundation, https://en.wikipedia.org/wiki/Wikipedia.

Williams, R.W., Herrup, K. "The Control of Neuron Number." *Annual Review of Neuroscience* 11 (1988): 423-53.

Wilson, David Sloan. *Darwin's Cathedral: Evolution, Religion, and the Nature of Society.* Chicago: The University of Chicago Press, 2002.

———. *Evolution for Everyone.* New York: Bantam Dell, 2007.

Wilson, Edward O. *Consilience: The Unity of Knowledge.* New York: Knopf, 1998.

———. *The Social Conquest of Earth.* New York, NY: Liveright, 2012.

Wranghan, Richard, and Dale Peterson. *Demonic Males: Apes and the Origins of Violence.* New York: Mariner Books, 1997.

Yong, Ed. *I Contain Multitudes: The Microbes within Us and a Grander View of Life.* New York: HarperCollins, 2016.

Zalasiewicz, J., and et.al. "Are We Now Living in the Anthropocene?". *GSA Today* 18, no. 2 (2008): 4-8.

Zorn, Carl. *Jefferson Lab* (2018). https://education.jlab.org/qa/electron_01.html.

Made in the USA
Middletown, DE
09 February 2019